··

LOOKING INTO HOUSING

A PRACTICAL GUIDE TO HOUSING RESEARCH

DOUGLAS ROBERTSON and **PAT McLAUGHLIN**

··

Chartered Institute of Housing
Policy and Practice Series

The Chartered Institute of Housing
The Chartered Institute of Housing is the professional organisation for all people
who work in housing. Its purpose is to take a strategic and leading role in
encouraging and promoting the provision of good quality affordable housing for all.
The Institute has more than 13,000 members working in local authorities, housing
associations, the private sector and educational institutions.

Chartered Institute of Housing
Octavia House, Westwood Way
Coventry CV4 8JP
Telephone: 01203 694433
Fax: 01203 695110

The CIH Housing Policy and Practice Series aims to provide important and valuable
material and insights for housing managers, staff, students, trainers and policy
makers. Books in the series are designed to promote debate, but the contents do not
necessarily reflect the views of the CIH. The Editorial Team for the series is:
General Editors: Dr. Peter Williams and John Perry, and Production Editor: Alan
Dearling.

ISBN 0-901607-92-4

Looking into Housing: A practical guide to housing research
Douglas Robertson and Pat McLaughlin

Published by the
Chartered Institute of Housing © 1996

Printed by The Cromwell Press, Trowbridge, Wiltshire

Contents

Introduction   Outlining the range and purpose of the book   1

PART ONE: PREPARING THE GROUND   4

Chapter 1   **Using Information**   6
The relationship between information and research   6
Operational Information   7
Strategic Information   10
Summary   15

Chapter 2   **The Development of Housing Research**   17
The focus of research   17
What is housing research?   18
Styles of housing research   19
How did housing research develop?   20
The future housing research agenda   27
Entering the policy arena: a cautionary note   28

Chapter 3   **Research Project Planning and Design**   30
The research process   31
Establishing a focus   33
Defining the research question   34
Selecting an appropriate research method   34
Negotiating and maintaining access   35
Developing the data collection instrument   36
Data collection   37
Analysing the data   37
Interpreting the data   37
Writing up and disseminating the findings   38
Timetabling and project management   39
Appraising existing research   40
Commissioning research or doing it yourself?   41

Chapter 4   **Commissioning Research**   43
Drawing up the research brief   44
Identifying potential contractors   47
Intellectual property rights   49
Negotiated contracts   49
Selecting the contract researcher   50
Research contract   51

PART TWO:	PUTTING THE PROJECT TOGETHER	52

Chapter 5	**Assembling Material**	**54**
	Library searches	54
	Other sources of information	57
	Planning the search	58
	Taking notes	58
	References	61
	Literature reviews	61
	Reading critically	62

Chapter 6	**Measurement**	**64**
	Measurement and meaning	65
	Quantitative versus qualitative measures	65
	Units of analysis	67
	Levels of measurement	67
	Validity and reliability	70
	Linkages	74

Chapter 7	**Sampling**	**76**
	Types of sampling	78
	Making choices	81

Chapter 8	**Questionnaires**	**86**
	Types of questionnaire	87
	Asking questions	88
	Question types	92
	Layout and design	97
	Piloting the questionnaire	98
	Administering the survey	99
	Response rate	100
	Questionnaires: strengths and weaknesses	101

Chapter 9	**Interviewing: Principles and Methods**	**104**
	Types of interview	106
	Interview techniques	109
	The causes of bias	112
	Recording and verification	113
	Special circumstances	114
	Interviews: strengths and weaknesses	114

Chapter 10	**Documentary Studies**	**116**
	Documentary research	117
	Practical issues in documentary research	119
	Documentary research: adopting a critical approach	123

Chapter 11	**Observational Methods**	**125**
	The Observer Effect	126
	Structured Observation	126
	The Naturalistic paradigm	126
	Participant observation	129

	Finding a setting	130
	Taking notes	130
	Problems of interpretation and generalisability	131
Chapter 12	**Case Studies**	**133**
	Types of case studies	134
	An evaluation of case study approach	135
	Type, quality and range of data	137
	Case studies: some practical issues	138
Chapter 13	**Information Technology and Housing Research**	**141**
	Using computers in research	142
	The role of the computer: a health warning	145
	The Data Protection Act	146
PART THREE:	**FINISHING OFF? – ANALYSING, THEORISING AND PRESENTING**	**149**
Chapter 14	**Managing, Analysing and Interpreting Data**	**151**
	Coding, data entry and data management	151
	Analysing quantitative data	153
	Using and abusing statistics	157
	Analysing qualitative data	158
	Theorising: making sense of findings	161
Chapter 15	**Reporting Research and Presenting Findings**	**163**
	Presentation and dissemination	163
	The need for different forms of presentation	164
	Presenting research results	167
	Structuring the research report	168
	Making presentations	170
	Using visual aids	174
	Conclusions	176
Chapter 16	**Concluding Remarks**	**177**
Appendix One	**Commissioners and/or Funders of Housing Research**	**179**
Appendix Two	**Information Sources on Housing**	**181**
Appendix Three	**A Sample Research Brief**	**184**
Appendix Four	**A Sample Research Contract**	**187**
Bibliography		**192**
Name index		**201**
Subject index		**203**

Acknowledgements

In drawing together the material for this book we are indebted to a number of individuals for their assistance and advice. Firstly we thank Gillian Young of Scottish Homes for, in effect, starting this venture off through her invitation to conduct a one day training session on drawing up a research brief. The material developed for this session became the initial stimulus to write this book. Gillian also provided useful comments on a number of the draft chapters.

Colleagues in the Department of Applied Social Science, at the University of Stirling, provided a range of information on both the theory and practical application of particular research methods. Given their varied backgrounds in fields of Housing, Social Anthropology, Sociology and Social Policy a broad range of knowledge and research experience was canvassed. A number, especially colleagues within the Housing Policy and Practice Unit, went further by commenting on drafts and proof reading the final versions of chapters. We would therefore acknowledge the invaluable assistance provided by Isobel Anderson, Nick Bailey, Alison Bowes, Angus Erskine and Jim Valentine. Particularly supportive comments and advice were given by both Duncan Sim and Mary Taylor.

Finally, can we thank Peter Williams, John Perry and Alan Dearling, for all the help, support and advice they gave throughout this venture. In particular, their comments on the first draft ensured the book was better focused to the practical needs of all researchers.

Douglas Robertson and Pat McLaughlin
University of Stirling
October, 1996

Introduction

This book is designed to be the essential guide for housing practitioners who wish to carry out a piece of research. The definition of research adopted is very catholic, encompassing the broad range of day-to-day tasks which are performed by all housing practioners. Research should not be solely viewed in 'academic' terms, where the task involves writing a thesis or dissertation, or being commissioned by government to evaluate a major housing policy innovation. Rather the research tasks addressed in this book involve the analysis and interpretation of information for the purposes of informing management change, encouraging the adoption of best practice, assessing performance in a variety of areas and enhancing staff development. Apart from these operational considerations, day-to-day research work within housing organisations also involves the production of a host of strategic information that is used to inform and justify future investment intentions or as an aid to planning a change of direction for the organisation. The target audience is, therefore, a broad church consisting of practitioners, students, researchers, and policy makers.

Over recent years there has also been an unprecedented growth in the market for housing research. With the emphasis of policy seeking to move local authorities from being direct providers of housing to that of 'enablers', there has been an associated growth in demand for monitoring and performance information as well as good quality policy research. The growth of new housing providers, within the housing association and private sectors, and their increasingly business-like orientation has also encouraged new research demands. All housing organisations are now expected to have a clear appreciation of their working environment through conducting tenant satisfaction surveys, local house condition surveys and, on occasions, tenant income surveys. Bids for capital resources now, given public expenditure constraints, require to be supported by a range of researched justifications outlining the impact such an investment would have. Amid all this change the student body has expanded greatly, reflecting the growing professionalisation of the housing sector. Both undergraduate and postgraduate housing courses typically demand a student project as a means of assessing the student's analytical and interpretative skills.

While the majority of this research work is still conducted 'in-house', there has been a growth in housing organisations commissioning research. More often than not, those managing such work are not research specialists, but practitioners with a specific interest in the commission. The book will be an invaluable tool for those charged with such a task as it provides the information necessary to assist them in the production of focused research briefs. Too often such commissions are not clearly thought through and, as a result, the resulting research report fails to address the key questions which the organisation wants answered. Those commissioning work need to have a working knowledge and understanding of the range of research methods available in order to draw up the brief and manage the resulting contract. Such knowledge is a prerequisite to ensuring the end product of this process is of use in addressing a specific practical issue. Further, only by better understanding the research process, in its entirety, can housing professionals be capable of evaluating the variety of research outputs which they encounter in the course of any working day.

The book is written in a style that makes it accessible to all users. It has three goals:

- firstly, to provide the basic information necessary to both understand and reflect upon the actual research process;
- secondly, to assist housing professionals understand the broad range of research literature currently available; and,
- thirdly, to enable the reader to use this knowledge to design and execute their own research work, and where necessary have the confidence to commission work from others.

Existing research books tend to emphasise either methods at the expense of practical issues, or vice versa. This book strives to strike a balance between methods and how they operate in practice. It seeks to discuss research issues in a way that encourages housing practitioners to think through research strategies, rather than to see them as a number of unconnected tasks. Recent examples of pertinent housing research are used to illustrate the key issues involved in using a specific research design.

To achieve these goals the book splits into three parts:

Part One sets the research issue in context. The four chapters explore the nature of housing research and its relationship to information. The basic concepts and procedures involved in planning a research design are outlined. This part also considers the development of housing research and how this activity has changed in response to the increasing demands of the housing profession. It is within this context that the crucial relationship between research and policy is considered.

Part Two contains nine chapters which consider the issues associated with a range of research methods. The emphasis here is on decision-making and thinking through the strengths and weaknesses of each approach, and their relationship to the overall research design. The uses of information technology in housing research are also discussed.

Part Three covers data management, the analysis of data and the presentation of findings. Consideration is given to the use and abuse of research findings. This is following by two chapters which focus on the the complex business of what to do with the data once it has been collected. Different research designs present the researcher with different interpretation issues. Spending time at the design stage working out exactly what outputs are expected from the project helps ensure that the key research objectives are kept clearly in mind. It also limits the likelihood of collecting unnecessary data.

Although there are many books available on various aspects of social research – from general introductions and practical step-by-step guides, to detailed explorations of specific approaches and methods – none deal with the issues as they relate to housing research. This book fills this gap, both by addressing housing research directly and by bringing together practical information on the key methods available to the housing researcher. Given the growing demands of housing organisations for both operational and strategic research information, as well as high quality evaluative research material, this book will prove to be a valuable addition to a surprisingly neglected area of housing literature.

PART ONE:
PREPARING THE GROUND

In order to build a house you first need draw up a plan which outlines your ideas and ambitions for that building. Having thought through what you want from the dwelling, and perhaps considered a number of different design solutions, you eventually opt for the optimal solution. This solution will then be constrained by time, money, and your own technical competence to carry out the work. It may be, however, that you opt to instruct an architect or engineer to assist you in developing the plan and managing the resulting construction phase. Another approach would be to opt for an architectural competition. To proceed with either a commission or a competition you would need to produce a brief, detailing your ambitions, so those responding can address your stated desires. Such a brief is also essential if you intend to carry out all the work yourself.

When on-site the eventual working plan may undergo revision and amendments. Design ambitions have a tendency to be revised in the light of pressing practical considerations. Door sizes may need to be amended in order to accommodate disabled access. The cost of certain items may be considered too expensive, and will require to be substituted for acceptable alternatives. Timescales may also have to alter. At the end of the day, the house that is eventually built will reflect the expertise of those involved with the project and their collective ability to accommodate a range of practical considerations. Housing research requires a similar blend of expertise, compromise and accommodation.

This book introduces you to research design through examining all aspects of the research process. Just as in planning a house, you need to have an appreciation of all the stages of construction and possible approaches available to tackling the project. Given this focus there is an expectation that you will read other books on methods, to gain a fuller understanding of the various approaches outlined here. The careful management of time, and ensuring the project is brought in within costs are critical considerations. You, therefore, need to ensure that your ambitions are adequately tailored to meet the constraints imposed by the available time and money. Again careful planning is critical in this regard.

Part One starts by considering the distinction between information and research, a distinction which is typically made on pragmatic grounds. Information is the building block of any research exercise. Yet, the fact that you have amassed a range of good quality information will not necessarily result in a good piece of research, just in the same way as a poor builder will not produce a good house from first rate materials. Information, or data, can never be a substitute for analysis and interpretation, the cornerstones of good research. Yet, without good information such analysis and interpretation is not feasible. Information monitoring involves reporting on figures and trends, to assist the operational management of organisations. Research, by contrast, is where this information, and data generated from other sources, is employed to either provide an interpretation of what is happening, or construct new arguments that will require further investigation. A key decision in any research exercise is deciding which problems can be investigated using existing information, and which will require the generation of new data. The first chapter, therefore, outlines the range of information used by housing organisations in their day-to-day work, and illustrates how such material is employed to address the broad range of research demands present within any housing organisation.

Having explored this range of information and research Chapter 2 goes on to examine the key phases of housing research to date. This chapter sets the book in context and shows how the policy focus has become stronger at a time when the task of conducting research has become a more universal phenomenon. From being a rare one-off activity, housing research is now a key component in the work of all housing bodies. Chapter 3 then goes on to consider issues associated with planning and designing research. Whether research is being carried out by yourself, or the work is being commissioned from consultants, the planning and design issues are the same. In order properly to manage your own research project, or that being carried out by consultants, you have to have a clear appreciation of the specific research question the study is to address and a good understanding of the various research methods that are being employed to explore that question. Such an understanding is invaluable in terms of ensuring the research achieves its stated objectives, and achieves them within a realistic timescale and within the cost estimate. Having outlined the various approaches to research design, the issue of research ethics is briefly touched upon. This introductory part concludes with Chapter 4 which considers the range of issues involved in commissioning research from external consultants. Central to this discussion is the significance of the research brief and the drawing up of an enforceable contract.

CHAPTER 1:
Using Information

Objectives of the Chapter

This chapter is designed to ensure that the reader:

- appreciates the distinction between information and research;

- recognises the central significance and importance of good information in conducting research work; and

- is aware of the wide ranging and growing information demands placed on housing organisations and how these relate to both information and research requirements.

The Relationship Between Information and Research

There is a distinction between collecting information and conducting research. Clearly while the two are interdependent, the collection of information does not, in itself, constitute research. Research is the systematic collection and interpretation of information applying a particular hypothesis or theory. Information, on the other hand, is any kind of data whether facts and/or figures. Housing staff frequently gather information but do not necessarily know how it will be subsequently used. Data collection is part of the research process, for without good information, analysis and interpretation are not feasible. To ensure good management practice housing organisations need to have good information. They also require to undertake, and be aware of developments in, housing research.

Within housing, there are a broad range of information requirements in order to carry out the range of day-to-day functions, whether operational or strategic. Within an operational context such information would include void periods, the number of allocations, specific waiting list details, property details in relation to size, amenities and services, arrears and bad debt levels. The range of financial information which informs both monthly cash flows and annual budgets is another useful source of operational data. To enable the execution of the various strategic functions, information could be required on house condition, current population profiles and future projections, as well as the previous investment patterns of a variety of housing providers. Information is also a prerequisite to meeting the broad range of public accountability requirements which pertain to most publicly funded housing bodies. Finally, as housing managers become more focused on developing a business culture within their organisations there has been a corresponding increase in information requirements necessary to satisfy, for example, performance monitoring in both an operational and strategic context (Catterick, 1994; Robertson and Bailey, 1994). This chapter will outline the range of information requirements which are common to all housing organisations and show how this material has been employed to produce the broad and varied range of housing research which is conducted day and daily within all housing organisations. The chapter is designed to illustrate the range and varied focus of what can be loosely termed housing research.

One of the most common problems in conducting research is locating information which is held in a format which suits your specific research requirements. A notable example is the fact that the Census does not hold data on actual income levels. The reason given is that including such a question could discourage respondents from completing the Census form. Researchers wanting to construct an income profile of a particular locality would, therefore, need to draw on other sources, or substitute proxies for income such as car ownership, or the proportion of the population in full-time work. The Census also contains information on socio-economic groups, which is constructed from information on employment type. Further, official information, or statistics, is more often than not held at a scale which is unhelpful to those interested in finding detailed local information. Official data on homelessness, or on council house sales for example, or on the use of improvement grants, is commonly held by local authority area. How this translates to the towns and cities within these administrative areas is rarely, if ever, provided.

The limitations inherent in certain types of information can also be a problem for individual housing organisations. For example, details about allocations may be held by area housing office, rather than by type of house or household, so any analysis of this data would not be helpful if you wanted better to understand particular household letting demand patterns. To conduct research on these topics you would have to find some other means of collecting the required information.

Operational Information

Monitoring

Measurement is critical to monitoring the performance of any housing organisation. It is crucial to achieving good operational management. Only by measurement can you decide whether the organisation is achieving its goals. Monitoring should cover all aspects of internal management. There is a vast array of information collected within all housing organisations to monitor day-to-day progress and overall performance. The analysis of this information helps inform most management decisions. Central considerations in this context revolve around performance and associated costs. There are, however, also issues of public accountability. Given that most housing organisations are in receipt of public funds there is a need to ensure probity at all levels within the organisation. Finally, monitoring also helps inform future strategic decisions.

At its most basic, operational systems should be capable of providing a range of information about the housing stock and the households resident within that stock. Such details are crucial when, for example, you plan to up-grade central heating systems. With such information you are able to isolate the properties which require the up-grade. From the household data, information could be generated which would help with access arrangements, such as telephone numbers. It is from this basic building block of information that a wide range of other pieces of data can be attached and then, subsequently generated, which helps inform the work of any housing organisation. Rent details can be added, and this can be analysed to see if particular types of property have different rent paying characteristics. Analysis from allocations may highlight high turnover in certain areas and time sheets on estate management may highlight heavier workloads. Good quality basic information analysed in particular ways could provide a clearer pattern of how particular neighbourhoods go into decline. If the information is held over a long period of time the pattern of change could be traced back to certain management decisions or broader changes that were occurring within the community or society in general.

The generation of monitoring information also helps inform the range of issues associated with performance measurement. To ensure the organisation is meeting its stated objectives, day-to-day performance in relation to a number of tasks is measured. One obvious means of measurement is cost, and this is still the main measure employed by most housing organisations, through the monitoring and reporting of cash flows and budgets. More recently some organisations have become concerned with generating more detailed cost analysis through the use of cost-centred accounting. The time taken to carry out specific tasks is measured via the completion of time sheets. By compiling this information the time taken and associated costs can be calculated. Again the operation of this type of approach requires planning and forethought to ensure that the information required can be easily provided. If time sheets are not thought through information can be lost. Yet, too high a level of sophistication might mitigate against the system, in that staff may find it impossible to fill in their time sheets.

Cash information may be useful to managers charged with bringing a service in on budget, but it does not provide a useful insight into the actual quality of service being provided. In property maintenance, for example, while you can measure spending against budget, and through cost-centred accounting, the execution of certain tasks can be more realistically costed. Neither approach provides an insight into the quality of the maintenance service being provided. To gain some insight into this aspect, a maintenance section might want to carry out a certain proportion of pre- and post-inspections for all repair work in a given period. They then might follow this up by asking the recipients of this service what they thought of current maintenance services and the quality of contractors being employed. Their views on the technical competence of the work may also be considered, but some people might not be in a position to offer a view. Only through analysing this range of information could you hope to get a broader appreciation of the cost and quality of service being provided. This base-line information could then be employed to both measure actual performance and set future targets for maintenance performance.

The work of the Priority Estates Project provides a useful illustration of the types of indicators that can be employed within housing organisations (Power, 1991; Gregory and White, 1993). In essence, housing management tasks can be broken down into various component parts, and then set against the constraints imposed by time, money and location. In pulling this type of analysis together you can attempt to compare the relative efficiency of different organisations. The Department of Environment (DoE) study into the quality and cost of housing management services concluded that while housing associations provided a better quality of service in certain areas, when compared with local authorities, particularly in relation to tenant participation, they questioned whether the differences in operating costs merited such a variation. (Centre for Housing Research, 1989). This study also stated that there were good and bad performers in both the housing association and local authority sectors, and that the type of organisation was not a determinant of overall performance. In a later study, which covered similar ground, the variation in performance was put down to the range of operating environments within which housing organisations function (Bines *et al*, 1993).

The above studies illustrate the fact that monitoring operates at a variety of different scales and is not just concerned with the performance of an individual housing organisation. Given the growing concern about affordability amongst housing associations, in part generated by a growing reliance on private finance to fund new housing developments, national monitoring systems were established to record a range of details about households entering the housing association sector. The Continuous Recording (CORE) system, and its Scottish equivalent SCORE, allowed housing associations both collectively and individually to keep track of the household and income characteristics of new tenants. This information was used to establish working measures of affordability for the movement as a whole. This, in turn, was used by the housing associations' respective national representative bodies to campaign for greater public, as opposed to private, funding in order to ensure the future affordability of housing developments.

Government, for its part, is keen to ensure that the national policy objectives it has set are being met. Take for example the government's long-standing policy ambition to revitalise the private rented sector. The Housing Act, 1988 and its Scottish equivalent, the Housing (Scotland) Act, 1988 were designed to de-regulate all new private lets, thus encouraging new investment in the private rented sector (PRS). Conducting research on the PRS has proved to be notoriously difficult given the small numbers involved when compared to other tenures. Such difficulties are further compounded by the dispersed nature of the stock. Identifying stock for survey purposes is always problematic and, as a result, is an expensive exercise. Thus, assessing whether or not the government's policy ambitions are being achieved has proved difficult. A recent innovative monitoring study has, in part, resolved some of these difficulties by recording changes in both the stock size and the rent levels charged through utilising landlords' newspaper adverts (Bailey, 1996). This information, which covers the four Scottish cities, is also available historically, given the data is derived from newspapers which are a key archive source. Analysis of this information has shown that while the supply of self contained private rented accommodation has expanded the rents charged, in real terms, have remained constant. At the same time the supply of bed-sit accommodation has declined.

Consumer Satisfaction

In line with the increased interest in improving overall performance there has been a marked growth in the number of local authorities and housing associations carrying out surveys of their tenants. Other factors which have contributed to this have been a developing interest in customer care policies; a desire to be more efficient given the tight financial environment in which most housing organisations now operate; and as a response to the Government's Citizen's Charter initiative. As noted above, certain aspects of performance measurement also require the type of user information which is generated through conducting tenant satisfaction surveys (Prescott-Clarke *et al*, 1993).

Such surveys attempt to gain an insight into tenants' views on a broad range of topics which could include rent levels, rent structures, the operation of the repairs service, the criteria used in the lettings policy and the operation of the local housing office. Within a development context it is not unusual to interview those who have recently moved into new or refurbished property to get user views on certain design solutions. What are tenants' opinions about overall space standards, for example, or the layout of kitchens and bathrooms, the ease of operation of the central heating system or the windows? User feedback is also common when certain design initiatives, such as the provision of disabled adaptions, have been employed. Such surveys can allow comparisons to be made with previous ones to see if there is the perception that the quality of service or the quality of the housing provided has improved through time. Comparisons can also be made between different areas to compare the performance of different local offices. Such comparisons would, however, have to acknowledge the different operating environments which might exist between local offices.

While it is common practice to conduct such studies on existing tenants, on certain occasions it may be helpful to gain information about those currently on the waiting list. Housing association studies on affordability have often attempted such a survey in order to gain an understanding of likely future tenant income profiles. These surveys have, however, proved to be difficult and expensive to execute given the time and effort needed to trace those on waiting lists. Similar difficulties have arisen when campaigning organisations have attempted to survey homeless people.

Feedback can be gleaned from issuing forms within the housing office. Use can also be made of short postal surveys, conducted either in-house or by independently commissioned survey. No matter which approach is adopted this type of work involves considerable time and effort to ensure good quality information is produced. To engage fully in this research process you need to have an understanding of the basic issues involved in questionnaire work. Measurement and sampling are covered in Chapters 6 and 7 respectively, while Chapter 8 considers questionnaires and Chapter 9 interviews.

Strategic Information

Housing Needs Assessment

At its most basic, strategic information is used to help inform investment decisions. Capital bids by local authorities through Housing Investment Plans (HIPs) – Housing Plans in Scotland – draw on a broad range of material to justify their case for consent to borrow capital resources. Typically these documents set the context within which the housing organisation is operating before making a case to fund particular projects. A similar pattern of investment justification has developed within the housing association sector. As the number of associations increase and resources become increasingly tight, there is a need to develop a more rational means of allocating resources. Resource allocation by government and its agencies can never be totally rational, given the broad range of views about what would constitute a rational housing solution. All investment decisions, therefore, represent a political compromise.

A key tool employed in this strategic context is the housing needs assessment. For a comprehensive discussion of this approach see van Zijl and David Couttie Associates Ltd (1993). This method, which draws on a broad range of information, seeks to illustrate what investment would be required to achieve a balance between the number of households and the stock of dwellings at a particular point in the future. In order to do this, estimates of current households need to be calculated, which include an allowance for concealed and overcrowded households. From this information, and making certain assumptions about what will influence local population growth, an estimate of future households is calculated. The resulting figure is then compared with the estimate for future stock which is calculated from existing stock figures, plus forecasts for completions less demolitions. By comparing future effective stock with the household projection, a surplus or shortfall of dwellings will be revealed. The next task is then to assess any surplus or shortfall in relation to both tenure and locations, or sub-markets. Again by making a variety of assumptions, figures can be further broken down by house size and type as well as by price and quality criteria.

There is a large amount of information required for this type of task, and it has to be available at a range of levels, both national and local. National data on topics such as households and tenure is readily available from official statistics, but it is often hard to get data at a regional or local level. It is also the case that attempting to disaggregate information is never as easy as it first seems. Census information is the key source in this type of work. Both household and tenure data is available from the 100 per cent survey, and changes through time can be calculated from one Census to another. There can be difficulties if the Census is getting out of date, but there are official projections available which attempt to update the basic household information. The Census, therefore, provides the starting point to which other data sources are added in order to produce an insight into the current housing and household pattern. Locally generated information on household formation rates and the pattern of in and out-migration are clearly crucial, as is data on births and deaths.

At one time house type information was well complemented by the Valuation Roll, which provided the basis for local taxation through the rating system. The demise of this useful local information source was a consequence of the introduction of the ill-fated Poll Tax. Now Valuation Roll information is solely of historic interest. Within Scotland the Register of Sasines can provide useful local information on house prices and the rate of transactions (Williams and Twine, 1991). Other sales information can be gleaned from the local authorities Right to Buy sales and those relating to any stock transfers. Information on recent new build housing would be held by the local planning department. Building Society house price data sets, the best known of which is provided by the Halifax, provide useful regional information on average price inflation or falls.

Complementary information, again typically at a regional level, is provided by the National On-line Manpower Information System, which provides data on local employment patterns. Other useful sources in this area are the Census of Employment and the Labour Force Survey. Actual income and earnings data, especially at a local scale, is more difficult to find. The range of issues associated with using official statistics is discussed in Chapter 5, while those relating to using documentary material are covered in Chapter 10.

Other useful sources are provided by local authority housing plans and checklists, the latter being the information specified by government for their own housing investment appraisal purposes. Locally-specific waiting and transfer list information is also helpful, although its validity as a measure of demand is highly questionable given the lack of updating such lists receive. Housing association annual returns and business plans are other useful resources, especially if they operate within a tightly defined geographic area. Sample surveys relating to specific aspects of local housing needs analysis can also be commissioned as a means of tracing past trends.

The types of issues these studies should examine relate to shortages and surpluses of particular house types, sizes or prices of dwellings. Consideration needs to be given to the concentrations of poor quality dwellings, and then some assessment of how these can be better used to help meet certain demands. Local house condition surveys are, therefore, a crucial information source in this context. Long queues in certain sectors are also an issue to focus on when examining waiting list data. High levels of dissatisfaction, as expressed through tenant surveys, property abandonment or high turnover rates are also a critical consideration. Frustrated housing choices, again revealed by surveys or other operational data, are a useful consideration.

Compiling the information is but one aspect of this work. Using the data to construct future projections and then attempting to synthesise the range of collected material is where research skills play a greater part. These are undoubtedly required when collecting the data, because the research method adopted to carry out the housing needs analysis has a clear bearing on the information that needs to be collected. These issues will be discussed in more detail in Chapter 3, which focuses on the issue of research design. To make any projections you need to assume the existence of certain conditions, and to be able to argue the case. This means being aware of alternative view points or perspectives and addressing these. Projection work, therefore, requires the ability to develop clear justifications, access to good quality data and a certain level of dexterity in data manipulation, guided by clear analytical skills.

In predicting, for example, the issues that will influence affordability, you need to make assumptions about the potential future growth in existing and new tenants' incomes. This will involve making assessments about the local labour market and longer-term changes in the welfare system. Consideration should also be made of the role of the market in both rented and owner-occupied housing to meet certain housing demands from this group. Understanding the way in which queuing systems for rented housing operate and the likely tenant profile this produces would be of relevance. Information on who currently lives in the social rented sector would also be of assistance. Consideration of special needs groups from the community care planning material would be pertinent, as would information on local homelessness. To undertake such analyses requires a good knowledge of both national and local housing issues and the economy as a whole. Being able to isolate a range of relevant data and have the capacity to interpret it in light of this broader knowledge is where the analytical skill comes in.

The main criticism of this approach to housing planning is that without the analytical skills it can end up being merely a mass data collection exercise which never moves beyond describing the range of assembled information. Data is not a substitute for analysis and interpretation. Yet, without good information analysis interpretation is not feasible. To try and synthesise the range of patterns that are present within the data is no easy task, but that, in essence, is what research is all about. Research is the systematic investigation of material in order to establish patterns and reach conclusions. More often than not such research raises a range of new questions which require systematic investigation.

Housing Systems Analysis

Housing systems analysis is seen as a development from the standard housing needs approach. The main differences are in respect of information and focus. Housing systems analysis has a greater demand for information and, therefore, requires greater analytical and interpretational skills. The focus is also different, in that it is used primarily by funders to provide a means of assessing competing bids by various housing providers, whether in the private or social rented sector, based on an assessment of local housing market functioning.

Scottish Homes, which has invested much time and effort in developing this approach to resource allocation, has broad funding powers encompassing both private developers and housing associations. Once the wide range of information is collected, which typically encompasses more than one local authority area, it is analysed to highlight what investment decisions would produce a better functioning local housing market. Housing systems analysis, as with housing needs analysis, has both an information and research capacity. It is designed to be used as a planning, monitoring and evaluation tool. As it is designed to improve understanding of how particular housing markets operate, in the long run, it should provide the means to assess the impact of specific investment decisions within that market area. As with housing needs analysis, the detailing and description of information has proved easier to achieve than its subsequent interpretation. Consequently, its potential as a tool for impact analysis has still to be proven, and in the interim other approaches are employed.

Cost-Benefit Analysis and Option Appraisal

Cost-benefit analysis is a technique which is employed to assess the worth, in financial terms, of a particular development. Option appraisal is used as a means of selecting a preferred approach which best achieves the stated ambitions of a funding organisation. A range of justifications can be made in support of any housing investment decision and in a climate where public expenditure is tight such justifications have become a prerequisite to securing funding. Most capital bids to fund a specific housing development list an array of potential spin-offs or impacts. These need to be examined by funding bodies who have their own invest objectives. In agreeing to fund a particular project some assessment of the potential spin-offs has to be made. That said, once the decision has been made it is rare for these justifications to be systematically appraised. Only on large scale, or innovative projects is some form of appraisal or evaluative study conducted. In discussing the changing nature of welfare provision in Britain, Hills (1991, 6), makes the observation that public policy is more concerned with, "... *'throughputs' (number of operations carried out or length of waiting lists) or 'outputs' (number of houses built) resulting from public spending, rather than on ... 'outcomes.'*"

Cost-benefit analysis was a key component in helping to resolve major planning decisions about roads, airports and other infra-structure projects throughout the 1960s and 1970s. It has only rarely been employed in the housing arena. The central consideration in this approach is to cost the range of benefits and disadvantages of any development going ahead, as a means of aiding the decision-making process. Unfortunately, breaking everything down into costs is no easy task. For instance, how do you price the amenity value of a wood scheduled for redevelopment? It is also the case that different people put different values on different components parts of any development. Current disputes over the development of new motorways or by-passes illustrates this only too clearly. As a result, the differences in interpretation have invariably to be resolved at a planning inquiry where an independent appraisal of various claims is attempted.

In the case of option appraisal the project's potential funders are encouraged to examine the scheme against their stated corporate objectives. The results of this appraisal are then compared with other competing proposals and an investment decision, or priority, is established between these various projects. Option appraisal is a planning tool which allows funders to look at the range of investment choices available, at one point in time, and at the range of policy instruments they have available to meet their objectives. The guiding principal behind option appraisal is that information is used intelligently to help make decisions. It is also the case that any decision is not solely based on cost, although this clearly plays a significant role. The prime consideration is to achieve good 'value for money'. That said, the previous comments about the role of political considerations in any investment decision are still very pertinent. What this method attempts to challenge is the dominance of administrative criteria in the decision-making process. For example, it may be better to redevelop an area but, due to the lack of spending in the rehabilitation budget, this solution is all that is on offer. The use of option appraisal is widely encouraged by government and its agencies, but it does not appear to have wide currency, and where it has been attempted it has not always been to best effect.

Scottish Homes, in developing a new grant to enable private developers to provide low-cost home ownership, insisted that their local offices employed option appraisal on each scheme seeking funding. This option appraisal process has a rigid points system which awards scores for specific attributes of the scheme. The final score is then compared to a ranking system which is designed to measure externalities, or spin-offs. A recent evaluation of the operation of the Gro-Grant scheme discovered that there were only limited attempts at conducting this option appraisal scheme, and where it was attempted, the approach was cursory at best (Kintrea *et al*, 1996).

Evaluative studies are the main means of tracing any post-development spin-offs. These types of studies also review policy and practice issues in relation to outcomes. Such studies are the mainstay of housing research whether conducted at a national or local scale. Government departments and agencies are charged with providing evaluations of innovation in practice. Hence, the strong policy focus of so much government sponsored research. The previously mentioned Centre for Housing Research (1989) study, which compared the performance of different housing organisations, was a classic piece of government sponsored evaluative research. Given the operational focus of so much local housing research, a similar focus prevails. Academic housing research organisations are also very closely tied into this applied area, given their close ties with practice and their teaching focus on the professional housing diploma. As a result, much housing research tends to be applied and retrospective in nature.

Evaluating the worth of different projects or management approaches to particular tasks and problems is fundamental to all housing organisations. There has been much emphasis placed on the need to ensure that all public bodies become thinking, rather than reactive organisations. To achieve such status any organisation needs to have access to good quality information. At the same time, it needs to have the resources to manage, analyse and interpret this information. Interpretation is the real skill, for this requires you to draw on a wide body of knowledge to offer meaning.

Summary

The critical consideration in relation to all information gathering exercises is its collection and subsequent management. For this to be successful it is vital that those collecting the information are made aware of what use will be made of the data by others. It is also the case that those who want to measure a particular aspect of organisational performance, whether at the micro or macro level, are clear about the type of information they require. Too often not enough thought goes into these issues and the monitoring or evaluation ambitions of a whole host of organisations are undermined by the inadequacies of the available material. The reverse is also true, in that on occasions too much information is generated and it is difficult to make much sense of what is happening.

There is a close link between good information, good management and good research. While the majority of monitoring work involves reporting on figures or trends, research is where the information and data generated from other sources is used to either interpret what is happening, or formulate arguments which will require to be tested further. Both monitoring and research, therefore, inform day-to-day management and management practice in a broader sense. Clearly, the dividing line between information and research is a grey area. Much monitoring could be considered research, and much which purports to be research is in fact information monitoring. The crucial point, however, is that the information requirements of all housing organisations have increased dramatically over the last few years, and that with these increasing demands more and more staff are being expected to have a working knowledge of data collection, its analysis and interpretation. As performance culture, for example, develops within housing organisations there will be a greater call on generating and interpreting meaningful management information. The collection, management and analysis of such information is a 'nuts and bolts' issue for any IT system. The issue of data management is considered in Chapter 14, while Chapter 13 touches on a number of relevant issues in regard to use of IT. The actual analysis and interpretation of information, based around a particular research design, is the key task addressed by this book.

Further Reading

Catterick, P., (1994), *Business Planning for Housing*. Coventry: Chartered Institute of Housing.

Gregory, S., and White, J., (1991), *Frontline Housing Management: A Summary of Progress on 21 PEP Partnership Projects*. London: Priority Estates Project Ltd.

Prescott-Clarke, P., Atkins, J., and Clemens, S., (1993), *Tenant Feedback: A Step-by-Step Guide to Tenant Satisfaction Surveys*. London: HMSO.

Power, A., (1991), *Housing Management: A Guide to Quality and Creativity*. Harlow: Longman.

van Zijl, V., and David Couttie Associates Ltd, (1993), *A Guide to Local Housing Needs Assessment*. Coventry: Chartered Institute of Housing.

CHAPTER 2:
The Development of Housing Research

Objectives of the Chapter

This chapter is designed to ensure that the reader:

- understands the distinction between 'pure' theoretical research and 'applied' policy research;

- appreciates the five distinct developmental phases of housing research;

- recognises the central significance and importance of 'policy relevance' to the development of housing research; and

- is alert to the constraints and limitations of conducting research within an active policy arena.

The Focus of Research

There are essentially two types of research. While the first, often termed 'pure' or theoretical research, is designed to extend knowledge for understanding, the second, termed 'applied' or policy research aims to provide knowledge for action (Majchrzak, 1984). Theoretical research is concerned primarily with causal processes and explanations. The factors considered are frequently abstract or theoretical constructs and the intended audience is mainly academics. Policy research, by contrast, works from the basis that it is better to change the world, than to understand it (Hakim, 1987). Given this broader remit, policy research encompasses theoretical work, at one end of the spectrum, and essentially descriptive studies at the other. What unifies this field is its operational focus. The intended audience is practitioners such as policy makers, decision-takers, pressure groups, managers of organisations or specific client groups.

The distinction, however, between 'pure' theoretical research and 'applied' policy research is not clear. Developments in theory can have a marked impact on how we view certain policy areas. Theoretical debates, which emanate from post-modernist concepts such as globalisation and de-industrialisation, have a clear impact upon policy discussions about the need to restructure welfare provision. This in turn impacts upon housing, given its key welfare role, and brings a broader understanding of the forces which act to residualise certain parts of public sector housing. Policy is always framed within a particular theoretical construct. That said, operational considerations ensure that policy research focuses on practical solutions to the problems of run-down estates, whether through capital investment in physical re-structuring or via the promotion of community self help measures. Theoretical studies would tend to explain why this physical and social deterioration occurred.

In terms of other distinctions Hakim (1987) notes that while theoretical research typically occurs within a distinct academic discipline, policy research is multi-disciplinary. As such it has a tendency to draw upon a range of academic disciples. Policy research also has a tendency to be multi-dimensional (Majchrzak, 1984). This means that a range of methods is used in the average study in order to produce a rounded and balanced picture of the topic. Hakim (1987) feels that this is a function of the interests of the audiences for such studies and the broad interests of funders.

Policy research can either focus on providing an explanation or understanding of problems. There is, therefore, a focus upon consequences: the desire to find the one variable that explains a particular pattern. This invariably gives way to multi-variable explanations. Alternatively, policy research can be used to evaluate the outcomes or impacts of particular policies or programmes. Within policy research it is critical to prove that something did, or did not happen, before going on to provide possible explanations. To get to that point requires much defining, description, and measuring. Policy research can also generate statistical material in order to substantiate the existence of certain relationships. Statistical significance is not, however, the same as practical significance. This is essentially a matter of judgement that cannot be determined mechanically by statistical techniques (Morrison and Henkel, 1970).

What is Housing Research?

What exactly is housing research? In the first place, the study of housing is essentially a component of social science research which covers the 'scientific' study of social conditions and problems. This type of research has a long history, starting with the public health campaigns of the 1840s. A certain element of housing research specific to the physical condition of property would, however, be classified under a technical heading. The term 'scientific study' is used to distinguish research from unstructured, or random enquiry. To qualify as research any study should have a defined purpose, be related to relevant theories and existing knowledge and be systematic and representative in its collection of data.

Housing research, as with social science as a whole, tends to be an applied interdisciplinary field drawing upon theory which comes from a number of disciplines such as sociology, geography, economics or psychology. Quantitative methods, encompassing numeric measurement and statistics to prove assumptions, also have a key role to play within housing research. More recently qualitative methods, which involve drawing assumptions from the basis of observation, have taken on a growing prominence. Housing research overall is best treated within the context of social policy, as the long term concern of most types of housing research focuses on the social consequences of the decisions made about the provision and management of housing.

Before tracing the development of housing research some consideration should be given to whether research can be what is termed 'value free'. This term implies that the researcher has a responsibility to ensure that they conduct any study in a neutral fashion, ensuring that the study is not contaminated by personal bias or ideology. There is a clear expectation that the results of research should be objective: not unduly biased by the views of the researcher or the organisation funding the study. There is a counter view which argues that 'value free' research is utopian and, therefore, quite unrealistic. Clearly the beliefs and attitudes of the researcher cannot be eliminated and will have an influence upon their research. After all, such beliefs and attitudes help to determine the choice of subject and the subsequent adoption of a specific research method. It is also inevitable that those commissioning the research are subject to similar influences. The old adage *"who pays the piper calls the tune"*, has a clear bearing in this regard. The counter argument to this, from proponents of 'value free' research is that the selection of topic is 'value relevant', both to your values and/or the values of the funders. Such 'value relevance' should not be confused with trying to achieve 'value free' research. Those that argue against the 'value free' perspective adopt a 'reflexive' position, in that they state clearly their ideology and thinking, and in doing so send clear warning signals to the reader that this piece of work has been influenced in this particular way. Both perspectives clearly see the dangers of bias negating the value of research; where they differ is in approach. In conducting or considering any particular piece of research you clearly need to be aware of these influences. In research work it is essential that you try and ensure such influences do not unduly bias the results of the study. Aspects of this issue are explored further in Chapters 3 and 14.

Styles of Housing Research

Bulmer (1978) provides a useful classification which helps relate housing research to the body of social policy research. This work suggests that there are five distinct styles of housing research, which should be thought of as a continuum, although the distinctions are not always particularly clear cut.

Basic Social Science

This is concerned with advancing knowledge, whether through theory building and testing or the satisfaction of curiosity. Such inquiry is not designed to have a specific practical use, although it may do so. A useful example of this style of research are the theories of sectoral urban growth developed by American sociologists working in Chicago in the 1930s (Burgess *et al*, 1925; and Hoyt, 1939).

Strategic Social Science

This type of research is grounded within an academic discipline, or subject, but is orientated towards a specific problem which has arisen in the society. The research does not aim to prescribe a solution to that problem, but rather explains the nature of the problem. An example of this style of research is the various metropolitan studies conducted to gain a better understanding the operation of housing markets (Maclennan *et al*, 1992).

Specific Problem Orientated Research

This is carried out for a customer – typically central or local government – who provides a specification for the research. The results of the research are designed to help deal with a practical operational problem. There are numerous examples: housing co-operative research for Scottish Office (Clapham and Kintrea, 1994); race and housing research for Glasgow District Council (Bowes and Sim, 1995); homeless research for the DoE (Anderson, Kemp and Quilgars, 1993); and housing management practice research in England and Wales, again for the DoE (Bines *et al*, 1993).

Action Research

In contrast, action research involves research as part of a programme of planned social change. Such investigation is designed to study the effects of change as it happens. It also has a tendency to directly involve those being studied in the design of the research. Such participative research can offer a degree of dialogue between actors and observers. Other versions include what is termed 'practitioner research', which is small scale research carried out by practitioners into their own practice. This is essentially a reflective activity designed to inform practice. A good example of action research is provided by the Priority Estate Project (PEP) (Power, 1987).

Intelligence and Monitoring

This refers to the collection of demographic, economic and social statistics in repositories of data that may be drawn upon, with expert guidance, by politicians and administrators to help formulate policy. Example of intelligence and monitoring are provided by the Housing Condition Survey, Halifax House Price Index, or the Scottish Office Housing Statistics.

While the above classification provides a useful explanatory tool, in the real world there are not always clear cut distinctions between these different types of research product. Further, most housing research fits within one of two categories, namely specific problem orientated research and intelligence and monitoring.

How did Housing Research Develop?

The development of housing research can be broken down into five distinct phases, although the dates provided are more arbitrary than fixed. Such a categorisation draws from previous work carried out by Hole (1972; 1979). While each of these phases contains a unique element, or focus, each builds upon what went before. It is also noticeable that the research requirements for individual housing organisations have grown markedly, especially over the last decade. As a result, the scale or focus of housing research has progressively become narrower with a strong management emphasis on information and monitoring. Interestingly, certain of the key research issues of earlier periods, particularly the relationship between poor housing and health, have re-emerged after a significant absence. It is also the case that, over the period, housing research *per se* has become more policy focused.

Phase One: 1840-1940

Research has always played a key role in promoting legislative changes within housing. Social reform, in particular, focused upon the link between public health, poverty and housing, a concern exemplified in the work of Edwin Chadwick, the famous nineteenth century Poor Law Commissioner. Later both Charles Booth, a shipping magnate and building entrepreneur, and Seebohm Rowntree, a chocolate manufacturer, began to show how social enquiry, in addressing similar issues, could become more reliable and accurate through the use of systematic and well designed research methods (Englander and O'Day, 1995). It is also worth noting that these two figures were among the founding figures of British sociology. This interest in housing issues also ties into the philanthropic housing developments of the late nineteenth century such as William Lever's Port Sunlight, George Cadbury's Bournville, and Joseph Rowntree's New Earswick (Burnett, 1986). Other bodies promoting similar housing research were the churches, the old regulators of social policy, and municipal government, the new regulators and the child of Chadwick's reforms. Scottish examples of such studies are provided by the *Report of Commission of the Housing of the Poor* (Presbytery of Glasgow, 1898) and the later *Glasgow Municipal Commission on the Housing of the Poor* (Glasgow Municipal Commission, 1904). Municipal commissions were appointed by the relevant municipal corporation, and mirrored the parliamentary equivalent, the Royal Commission.

Government itself, through the Royal Commission mechanism, conducted most of the major housing studies of this period. The *Report of the Royal Commission on Housing* of 1884-85, resulted in legislation (initially for London boroughs but was later extended) enabling local authorities to buy land for long term improvement plans. It also insisted that half those displaced by demolitions were rehoused. The later 1890 Act also made it possible for local authorities to provide housing for sale, and to carry out improvements to existing stock. Similar powers had been granted to Glasgow in the 1860s to facilitate the renewal of the city's medieval slums (Worsdall, 1979). The view that private enterprise could not provide adequate housing for the working class developed during the First World War. In Scotland this view was articulated by another Royal Commission Report, this time covering the housing of the working classes (Royal Commission, 1917). The resulting report mirrored the conclusion drawn by the Advisory Housing Panel, in which Seebohm Rowntree is credited with making the case to Government that a direct subsidy to enable council house construction was essential if housing conditions in Britain were to improve (Burnett, 1986). This in turn fed directly into the famous Tudor Walters Report of 1918, which set down the technical standards expected of inter-war local authority housing. This work was also strongly influenced by the newly established planning profession, and its crusading desire to develop the 'Garden City' philosophy of Ebenezer Howard and Raymond Unwin.

Government's role in housing provision steadily increased during the inter-war period, as was the case with other social services. As a consequence of this Royal Commission antecedence, the housing research conducted in this period focused almost exclusively upon the technical and financial issues associated with the provision of new housing. A major area of activity was the production of technical manuals to assist local authorities in the construction of council houses. There was also an ongoing interest in monitoring the operation of the Rent Restrictions Acts, which were initially introduced in response to the Glasgow Rent Strikes of 1915 (Melling, 1983). Rent restrictions were reviewed five times between 1919 and 1945 and these reviews encouraged a research interest in the topic (Holmans, 1987). Government continued to review general housing conditions, with useful examples of such studies provided within the *Report of the Committee of Scottish Health Services* (Scottish Health Services Committee, 1936), and a study of rural housing in Scotland (SHAC,1937).

At local, as opposed to a national, level there were a number of interesting studies which outlined the future direction of housing policy. Both medical officers of health and city engineers conducted extensive statistical and monitoring work identifying slums and associated overcrowding. The development of major slum clearance programmes, under the auspices of public health legislation, in the late 1930s was interrupted by the outbreak of the Second World War. An interesting study from this period, which goes beyond the basic statistical analysis of the slums, is the Manchester University Settlement (1945) examination of the slum district of Ancoats. This study, a precursor to the famous Young and Wilmott (1957) study of Bethnal Green in London's East End, not only provided a detailed social and physical survey of this district but also attempted to assess the impact rehousing would have on the slum residents. Unfortunately, the follow up study had to be abandoned due to the war. Malpass (1995) details other similar studies in both Bristol and London (Young, 1934 and Durant, 1939). Housing was inextricably linked to the issue of public health throughout this early period and the research output reflects this focus.

Phase Two: 1940-1960

After the war there was considerable research activity in the fields of education, health and social welfare services, but little was directly conducted on housing. Donnison (1967) has argued that this was because the housing problem was seen as being so obvious and urgent that there was little need to identify and research the topic. The only major Government investment in housing research in this period was confined to the creation of the Building Research Establishment (BRE), which focused on the technical problems associated with mass house construction. Government housing research continued to be focused on an essentially technical agenda and was dominated by the production of the Ministry of Health's Housing Manual. A similar pattern was pursued in Scotland, but there was also evidence of a widening research agenda.

The establishment, in the years immediately prior to the war, of the Scottish Housing Advisory Committee (SHAC) as a Scottish Office standing committee ensured a regular stream of technical publications such a *Planning Our New Homes* (1945), *Modernising Our Homes* (1947) and the *Distribution of New Houses in Scotland* (1947). While in large part technical documents, they do articulate a broadening housing agenda; interspersed within the manuals outlining best design practice, the specific housing requirements of particular special needs groups such as the elderly, single people and 'spinsters' were detailed and argued.

Following the cessation of hostilities in 1945, there was a second major burst of re-construction activity. Not only was there a need to address the physical damage inflicted upon London, Coventry, Hull, Plymouth and Clydebank, but there was also a desire to pursue a housing reconstruction agenda which encompassed more than just public health considerations. Rather there was a clear economic and social agenda underpinning the ambitions of the immediate post-war planning exercises. These ambitions are best articulated in the regional plans which emanated from the Barlow Commission Report of 1940. Patrick Abercrombie produced a significant number of these documents, most notably the London and Clyde Valley Plans (Abercrombie, 1945; Abercrombie and Matthew, 1949). These land use and economic planning documents tended to view housing as an adjunct of economic restructuring (Robertson, 1996). A central feature of Abercrombie's work was the creation of New Towns on green field sites with fresh air, gardens and open space. Town planning in Britain had long held a strong anti-city agenda. Only through good housing, in clean environments, could the people be expected to reach their potential. Victorian industrial environments were to be cleared away. The research focus was, therefore, upon calculating population densities and generating complementary and supportive statistics to facilitate this economic and social welfare programme. At the same time, there was still a strong public health focus, through slum clearance and the provision of new family accommodation.

Few academics were interested in this applied research field. Notable exceptions were Bowley's (1945) study of housing policy and that of Jarmain (1948) on council rent structures. The afore-mentioned study on Bethnal Green by Young and Wilmott (1957) became a seminal work in sociology. Interestingly, a very similar type of study conducted in the slum districts of Liverpool did not gain the same prominence (Liverpool University, 1954). Housing research was perceived as a civil service function, rather than that of the academic. At the more local level there was nothing that would resemble a comprehensive housing service. Housing, as noted above, was largely a technical production issue involving architects, engineers and the sanitary department. The slums were to come down and new homes were to be put up. It was purely a technical issue. Local government generally employed few professional research staff, and as a consequence, policy was made solely on the basis of local politics and adhering to centrally generated guidance. Housing need was measured either through housing waiting lists, levels of overcrowding, or by the incidence of insanitary housing. Construction targets and ensuring particular density levels acted as the key planning tool. When Donnison (1967: 351) published his famous book *The Government of Housing*, the first comprehensive coverage of the broad range of housing issues he noted in the introduction that, "... *less than a decade ago the Ministry of Housing and Local Government did virtually no research on the issues covered in this book*".

Phase Three: 1960-1974

As the massive problem of slum clearance began to decline, both in a physical and political sense, the housing research agenda began to broaden out. There was also a change in general political climate. The Conservative Government brought Macmillan in to refocus the Party, after the Suez fiasco. Macmillan, who was probably Britain's most successful Housing Minister if construction figures are used as the measure, was determined to extricate government as far as possible from its responsibilities within the field of housing (Merrett, 1979). The mass provision of housing by the State was also being challenged by the incoming Labour Government of 1964. While Labour was ideologically committed to the provision of public housing, it also appreciated the need to adopt a more pluralist agenda which demanded a broader and better thought through housing policy. Labour, at the same time, also brought with it a crucial change in the climate for research, because as a Government it stressed the need to base policies on a considered evaluation of the facts. Harold Wilson, the Prime Minister, was critical in this regard, given his background as an Oxford scholar and a Civil Service statistician (Pimlott, 1992). Housing research flourished in the Wilson years.

During this period housing gained academic acceptance through the work of two key social scientists Richard Titmuss and Peter Townsend. Nevitt's (1966) seminal examination of housing finance is also worthy of a mention in this regard. The influence of town planner Barry Cullingworth was also considerable. Cullingworth later became the first Director of the Planning Exchange in Glasgow, a key library and information source for planning and housing issues. Specific academic studies in the field of housing became focused at the Centre for Urban and Regional Studies (CURS), which was established at the University of Birmingham in 1967. The fact that the Rowntree Trust started funding social policy research in the late 1950s, with a particular emphasis upon housing undoubtedly contributed to growing academic interest in the topic.

The 1960s also saw the creation of a nucleus of social research within central government. Both the Centre for Environmental Studies (CES), under David Donnison, and Social and Community Planning Research (SCPR) were effectively government 'think tanks'. They had been created by the Wilson Government to come forward with a broad range of social policy suggestions.

These dramatic changes in relation to housing research were, in part, a direct response to the conclusions of the Milner Holland Committee's Report of 1965 which demanded more systematic information collection:

> "We hope that strong and capably manned intelligence units will be maintained, both at central and local levels, able to collect and collate information on housing from all angles and employing skills in the economic, sociological, statistical and demographic fields."

Interestingly, this committee was established to examine housing conditions in Greater London, following the publicity given to notorious landlord Perec Rachman after the Profumo Affair of 1963 (MHLG, 1965; Short, 1982).

At the local government level, from the basis of his work in trying to move housing and planning policy away from clearance and towards a greater reliance upon improvement, Cullingworth (1966: 193) argued, that:

> "...our review of current local policies convinces us that local authorities need to have a clearer, deeper and more detailed understanding of the housing situation in their areas. The development of national information has had a major impact on national policy-formulation. But we no longer have a national housing problem...We have a larger number of local housing problems of great variety. It is therefore essential that local policies be based on a well-informed understanding of the problems of individual areas and the context in which they arise. Our first recommendation is, therefore, that local authorities should take steps to ensure that they are better informed of the housing situation of their areas."

This shift in emphasis was also encouraged on economic grounds given the impact redevelopment expenditure was having on Britain's fragile economy. The social impacts of clearance remained a central research theme, as illustrated by the work of Dennis (1970). Similar social impacts were also shown to exist with the supposedly more social sensitive improvement policy, as revealed in the informative and insightful study on Newcastle by Gower Davies (1972).

Phase Four: 1974-1980

The development of localised research and information capacity was greatly assisted by local government re-organisation in 1974, for England and Wales, and 1975 in Scotland. With the creation of larger local government units, local authorities were financially able to create in-house research capacity dedicated to addressing local housing issues. While this was initially focused within planning departments, some of the larger housing authorities started to establish distinct research and information sections.

Government legislation emanating from the Green Paper on Housing (HMSO, 1977) helped this development along, given that local authorities were now expected to produce, on a regular basis, a Housing Investment Plan (HIP). The equivalent within Scotland was called a Housing Plan. Comprehensive housing planning, at a district scale, is still a central feature of local authority resource planning, given these documents act as resource bids to central government. This practice, advocated by Cullingworth, became an accepted tool of local authority housing practice. This development also brought with it a burgeoning of local authority commissioned research work in the housing field. Contract housing research was now a discernable market for academics and consultants alike. The School of Advanced Urban Studies (SAUS, now the School for Policy Studies) at the University of Bristol was established in 1974 and built a reputation in this area along with CURS. It is also worth noting that SAUS was originally a joint venture between the University of Bristol and the Department of the Environment, again illustrating the close relationship between housing research and policy, whether at a local or central government level.

Also at this time the Government sponsored a series of research projects which were designed to explore the causes of urban decline. The results of the work by the various Community Development Projects (CDP), funded by the Home Office, and the Inner Area Studies (IAS) funded by the DoE, challenged many of the preconceptions held about Britain's 'Urban Crisis' (Lawless, 1981). To an extent, these studies helped ensure that renewal projects became to be seen primarily as local economic ventures rather than redistributive mechanisms for poorer households.

Phase Five: 1980 – 2000

This later period is of considerable interest as it represents in large part the current pattern of housing research. It started dramatically enough with the Government closing the Centre for Environmental Studies (CES) in the early 1980s, as part of the Conservative Government's rationalisation of quangos. This closure was also symbolic, in that it signalled a separation between government and semi-independent 'think tanks'. The move was also a clear statement that Government was less enthralled by research, for research's sake. By this stage both the CDP and IAS had run their course.

That said, the demands of both national and local housing policy generated a considerable amount of direct housing research, funded through the DoE, the Scottish and Welsh Offices, The Housing Corporation, Scottish Homes, Tai Cymru, the Northern Ireland Housing Executive and many local housing authorities. Add to this the funding made available via the Economic and Social Research Council (ESRC), the Joseph Rowntree Foundation (JRF) and other charities. So despite this inauspicious start, housing research has boomed under the Conservatives. Academic research, in particular, has boomed. Most notable was the designation by the ESRC in 1984 of a research centre dedicated to housing, the Centre for Housing Research (now Centre for Housing Research and Urban Studies). An interdisciplinary team of housing researchers was assembled under the housing economist Professor Duncan Maclennan. A Chair of Housing Policy was also created in York, funded by the Joseph Rowntree Foundation in 1989, building on similar development at both Cardiff under Professor Peter Williams and Salford by Professor Valerie Karn. Since then a number of other academic institutions which run housing courses have created Chairs in housing, thus heightening the academic profile of the subject. The development of professional housing courses was inextricably linked to this development, and this perhaps accounts for the strong policy focus of so much current housing research work.

Part of this growth and the strong policy emphasis of the research work was also a consequence of the adoption of new procurement methods for all government services. Competitive tendering became the order of the day in all fields of public policy, and with it competition was generated for research funds. By testing the market, a broader variety of researchers came into being, both from academic institutions and the growing body of private housing consultants.

Perhaps the key player in heightening the profile of housing policy research has been the Joseph Rowntree Foundation, under the Directorship of Richard Best. Best, who was previously the Director of the National Federation of Housing Associations, wished to promote a new welfare agenda programme, in which housing is seen as a key part of the wider welfare system. Much of the Foundation's focus on housing has been in the field of housing finance, with a particular emphasis on reforming the current iniquitous housing finance system. Owner occupation and the impact it has on the national economy has been another theme, as has the need to generate a new accord with private renting. The Foundation has a clear agenda of influencing policy, so it operates, in part, as a pressure group on government, suggesting amendments rather than radical reform in the main. The JRF has been able to fund this substantial research programme because of its windfall when Rowntree was taken over by the multi-national Nestlé Corporation in 1985.

In terms of more local scale research the growing pluralisation of provision within the rented sector, largely through the expansion of housing associations, has brought with it a further growth in the demand for research and information from within the housing profession. As noted in the previous chapter, local authorities and housing associations, in order to justify future funding and be seen to be accountable, need to produce far more information. Both types of organisation have to create and appraise the implications of a wide range of new information provided by business plans, community care plans, housing plans, local investment plans, housing agency investment plans and the like. Further, with the development of a more business orientated focus in the provision of rented housing there are growing demands for information which can measure on-going performance, to ensure stated management targets are being achieved. This information explosion, aided and abetted by the recent developments in information technology, has blurred the dividing line between research, market research, monitoring and information. These developments have also raised questions about the value of such work; the assembly of information to justify a capital investment, for example, may not produce a rational response by funders who have a broad range of suppliers to service and a set of overriding political imperatives to meet. This in turn can create conflict internally with housing organisations about the value and purpose of the research function.

Housing research has become far more ubiquitous during this later period. It has also become very much more policy focused, moving down from providing research that informs the national policy agenda to providing a similar capacity at a local operational scale. Research, in one sense, could now be viewed as the servant of the housing profession, and the wider housing 'policy community'. Rather than helping to set policy agendas, however, in its new operational role research rarely challenges the constraints in which policy operates. There has also been a move away from researching issues to evaluating operations. Such an approach certainly has merit, in better informing those working in housing, but it also has clear limitations. This issue is explored in more detail in the following two sub-sections.

The Future Housing Research Agenda

Housing has always had a very close relationship with policy evaluation and development. As noted above, this tendency has become more pronounced in recent years. Housing can never be an academic discipline in its own right. It is a multi-disciplinary field that draws from other fields. According to Malpass (1995), over the last twenty years, housing has moved from an academic grounding in sociology and social policy, towards that of geography and economics. This in part reflects the broader political changes within society which have occurred over this period. At the same time there is an implication that the theoretical basis of housing research has weakened as a consequence of its policy focus and the dominance of contract research. Yet, it should also be recognised that the theoretical underpinning of housing research has always been weak. Both sociology and social policy within Britain has a strong empirical, rather than theoretical tradition.

Housing has become something of an intellectual ghetto: in developing a distinct profile it has cut itself off from the debates and discussions in other academic disciplines. With the development of housing studies, being closely tied to the growing professionalisation of housing training, this isolation was perhaps not surprising. Yet, with the creation of more multi-disciplinary arenas, in which housing research is discussed, a re-think as to the direction of housing research is likely to occur. Forums such as the Housing Studies Association and the European Network of Housing Researchers (ENHR) involve researchers who work within a stronger theoretical tradition which has helped illustrate the limitations of 'policy relevant' studies. This interplay has also created an interest in explaining the broad similarities in both circumstance and policy response which were evident within different European countries.

Trying to find better theoretical frameworks to explain the broader changes occurring within society, and the bearing these have on housing, is clearly a function of academic study. But academic study should also provide the policy community with considered research on which they can amend or create policy responses. This after all is a key function of academic work. Central government perceives a problem and commissions research to understand that problem. In the light of these findings policy is either changed or reviewed. Opposition political parties commission research with a view to challenging established policy and practice, or to bring forward new polices should they gain power. The Conservatives' Housing Act, 1980, which introduced the Right to Buy is perhaps the classic example of this later approach. Similar practices exist within local government. Research has to examine and evaluate existing practices in order to refine and improve public policy. Yet, it should also contribute to a wider understanding of the various changes occurring within society. The problem at present is that there is not a proper balance between these two positions.

Entering the Policy Arena: a Cautionary Note

As central and local government fund the vast bulk of housing research, they effectively set the research agenda. These bodies decide what is to be investigated and in what way the resulting research is to be carried out (see Appendix One for a list of key commissioners and/or funders of housing research). Problems or issues, therefore, must loom large to be deemed suitable for further investigation. Clearly, it would be naive to ignore the party political and organisational interests which have a bearing on all research. Again this relates to the earlier discussion of 'value free' research. Politics will always have a bearing on the execution of research.

Pressure groups use research as a means to heighten the profile of particular issues. They use their limited resources to try and bring issues onto the agenda. Recent examples are provided by CHAR: the Housing Campaign for Single People, on *'Care in the Community for Single Homeless'*, Shelter Scotland's attempt to highlight the need for a Rough Sleepers Initiative within Scotland, or their work detailing the high incidence of permanent caravan residence in certain rural areas. It is also worth bearing in mind that one of the most significant pieces of housing legislation in the last 30 years, the Housing (Homeless Persons) Act, 1977, was introduced by Stephen Ross, the Liberal MP for the Isle of Wight, on the back of substantial voluntary sector research. The Joseph Rowntree Foundation also acts as a pressure group, trying to influence government to adopt its vision of a new welfare accommodation. At the same time, it has to accept the broad policy tramlines set by the current government.

Central and local government research, therefore, falls into two distinct camps:

1. 'Rational': the policy maker decides what extra information is needed to assist in the formulation of policy.

2.   'Political': the policy maker either perceives certain problems and wants research to find the answer, or is inclined to a certain course of action and wants research to reinforce this, or asks for research to cool the issue off.

Policy makers seek information from a broad variety of sources, which collectively have been termed a policy network or community (Marsh and Rhodes, 1992). Researchers are not the exclusive source of advice on policy matters, nor should they be. Any policy debate will involve a number of overlapping and interlocking social groups. These debates also depend very heavily upon personal, often accidental, contacts with a range of sponsors who may themselves play little or no part in the actual policy debate. The policy reaction to research may not, therefore, bear a close relationship to the either the conclusions or recommendations. This is one of the major drawbacks of operating within an active and ever changing policy area, whether at a national or local scale.

CHAPTER 3:
Research Project Planning and Design

Objectives of the Chapter

This chapter is designed to ensure that the reader:

- **understands the various stages involved in planning and designing a research project;**

- **fully appreciates the significance of each individual element of the research process; and**

- **is able to use this approach to evaluate published research findings.**

Introduction

The secret of good research, as with many other activities, lies in its conception, good planning and careful preparation. Conception is about being able to define, and then refine the specific research question which you want to address. Planning involves matching the demands of the research question to the available resources, in the best way possible. Essentially, planning represents a compromise between idealism and pragmatism: between the aims of the research and the resources available. There is, for example, no point in planning a comprehensive study of council house sales, if you have neither the time nor resources to carry the task through. Preparation is about ensuring that a range of practical difficulties, which could impact on the execution of the research project, are considered and addressed as part of the planning process. In a study of council house sales, gaining access to sales records, or gaining access to purchasers for interview purposes, would have to be considered carefully. The phrase 'research design' attempts to cover the whole process of planning, execution, recording, reporting and dissemination. This is a process which should always be thought of as a whole, but all too often is not. The chapter is, therefore, designed to assist in understanding the complete process that is research. Consistency between these various stages is critical to achieving quality research.

By working through the research process, as outlined in Figure 3.1, you will also be able to assess the significance of the research findings produced by others. This will enable you to see the relevance of other pieces of research, or to your own job, or to the work carried out by your organisation, or to your own studies.

This chapter considers the various aspects of planning and design that have to be addressed when carrying out your own, individual piece of research. The assumption here is that you will be conducting your own small scale research project, by yourself. However, if you are charged with the task of commissioning a major study, you will need to go through exactly the same planning and design exercise. A full consideration of all aspects of such a project will still be required, even although you will not be carrying out the research work. Both understanding and appreciating the various aspects of any research project is critical not only in terms of designing an appropriate brief for the work, but also to ensure adequate project management. The following chapter provides a more detailed discussion of research commissioning and contract management. The issue of deciding whether a particular study should be commissioned, as opposed to being carried out by yourself, is considered within this chapter.

The Research Process

Conducting research is a dynamic process, which can be represented schematically as a continuum of seven distinct stages. Each stage in this planning and design process will be outlined within this chapter. Detailed consideration of each stage is the focus of the subsequent chapters in this book.

Classifying each of these stages in this manner implies that planning and design are both sequential and straightforward. This is unfortunately not the case. The progression from one stage to next is not necessary linear. In practice, the process usually involves many revisions in the light of the decisions that are made at a later stage in the process. If particular assumptions about how to conduct the study prove invalid, then a revised or completely new approach will have to be planned and designed. Alternatively, you may be forced to revise the specific focus of the research question if the initial research method proves unworkable. Research and design, depending on the nature of the specific research question, can become a very complicated exercise. It can, on occasions, resemble the old adage of one step forward and two steps back. Hence the significance of properly acknowledging the importance of the feedback mechanisms detailed in Figure 3.1. Revisions and a certain amount of repetition may seem tedious at times but planning and design is the critical investment in any piece of research. If properly executed, it can save considerable amounts of time, money, and personal energy as the project progresses. Just as important is the fact that by working through the various issues thrown up by planning and design, the quality of the final research product should be greatly enhanced. Research tends to be a more messy exercise than this logical and rational sequence implies. It is, however, important to try and work in a logical and sequential manner bearing in mind the knock-on consequences of all decisions made within the planning frame.

Figure 3.1: The Research Process

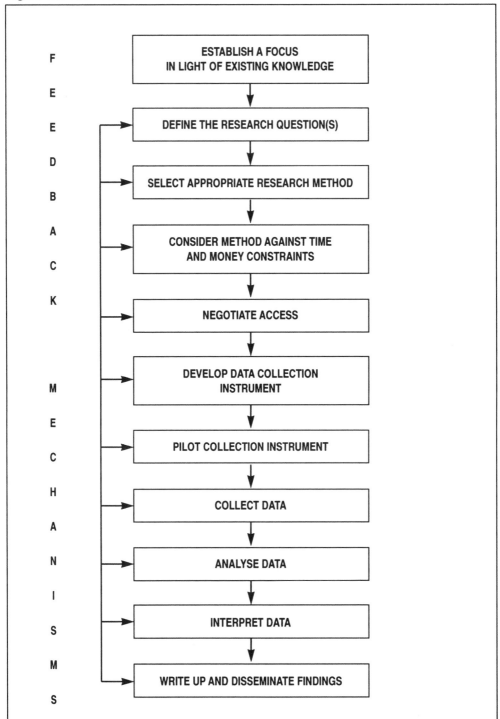

Establishing a Focus

Research design typically starts with either a specific query or problem. It can also arise as the result of a request to conduct a specific piece of research. The particular research agenda will, therefore, reflect either your own personal interest, or that of your employers. It is also likely that the topic or issues under consideration will be broadly defined.

The first step in the research process is to establish a clear focus for the research; to identify a general problem area which would benefit from further study. For example, you might be interested in a number of issues: the problem of youth homelessness; customer satisfaction with the housing service provided by your housing association; or assessing the impact of a specific government policy decision such as the Right to Buy. While all these topics are worthy of further investigation, let's examine one in greater detail.

The implications of council house sales have been an important strand of housing research over the last decade (Foulis, 1985; Forrest and Murie, 1988; Murie and Wang, 1992; Twine and Williams, 1993; Cole and Furbey, 1994; Rosenburg, 1995). Selecting this broad topic is a beginning, but more thought is needed to establish a focus. What aspects of council house sales do you wish to explore? One focus would be to examine the importance of stock type in determining the actual rate of sales. Another dimension might be the financial implications of council house sales, in terms of capital and revenue expenditure, for the local authority. The implications of council house sales for the management of mixed tenure estates could offer another avenue of enquiry. Or perhaps you would like to adopt an international perspective, in which you conduct a review of the various policy and fiscal environments which encourage the privatisation of public sector housing within Europe. Spending time thinking about the broad range of issues or problems associated with your chosen topic and supporting this process through appropriate reading, will help you to narrow the focus of your study. Clearly, you cannot research all aspects of your chosen topic; that is not the object of the exercise. Rather what you should be trying to do is to narrow the scope of the study to the point where it can be expressed clearly in a sentence or two. Once this is accomplished you will be ready to move on to the next stage of the process.

At this initial focusing stage you should also give some thought to the practicalities of conducting the proposed research. You might start by asking yourself whether your chosen topic is really worth the effort? Does it justify being a one-off research study, or is it more appropriate to instigate a monitoring study? Has the subject already been comprehensively studied, or is new research justified? What would your project add to the existing literature? Who, for example, might be interested in the results; are they likely to have any important professional, ethical, policy or scientific implications? What resources, in terms of time, finance and any other support can you reasonably expect to call upon? Given such a level of support, can the proposed research be tackled adequately? If the study has to be scaled down will it still be capable of answering the question or questions which interest you? These are just some of the practical questions that need to be addressed right from the start. At this preliminary stage, attempting to clarify the nature and objective of the research is the critical issue. Too often those conducting research have clearly thought through both the approach and methods they intend to employ, but have been unable to establish a clear focus for their study.

Defining the Research Question

The research question should provide a brief, clear and realistic statement of the purpose of the research. It is the foundation on which you build your study: it helps you decide upon the sort of data you will require, how best to collect that data and the particular focus analysis will take.

Having narrowed down your general focus, as described above, and supporting this exercise through a preliminary literature review (see Chapter 5 for more details), you should be in a position to formulate a specific research question, or set of questions. This might be in the form of a question, such as, *"... what have the financial implications of the Right to Buy been, both in capital and revenue terms, for English metropolitan local authorities?"* Or it could be a simple statement of intent, *"The Right to Buy has radically altered the financial position of metropolitan local authorities."* Either approach will suffice, for the important thing is that you have a clear statement of the problem which identifies (i) the focus of the research – the dependent variable, financial changes caused by the Right to Buy, and (ii) the limits of the population – council house sales within metropolitan local authorities.

Many research projects, however, begin not with a question, but with an hypothesis; a tentative statement in the form of an assumption which is subject to verification or refutation through subsequent research. An hypothesis can be written as a simple declarative statement; for example, *"... the financial position of metropolitan local authorities in England has been seriously undermined by the financial repercussions of the Right to Buy legislation."* Alternatively, such a hypothesis can be expressed in a slightly different way, namely, *"... council house sales, as exercised through the Right to Buy legislation, act to further residualise and polarise the remaining council housing stock by seriously weakening its financial basis."*

Formulating a research question, however phrased, also involves defining concepts and variables. In the above examples, the concepts 'privatisation', 'residualisation' and 'polarisation', are all pertinent to such a study. Each would require a working definition which is coherent, unambiguous, and is framed in a way that makes it possible to measure the relevant variables. As part of working through such definitions you would need to consider what data would be required to adequately explore these concepts. It is crucial that such definitional aspects of any study are carefully thought through, given that they have a major bearing on how you subsequently structure the study.

Selecting an Appropriate Research Method

Once you are clear about what it is you want to study, the next stage is to think about the research strategy; how you will go about carrying out the investigation needed to answer the research question. In an ideal world you would choose the research method that was most appropriate to the particular research question; that is you would select a strategy that seemed most likely to address the question, and thus produce the answer in most detail. In practice, however, research design is often influenced by practical considerations. Certain methods might be ruled out because they are too costly, or because there is not sufficient time available to carry them out.

The best method for studying the financial impacts of council house sales within metropolitan authorities, for example, might be to conduct a detailed financial appraisal of all metropolitan authorities over a ten year period. This strategy might have to be ruled out simply because of the high costs involved. To get round this resource difficulty, you might opt to conduct three or four case studies over a five year period. Bear in mind, however, that in scaling down the study, there may be implications for the quality of the research and its ability to explain broader patterns.

Resource considerations, however, are not always paramount in selecting a particular strategy. You may choose a strategy because it is one you know particularly well and are confident in using; it may simply be the only method you feel you have any knowledge of, particularly if you are new to research. The danger here is that by restricting your choice of research method, you also influence the definition of the research problem. Again this can have a bearing on the quality and applicability of the subsequent research output.

Part Two of this book is designed to give you an idea of the range of research methods that can be employed. But before you get to that stage both the purpose of research and the likely availability of data should have been considered, as these have a clear bearing on the eventual method or methods selected. The purpose and eventual use of research should govern the research method. Bear in mind that it is all too easy to become immersed in the details of research methods and, in the process, lose sight of the initial aim of the study.

Negotiating and Maintaining Access

Getting access to the research site, or the people you particularly want to see can take time, so it is best to begin the process as early as possible. When you are clear about the research problem, the method, and about what you want from individuals and/or organisations, that is the time to start negotiating access.

The first task is to find out exactly with whom you need to negotiate. Many organisations, especially departments of local and central government, have structures in place for dealing with requests for research access. You may have to get permission from senior managers, administrators, or other so-called 'gatekeepers', before you can approach the individuals you want to participate in the study. Negotiating access through gatekeepers can present problems. In the first place, as gatekeepers act on the management's behalf, there is always a danger that your research may be identified with the direct interests of management. That is not always helpful, and you always need to make it clear, when introducing the research to any respondent, that you act independently. The second problem concerns the gatekeeper's ability to control what aspects of the organisation, or which individuals you eventually meet.

The detailed negotiation of access will of course differ from one research project to another. Whether you have to negotiate through gatekeepers or can deal directly with respondents, there are four main points on which you will have to satisfy any prospective respondent. These are:

- Significance – illustrating why the research is important.

- Reason for choice – why is co-operation being sought from this particular person or organisation, and what do they gain by taking part: put simply, what's in it for them.
- Purpose – what sort of information are you seeking, why do you want it, and what use will be made of it.
- Confidentiality – what degree of confidentiality, or anonymity, can you guarantee respondents?

You might also think about exactly what it is you are asking of the respondents. The acid test, as Bell (1994) suggests should be whether:

> *"If at some time in the future colleagues or other research workers ask you for cooperation with a project, would you be willing to give the same amount of time and effort as you are asking for yourself? If not, perhaps you are asking too much!"*

(Bell, 1994, 47)

If access is eventually granted, and there is no guarantee that it will be, there may be conditions attached. Gatekeepers, for example, might demand the right to vet any material prior to publication. In such instances, you will have to decide whether these conditions are acceptable and consistent with the aims of the research. While you might be happy enough for the gatekeepers to check a draft of the report for factual errors, granting them an effective veto over publication may be harder to accommodate.

Requesting access can sometimes be a straightforward once only activity. Postal questionnaires, for example, typically address the issues of access, through either an introduction or via a covering letter. In other situations, and particularly where observational methods are being used, access is something that has not only to be negotiated, but also requires to be maintained over a period of time. Ultimately, however, all researchers depend on the good will of those who are the subjects of their studies. Access is a privilege, not a right, and all researchers have an obligation to do everything they can to maintain the goodwill of respondents throughout the course of any study.

Developing the Data Collection Instrument

The next task is to develop a research instrument. Some of the most commonly used quantitative and qualitative instruments are discussed in Part Two of this book. In some cases, you may be lucky enough to find an existing instrument that can be readily modified to suit your specific purpose. For example, in carrying out a customer satisfaction survey, you might simply collect a number of customer satisfaction questionnaires which have been employed by other housing organisations, and then use that information to construct one for yourself. Or you may have to start from scratch and develop a research instrument of your own. In either case you should take the time to 'pilot' properly the data collection instrument to ensure it fits the purpose. In the case of a questionnaire, for example, a pilot study should help clarify any ambiguities in the wording of questions, identify gaps in the information being sought, and finally give you an indication of how long it will take a respondent to complete the questionnaire. If you are using a more qualitative method, such as an open-ended interview, a pilot may be of less importance, since the instrument can be developed or adapted as the study proceeds.

Where questionnaires or structured interviews are being used the feedback that comes from a pilot may prevent costly errors. Bear in mind, a misunderstood question will negate all the answers to a given item.

In deciding upon the research instrument you should also consider what sort of analysis is likely to be employed on the data once it has been collected. This might appear to be putting the 'cart before the horse', but if you don't give some thought to the analysis of data at this stage you may find that you have omitted to ask an important question, or that the question has been asked in an inappropriate manner. This is of critical importance if you intend to conduct cross tabulations, that is comparing one set of answers to another, to see if a particular pattern arises.

Data Collection

The next step is conducting the actual fieldwork – going out and collecting the required data. This is the public face of research. Most people equate research with the ubiquitous market researcher who operates in town centres, clipboard in hand, asking questions of unsuspecting passers-by. What your actual fieldwork consists of, will, of course, depend upon the specific research topic and the research instruments used. In most cases there will be a range of existing data sources, either existing locally or nationally, which should shed some light on certain aspects of your chosen topic. Again the existence of such material stresses the importance of conducting a rigorous planning and design phase. There can be nothing more disheartening than finding out that the data you have been trying to generate is readily available from an easily accessible public record.

Analysing the Data

Having collected the data you require, by whatever method, the next stage is to organise and analyse this material. The data may have to be organised, classified and collated, in preparation for subsequent analysis. With the recent advances in computers it is likely that this technology will be employed in the data analysis task. This is true not only of quantitative data – such as that derived from questionnaires – but also for qualitative information which is increasingly being stored and analysed using computer software. Chapter 13 examines the broadening application of information technology within housing research.

Organising the data is, however, important for other reasons. In the first place, it enables you to get a better overall feel for the data. This is important because it can help you to avoid making ill-informed judgements based on partial information or atypical incidents. Secondly, it makes your research material accessible to others who might want to conduct a secondary analysis. Remember, data collection is an expensive exercise, and if it can be reworked for related or other purposes the output from fixed costs is enhanced.

Interpreting Data

As was mentioned earlier, the framework of the data analysis should have already been well thought through, if not actually decided at an earlier stage. The important point here is to leave enough time not merely for the mechanical operation of data analysis *per se* – often affectionately referred to as 'number crunching' – but rather for the time consuming task of interpreting the findings. It is the interpretational skills that are central to research. However, without good quality data focused on particular topics interpretation becomes a very difficult task. Findings need to be tied back to the original research question and the theoretical concepts which informed the research. In formulating the argument it is critical that the conclusions are justified from the data. This is the basic error of so much research. To avoid this problem you should always ask yourself what conclusions are justified from the evidence that has been obtained, and how does this relate back to the research question?

Writing up and Disseminating the Findings

This stage, as detailed in Figure 3.1, is somewhat misleading, since it gives the impression that writing up can be safely left to the end of the research process. That is certainly not the case. Whether you are doing research for your employer or for yourself, you should always plan to be writing earlier drafts as each stage in the research process proceeds.

The essential element in writing an effective research report is being clear about your audience and communicating to them the main features and the significance of the research findings. It helps, therefore, to know something about the likely users of the research, right from the outset. How you envisage the research being used, and by whom, may influence the presentation and the dissemination of the findings.

Mention of writing up the research also raises the question of dissemination. You should not plan research on the assumption that no one will read the finished account. Even if all you intend to produce is a research report you should give some thought to promoting its wider dissemination. Such dissemination may take a number of forms. There will be the ubiquitous research report of course, or, if you are doing the research as part of an academic qualification, the bound dissertation. Beyond this, you might consider publishing a research article in an academic or professional journal such as *Housing, Voluntary Housing* or *Roof* (for a fuller listing of various housing related publications see Appendix Two). Alternatively, your work could end up as a chapter in an edited book. However, to achieve that end, the editor of the book has to have heard of your work. One means of getting this wider audience is to use your research findings as the basis of a conference presentation. It pays to think about such matters, at the planning stage, as some forms of dissemination can take a considerable amount of time to come to fruition.

Another consideration is how to inform the respondents about the outcome of the research. It may be that you have agreed some sort of feedback as part of the access negotiating process: as noted above it is quite common for gatekeepers to insist upon the right to comment on a draft of any material prior to publication. Even when they do not, it is good manners as well as good PR to ask them to comment on matters of accuracy. The gatekeepers are not the only ones involved in the research, and you cannot assume that they will copy your report to other respondents. A short article for the in-house newsletter, if there is one, might well prove a more effective method of dissemination. The point is that, if possible, you should try to make the findings of your research accessible to all those who gave you the information in the first place. As with all aspects of research process, the time involved in dissemination needs to be built into the research plan.

Timetabling and Project Management

> "Alice sighed wearily. 'I think you might do something better with the time,' she said, 'than waste it in asking riddles that have no answers.'
>
> 'If you knew Time as well as I do,' said the Hatter, 'you wouldn't talk about wasting it. It's him.'
>
> 'I don't know what you mean,' said Alice.
>
> 'Of course you don't!' the Hatter said ... 'I dare say you never even spoke to time!'
>
> 'Perhaps not,' Alice cautiously replied, 'but I know I have to beat time when I learn music.'
>
> 'Ah! That accounts for it,' said the Hatter, 'he won't stand beating. Now, if you only kept on good terms with him, he'd do almost anything you liked with the clock ..."

(Carroll, 1865, 97)

Keeping on good terms with time is one of the most demanding tasks in conducting research. There are always deadlines which have to be met and there never seems to be enough time to do everything that has to be accomplished. Careful planning can help greatly, especially if you follow three simple rules:

- Construct a realistic timetable and stick to it. Make sure you know when the various deadlines fall, what has to be done to meet them, and what time you really do have available. Never work on the basis of an idealised notion of the time you would like to have.
- Plan a sensible sequence of activities. Think carefully about when things have to be done. There will be occasions, for example, when it is more efficient to be doing two or more tasks at the same time. Pay particular attention to external factors that put constraints on your schedule. If you want to interview housing association committee members, for example, you may be limited to the dates of committee meetings, and in some cases that may be just six a year.
- Monitor progress and don't let the schedule drift too much. That said, your timetable cannot be set in stone. Sometimes it will be impossible to stick to the schedule and you will have to make alterations to cope with delays, or unforeseen events. Nevertheless, try and deal with any problems as soon as possible and restructure your timetable, rather than let it drift.

Displaying your timetable graphically makes it is easier to monitor actual progress. Using a bar chart such as the one in Figure 3.2, for example, can tell you at a glance what stage the research should be at, what progress has been made to date, and what remains to be achieved.

Figure 3.2: An Example of a Research Timetable

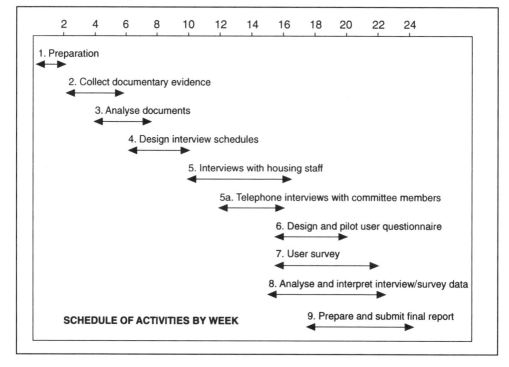

Appraising Existing Research

Much of what has been outlined in relation to research planning and design can also be employed in appraising existing research material, whether published or not. Bear in mind that research appraisal is also an integral part of the research planning process. Such a skill is also helpful in your day-to-day work, as research output could have a direct bearing on your work, or the work of your organisation. Appraisal can be broken down into four distinct stages, each of which contains a set of pertinent questions. Through answering these questions you gain a clearer insight into the true value of the research.

Clarifying the nature of the research

- Who did the research and when?
- What were the objectives of the research and why are the issues raised at this particular point in time?
- Who wanted to know the answer?
- How were the results to be presented?

Deciding whether new research should be carried out

- Are there existing studies which could provide the required information, or could have served as a model?

- Was there other existing data that could be used?
- Was a special study needed, and if it was should this have been one-off research study or a monitoring exercise?

Deciding upon appropriate methods

- What methods were employed, and why?
- How well were the actual research methods applied?
- How were the results analysed?

The Argument

- Does the evidence and the argument presented justify the conclusions reached?

Using the same set of questions as a quality control mechanism as you work through your own work should ensure a sharper focus in the resulting work. Some of these questions should also be incorporated into your planning and design work, given they repeat many of the points raised above.

Commissioning Research or Doing it Yourself?

Until now the assumption has been that you will be doing your own small scale research, either in connection with your work or as part of a housing course. You may find, however, that some important issues arise which your organisation should have investigated, or evaluated, but without full-time research back-up, or greater experience on your part, such tasks will not be readily undertaken. If you can secure funding from your own organisation, then one option is to commission a contractor, such as a university department or private consultant, to conduct the research on your behalf. The other is to try and secure the necessary funding from a charitable trust or foundation, which specialises in housing research (see Appendix One). It is, however, important to bear in mind that although such organisations fund housing research in general, they may not be interested in your specific project. All trusts and foundations operate an agreed programme of research activity which reflects their particular priorities at that point in time.They are also keen to ensure that funded research has wide policy relevance. It is, therefore, crucial if you are thinking of going down this road, to obtain a copy of the various research programmes operated by such organisations. Details of how to apply for monies and the timescales which the organisations operate in respect of awarding funds are also provided and must be adhered to stringently.

Research projects vary, of course, but commissioning research typically involves a competition between two or more research contractors. The competition is based upon a research brief provided to the researcher by the customer, which is typically either a government department, a government agency, a local authority or a housing association. This brief should outline the nature of the research problem, why it is perceived to be important and what the customer expects from the contractor. It is, in effect, the brief which provides the basis for the contractors research planning and costing exercise. It is crucial, therefore, that the brief is comprehensive, clear and precise, and that the research objectives are feasible, within the time and financial constraints imposed on the proposed project. While it is usually open to the contractor to make their own recommendations in respect of research methods, it is always open to the customer to specify the preferred method in the brief. The brief should be the end result of a research planning and design exercise, as opposed to something cobbled together late on a Friday afternoon. If you should find yourself commissioning research, and having to write a research brief, you will find it useful to think through each of the planning stages in much the same way as you would have to if you were conducting the research yourself. The following chapter explores this theme in greater detail.

Further Reading

Bell, J., (1993), *Doing Your Research Project*, (Second Edition). Milton Keynes: OUP.

Berry, R., (1986), *How to Write a Research Paper,* (Second Edition), London: Pergamon.

Carroll, L., (1865), *Alice's Adventures in Wonderland*, London: Norton.

Phillips, E., and Pugh, D., (1987), *How to Get a PhD*. Buckingham: Open University Press.

CHAPTER 4:
Commissioning Research

Objectives of the Chapter

This chapter is designed to ensure that the reader:

- appreciates the range of issues associated with commissioning and managing contract research;

- understands the various elements which ensure the production of a well considered and professional research brief; and

- is aware of the various approaches that can be used to select a research contractor.

Introduction

The working assumption throughout this book is that you will be undertaking the research yourself, either alone or as part of a small group. There may be situations, however, when some or all of the research activities within your organisation will be contracted-out. Many organisations, including national and local government agencies, commission research, even when they have their own 'in-house' research staff. A recent survey of the research function within local government (Boddy and Snape, 1995) found that external researchers tended to be used when:

- the necessary substantive or methodological expertise was not available in-house;
- in-house staff could not complete the work within the allotted timescale;
- 'independent' analysis was required to lend greater weight and validity to the research findings (particularly in relation to jointly commissioned work, when having one of the organisations involved undertaking the research might be viewed as problematic);
- the research project involved large scale survey work and, therefore, requires more staff than are available in-house;
- the experience and reputation of a particular organisation or individual was sought to inform the research; and

- contracting-out of some or all of the in-house research function was a policy stance of the local authority or was seen as a more cost effective use of staff resources and facilities.

In practice, the choice will be determined by organisational policy, the nature of the research and, as always, by the available resources. Having regard to the possibility that you may find yourself in the position of commissioning rather than conducting research, this chapter will explore some of the issues involved. These include drawing up the research brief, finding a research contractor, and managing the resulting research project.

Before considering the details of commissioning it is worth noting that, to cover the high costs involved in funding research projects, organisations may opt to form partnerships with other interested parties. For example, a local authority and the housing associations operating within its geographic area may have a collective interest in the results of a local housing needs study. Similarly a group of local authorities and a government housing agency may wish to jointly commission a study into the application of community care policies. The issues involved are the same as commissioning any piece of research, the major difference is in relation to ensuring that all parties feel they have ownership of the study. This relates not only to drawing up the brief but to the subsequent management of the contract. While on paper achieving such accommodation can appear easy, competing organisational interests and priorities can result in much tension. That said, spreading the cost of research, while at the same time ensuring the results of the study reach a wider audience, is a strategy well worth pursuing.

One other means of covering the cost of research is to draw up a proposal, which in effect is a research brief, and try and get either a charitable trust or another interested body to fund the work. (A list of possible funders/commissioners of research are provided in Appendix One). Current details of how to apply for funding from such bodies are usually readily available from each one on request.

Drawing up the Research Brief

Designing the research brief is the most important part of the commissioning process: it needs to be well thought out, detailed, clear, and practical. If this is not the case, the research objectives may not be realised and valuable time and money will be wasted. The brief itself is similar to the research plan discussed in the previous chapter, except that in this case you must specify even more carefully and clearly what the contractor is being asked to do. The first step, therefore, is to be clear about the purpose of the proposed research. This involves you in focusing the research question as discussed in the previous chapter.

Unlike your own project, the ideas for commissioned research will more often than not come from people who have little or no direct involvement with the study; from local government officials, departmental heads, or councillors. Such groups may be more interested in policy making than in the 'nitty-gritty' of research design. Ideas for research projects that have originated in this way have a tendency to be presented in rather vague terms. Before you can begin the task of drawing up a research brief, therefore, you will have to translate these imprecise, contradictory or loaded ideas into a meaningful and viable research question(s).

At this early stage you should always try to consult with others who might have an interest in the area being investigated, or who may become potential end users of the research findings. For example, if you were proposing to commission a survey of customer satisfaction with housing services, you might find that another department such as cleansing, or building and works, would also like information or perhaps an input into the topic of customer satisfaction. Combining two surveys might be a more efficient and effective use of resources. At the very least, informing others of what is being planned should minimise future criticism that someone or some department was not properly informed.

The precise details of the research brief will vary from project to project and organisations may have their own particular house style. In general, however, a good research brief should contain detailed information on the following:

The Background

The background to the project, including the policy context where appropriate, should be briefly outlined. The aims and objectives of the research should then be clearly stated. Aims can be described as the general goals to be achieved by the project. These aims have then to be translated into objectives which describe specific activities to be undertaken in order to answer the research question. In thinking about the aims and objectives, indeed in thinking about all aspects of the project, it is important that you are realistic about what can be expected within time and financial constraints. Perhaps the most common mistake in research briefs and in the proposals that are submitted in response to them is underestimating the resources required to undertake the project.

The Research Design

The research brief should be comprehensive, but that does not imply that it needs be too tightly specified or inflexible. The question here is really about how much flexibility prospective researchers are to be allowed. Some researchers, of course, take the view that they are best placed to decide upon detailed design issues; that, *"... the researcher and only the researcher, should decide"* (Denzin, 1978, 331). Those commissioning the research may take the opposite stance. A more constructive approach would be to see research as a collaborative venture. Certainly you have to be clear about what you want and you may have an idea about how this might be achieved; but it is still possible, and desirable, to be flexible and allow the contractor to modify the design or to suggest alternative approaches to the research problem. You may need to allow more time at the start of the research development stage to work through the details of the project in this way. That said, you can also save a great deal of time by avoiding possible areas of conflict and confusion as the work progresses.

The Research Outputs

The outputs that the contractor will be expected to provide, such as reports and presentations, should be clearly specified within the brief. These expectations should be clarified at the commissioning stage because they may have cost implications and such information may be important to the researchers. For example, the researcher will want to know whether or not the research report will be published. Similarly, any restrictions that might be placed on reporting should be clearly spelt out within the brief.

The Timetable

The pressure on timescales is an increasingly important factor in all research. Organisations which commission research are, perhaps understandably, anxious to act on the findings. But there is a need to be realistic about timescales. It takes time to produce a good research brief, particularly where exploratory work is needed to decide upon the feasibility of the project and whether the necessary data is likely to be available. It also takes time for the contractors to prepare good quality proposals in response to the research brief. It takes time to properly scrutinise the bids and award the contract. Then there is the time taken by the selected contractor to conduct the research and to prepare reports and for other research outputs. Deadlines for interim and final reports need to properly acknowledge the requirements of the research, rather than the policy or financial imperatives. Too often, for example, research is commissioned in January with an expectation that it will be completed by the end of the financial year, that is by 31st March that year.

There can be no hard and fast rules about timescale. If tendering is being used, however, you will have to set aside sufficient time to conduct the tendering process to allow potential contractors to discuss the brief prior to submitting a bid and so on. Four to six weeks would be a reasonable timescale for most projects. On fairly small, straightforward projects a shorter timescale may be feasible, but you must be satisfied that the contractors will have sufficient time to put together a fully considered bid.

Management Arrangements

The contractual arrangements and conditions, including the arrangements for monitoring and supporting the project, should be clearly specified at the outset. You will want to monitor both the progress and the quality of work, to ensure that high standards are maintained throughout and that you get 'value for money'.

The precise arrangements for monitoring contracts will vary from project to project and from organisation to organisation. Most contract research of any size, however, will have a steering committee, or a small management group of some sort, which meets at regular intervals to review progress, sort out difficulties and provide support and advice on the implementation of the research. Membership of steering committees should be limited to a small number of people, typically no more than about six, who have some expertise in the area or who can facilitate the work of the project in some other way, most commonly in facilitating access. Such steering groups can also help in dissemination, a topic touched on in Chapter 15. The disadvantage, of course, is that steering committees involve time and other resources. If you require to establish such a management group remember that some provision will have to be made for this in designing and costing the project. Steering group approval of various stages of the research work can also impact on the project timescale if the steering committee fails to meet its deadlines.

If you have any concerns about the feasibility of a study, you may decide, in addition to the usual monitoring, to phase the contract. By separating out the distinct stages of the project, you have the option to terminate the contract at the end of a given stage, if results suggest there is only limited scope for further work. Phasing may also be useful when using new contractors for the first time, as it leaves you the option of employing a different contract researcher in the latter stages of the project should major problems arise.

Funding

You need to be aware of the likely cost of the proposed research and, just as important, of the budget available. Whether or not you include an indication of the funding available for the project in the research brief will be dependent on current practice within your organisation, and on the nature of the project. On the one hand, giving some indication of price may be expected to increase the prospect of getting comparable bids, leaving the quality of proposal as the main criterion for deciding a particular contractor. On the other hand, as a result of difficulties in estimating ranges of cost, it may artificially inflate or deflate costs. Some organisations take the view that it is more appropriate not to include funding information where the project can be clearly defined. This typically applies to work involving the use of standard methods. Where the possible methods are more open-ended, funding information may to be an essential part of the research brief.

The cost of any project will depend on such items as travel, staff costs, liaising with the research funders, preparing reports and other outputs such as giving presentations. It is difficult to make precise calculations, but it helps if you have some idea as to the likely range of costs. Even if you decide not to share this information in the research brief, you will need to have a good idea of the costs of the various elements to help you appraise rival bids.

Once you have completed the draft research brief it is useful to have someone with an interest in the topic area to comment on it, before it goes out to potential contractors. Often in being too close to a project topic, over a period of time, it is easy to miss some basic points or details. An example of a research brief is contained in Appendix Three.

Identifying Potential Contractors

Once you have drawn up the research brief, how then do you find a suitable contractor to carry out the research work for you? You might chose an academic institution such as a university housing department or a private consultancy. There are advantages and disadvantages to both, as Hakim (1987) points out:

> "The main advantages of university based research are that a greater depth of theoretical work will be brought into a project ... But because academics have competing teaching responsibilities, being in effect part-time researchers, the work may be subject to long delays, and the individualistic ethos of the academic community impedes team research... The main advantage of the research institute and of specialist agencies are that their full time research staff can complete studies more quickly, and they are able to retain a variety of specialist and general support staff who are needed only on an ad hoc basis

for particular aspects of a study – such as sampling experts, statisticians, data processors, or clerical support staff."

(Hakim, 1987, 168)

Most commissioned research, certainly most research of any size, is awarded using some form of competition. The advantages of the competitive process are that it (i) affords the widest choice from a range of expertise, including new potential contractors, (ii) helps prevent contractors and customers drifting into a cosy long-term relationship in which familiarity can breed, if not contempt, then staleness or complacency, and (iii) it helps ensure that the research is as cost-effective as possible. This last is an important consideration, particularly where accountability for public funds in involved. For this reason, tendering is the prescribed means of competition for the majority of public sector work.

When tendering, rival contractors are required to make sealed bids in response to precisely the same specification. The process is characterised by a high degree of confidentiality and a formal relationship between the buyer and the contractor. The research is awarded to the contractor who submits the lowest acceptable bid. This strict legalistic approach to tendering can be counter-productive in that it hinders effective discussion and gets in the way of researchers developing a real understanding of the research problem. In practice, then, the approach is often modified in some way, perhaps to encourage researchers to suggest alternative methods and/or to allow them to discuss the brief before submitting a bid. It is not uncommon for commissioners to get in touch with a number of potential research organisations prior to a specific topic being officially tendered. This allows these researchers to undertake some preliminary work prior to the tender being received.

The most straightforward way of ensuring fair competition is simply to advertise the project as widely as possible: any and all interested researchers can then apply. In this way, everyone gets an equal chance to enter and you can pick and choose at will. In practice, however, this sort of wide open competition may prove to be an expensive and unwieldy process for all concerned. You might attract a great deal of interest with your advertisement, which is good. Sorting through and making a selection from a large and varied number of rival bids will, however, take time and may not be as manageable in that you are not always familiar with the respondents track records. You should also take into account the possibility that some suitable researchers may be put off because they are not convinced that the cost and time involved in preparing a bid is justified by the chances of success.

Some public sector agencies tend to favour open competition, perhaps because it offers the most convenient way of ensuring that all researchers within their constituency of interest have access to funding. It is more usual, however, to restrict the numbers being invited to bid to a short list of suitable contractors. This form of restricted, or closed competition, may seem less democratic, but it is likely to be more efficient and cost-effective. A short list of potential contractors is usually drawn up in one of two ways:

- An open invitation may be issued to researchers to express an interest in a specific project, or a programme of research priorities. Researchers may be asked to provide a brief outline of their ideas and credentials to help with short listing. This keeps the work in the first stage to a minimum. Those short listed in stage one are then asked to submit more detailed bids for fuller consideration. This two stage competition also has the advantage of ensuring that the new contractors are not excluded from the bidding process.

- Alternatively, organisations and agencies which commission research on a fairly regular basis might build up a database of 'approved contractors'. The database might contain information about contractors' knowledge of research areas and/or particular types of survey; their technical or specialist qualifications; their ability to mount an effective field-force; and their credibility and reputation based on their performance on previous projects. This information can then be used as the basis for drawing up a short list of contractors who will be invited to bid for a given project.

Whatever method is used to identify a short list, it is best to keep the numbers invited to bid to a minimum. This usually means keeping the list down to six, or preferably fewer. Don't forget large numbers waste time as most contractors will be unsuccessful despite having spent time in preparing bids:

> *"The more players, and the more elaborate the process, the higher that cost will be. At 1994 prices it might cost a research supplier anything between £1,000 and £5,000 to submit a fully worked-out and costed proposal, depending on the nature of the project. Taking a mid-range cost of £3,000 this means that inviting four suppliers to compete would in gross terms absorb £12,000 of research resources; inviting 10 people would absorb £30,000 – of which nine-tenths would by definition be wasted."*

> (SRA, 1994, 11-12)

If you are new to commissioning research and you don't know the market, increasing the numbers invited to bid might seem like a safer option, but bear in mind that you will also be wasting your time in managing and evaluating the unsuccessful bids. If you don't know the market the best option is to get advice from someone, perhaps a more experienced colleague, who does.

Intellectual Property Rights

Similarly, avoid the temptation to use the competition as a means of trawling for ideas or alternative solutions to your specific research problem. There will be times of course when one or more of the rival competitors makes a suggestion which improves the research design; indeed suggestions and modifications to the brief are to be encouraged. Using such suggestions, however, may raise the question of intellectual property rights. If the originator of an idea is unsuccessful – and having a good idea does not guarantee success – who, then, owns the idea? Is it ethical to use an idea, by passing it on to the successful competitor, for example, without indemnifying the unsuccessful researcher for their contribution? There is no simple answer, but if you have a project in mind and you feel it is necessary to draw on the expertise of a number of researchers, you should consider buying consultancy time from these researchers before finalising the research brief.

Negotiated Contracts

Not all research projects go out to tender. There will be circumstances where it is not necessary and/or desirable. Where it is clear, for example, that only one contractor has the particular expertise or experience necessary to undertake the project, direct negotiation may be the preferred option. Direct negotiations may also be pursued where an academic institution or a research company has exclusive access or ownership of data or specialised facilities. With small scale projects, contracts worth less than about £10,000, the costs involved may also argue against tendering. In negotiating the price for a particular project, however, you might use costs from similar recent competitive projects as a 'benchmark' for negotiating costs.

Selecting the Contract Researcher

How do you choose the most appropriate researcher from amongst the bids you receive? In formal tendering the choice is apparently simple; you take the lowest bid. It may be unwise, however, to make the decision on cost considerations alone. The lowest bid may not be the most appropriate. There is always the possibility that a bid which is significantly lower than the others reflects not cost-efficiency so much as a misunderstanding of the research brief. If you are concerned that a bid is abnormally low, the resources detailed in the bid should be examined and re-examined carefully and then compared with the other proposals. If the bid is acceptable on quality grounds, the potential contractor could be asked about any serious discrepancies in the proposed resources and if satisfactory explanations are not forthcoming it is probably best to reject that bid.

In general, bids will be evaluated against a range of criteria which include competence, quality and imaginativeness, as well as cost. In considering a bid you should ask yourself the following questions:

- Does it demonstrate a clear understanding of the requirements of the project?
- Does it demonstrate the level of ability needed to undertake the analytical, technical and data handling aspects of the project?
- Does it comment constructively on any conceptual, methodological and/or data related problems that might be anticipated and on how these might be addressed?
- Are there suitably qualified and experienced staff available for all aspects of the project?
- Do the researchers seem prepared to work closely with you (and you with them)?
- Does the proposed timetable appear to be realistic and achievable?
- Are the costs, staffing and other resources clearly specified and adequate?
- Do the researchers appear likely to produce high quality results and be able to present and communicate findings clearly and succinctly?
- Does the proposal conform to the Chartered Institute of Housing's Code of Conduct?

If in doubt about a researcher's suitability, ask for and take up references and ask for examples of previous research reports. In some cases you may decide to interview the prospective contractors, perhaps to clarify some aspect of the design. Such interviews should only be conducted when the contractor has a reasonable prospect of being awarded the contract. If you intend to ask all potential contractors to an interview, or to make a presentation in support of their bid, this should be stated within the brief. If possible, the date and format of the interview or presentation should also be stated in the brief.

Finally, successful and unsuccessful contractors should be advised of the outcome of the selection process as soon as possible. Contractors may find it helpful to have some feedback on the perceived strengths and weaknesses of their bid, but the details of their competitors' bids should, of course, remain confidential.

Research Contract

Having selected a contractor, the commissioning organisation usually formalises this through issuing a legally binding contract. This document typically sets out the purpose of the research study, the respective role of contractor and customer, its timescale and any other contractional conditions which are relevant, such as fee management arrangements, expected outputs and the ownership rights in respect of the research data and products. An example of such a contract is provided in Appendix Four.

Further Reading

Boddy, M., and Snape, D., (1995), *The Role of Research in Local Government.* Wokingham: Local Authorities Research and Intelligence Association.

Denzin, N., (1978), *The Research Act in Sociology.* London: Butterworth.

Hakim, C., (1987), *Research Design: Strategies and Choices in the Design of Social Research.* London: Allen and Unwin.

Social Research Association, (1994), *Commissioning Social Research: A Good Practice Guide.* London: SRA.

PART TWO: PUTTING THE PROJECT TOGETHER

The previous section considered the preparation and planning of a research project. This second part discusses the next phase, namely, how to assemble the evidence required to answer the research question. The following nine chapters are designed to get you thinking about the range of methods that might be employed to collect data. The topics covered include: how you go about undertaking a literature review; what issues you need to consider in relation to measurement; and what considerations should be taken when drawing up a sampling frame. A range of the more common data collection methods are then considered in separate chapters. The increasingly important role of computers and information technology in research will also be discussed.

Choosing a Method: a Tool Kit Approach

Selecting the most appropriate research strategy for your needs is dependent on the nature of the data you want to collect. Such a comment should reinforce the need to be clear about the research question you are trying to answer. The research question determines the types of evidence you need to collect and to some extent the methods you can employ. Consequently, the theory and concepts that underlie that question also have a key influence. The relationship between the research question and research design is, therefore, critical. Careful thought needs to be given at the outset to ensure that the research design will allow for the collection and analysis of the required data within the timescale. An equally crucial consideration is that the collected data can be analysed and interpreted in a way that addresses the research question.

The first thing to say about choosing a method is that no one approach is inherently better than another. The important criterion is that the chosen method should be viewed as the most appropriate for that given purpose. In might be helpful to think of the various research methods as a sort of tool kit: some tools are more appropriate for one task than another. If you wanted to put a nail into a wall you would choose a hammer in preference to a screwdriver. While you could put a nail into a wall using a screwdriver, the result would not be as good as with the hammer. Similarly, if you wanted to know about how people behave in given circumstances you might feel that observation was more appropriate than a self completion questionnaire.

The decision about which method to use will also involve adapting to other more practical constraints. Inevitably, there is the question of time and resources. If resources are limited there is little point in designing a sophisticated longitudinal study, covering say a five-year time span, when all you can hope to administer is one short questionnaire. Time constraints can work against the research in other ways. If, for example, you want to observe the meetings of a local authority housing committee, there will only be a limited number of opportunities available to do so during the life of the project.

The resources to be expended on your behalf by those who are the focus of your study will be another consideration. A housing department may be willing to let you distribute a brief questionnaire to their staff. They may be more reluctant to allow you observer status and unrestricted access to the department's work or records. These logistical factors will, inevitably, have an influence on the final choice of methods.

It should be acknowledged that the personal preferences of the researcher may also have a part to play. For whatever reason, some researchers seem to favour one method as opposed to another. There might be a temptation, either consciously or unconsciously, to frame the research question in a way that suits this preference. This section is designed to expose you to a wide range of methods. To help in better appreciating their value, specific examples of research work using these approaches are provided.

Combining Methods and Triangulation

While the following chapters describe methods in a way that might suggest that only discrete choices are available, it is often more useful to consider combining methods. These different tools can often be employed to complement each other and make the job easier. In studying how the local housing department operates, two distinct approaches could be employed. To get a better understanding of how the organisation functions, on a day-to-day basis, in relation to rent arrears practice or homeless advice, participant observation might be the most appropriate method. To explore the policy-making involved in delivering these local housing services, interviews might be preferred with the key players such as councillors and housing officials. By combining research methods in this way it is possible to study the same events from several different points of view. As a result the conflict and contradictions thrown up by the interplay between policy and practice should become clearer. This process of combining methods is called triangulation and is a useful means of establishing the validity of data.

Finally, when you think you are clear about your research question and the method to be adopted, a useful quick check is to try to summarise both, for either a colleague or your supervisor. If you cannot achieve this satisfactorily in about five minutes or less, you need to give the matter some more thought. The following chapters, therefore, provide a review of the key building block for any research project.

CHAPTER 5:
Assembling Material

Objectives of the Chapter

This chapter is designed to ensure that the reader:

- understands how to access the various literature sources required to undertake a research project;

- knows and understands how to read critically a range of published material; and

- knows the steps necessary to prepare a literature review.

Introduction

Reading and familiarising yourself with the available literature in your area of interest is a critical part of the research process. Reading helps you to focus on the research question. It also helps in the development of theories and in thinking through particular research designs that could be employed in addressing the research question. Within this context what does not exist within the literature may be just as important as that which other researchers have already written about. It is, therefore, important to conduct such searches systematically, ensuring you take concise notes that can be referred back to at a later stage. Having sought out the available written information it is then necessary to make sense of it through conducting a literature review. This chapter outlines the key steps involved in carrying out all of the above tasks.

Library Searches

How then do you find published material? The best and the most obvious starting point is the library. Libraries, according to Bell (1993), can seem like an *"Aladdin's cave for students and researchers."* Yet, among such riches it is easy to get lost. You therefore need to get to know how your library is organised. First, find out about the reader services the library provides. This will help you assess what published materials it holds and how exactly you can access this material. It is unlikely that the library will meet all your immediate needs, but it should have borrowing arrangements with other libraries which may collectively offer a better selection of materials in your chosen subject area. University and other specialist libraries are the best sources for research literature but access may be more restricted. It is therefore worth checking with the library beforehand about their requirements in relation to access. If you are not a registered student, for example, you may be granted only limited reading and/or borrowing rights. Further, there is likely to be a charge for using these services.

Library staff are an invaluable aid to locating the hidden gems you are seeking. Their guidance and skills can help greatly in finding published material. Vaughan's advice, *"... that you should make friends with the relevant library staff and always be polite, patient and remember to thank them,"* is worth taking to heart, (Vaughan, 1982).

Libraries contain a wealth of sources that are useful in conducting research. These include:

1. The catalogue lists of the stock held by the library. For each publication held, the catalogue details the author, title, date of publication, place of publication, and a set of keywords or brief text about the subject area covered by the publication. Increasingly catalogues are accessed on-line which makes searches far easier. Almost all such on-line catalogue facilities access material through a keyword system. These replace the previous paper and micro fiche systems. Library catalogues have, as a result, become more standardised but there are variations in how they operate. This standardisation has the advantage that through the catalogue in one library you can access the catalogues of other libraries.

2. Books are typically organised on the shelves by a subject-based catalogue system, such as the Dewey decimal system. Below are listed the catalogue entries from the *Dewey Dictionary* for the main housing topics. To aid in such searches the *Dewey Dictionary* is now available on-line.
   Housing and Sociology   307.336
   Housing and Local Government   352.75
   Housing and Social Services   363.5
   It is important not to limit your search to the use of the word 'housing'. Housing renewal, for example, is listed with area planning under architecture which is 711.59, and not under housing.

3. Journals and periodicals are a major source for research and are referenced in appropriate abstracts and indexes. Refereed journals – those in which the articles have been subjected to review by persons with some expertise in the field – are usually considered more authoritative than non refereed journals. The latter tend to be the professional journals while the former are academic. The main refereed journals in the housing area are *Housing Studies, Urban Studies*, the *Journal of Social Policy, Policy and Politics* and *Environment and Planning*. Professional journals include *Roof, Housing, Housing Review, Voluntary Housing* and *Housing and Planning Review*. (A full list of relevant publications can be found in Appendix Two.)

4. Abstracts provide bibliographical information and summaries of published journal articles. An index classified by subject area can also help you find relevant work. While the catalogue is the primary means of finding books, in a particular subject area, abstracts are essential for finding journal articles and other periodical sources. Undoubtedly the best source for accessing housing material is the *Applied Social Science Index and Abstract* (ASSIA). ASSIA is continuously updated and bound in yearly collections. The *Social Sciences Citation Index* (SSCI) is another useful index, and is now also available on-line through BIDS (Bath Information and Data Service). Housing is also covered in the *British Humanities Index*. Each index draws from a set of specified publications (academic journals, professional journals, magazines and newspapers) which are detailed in the publications. To illustrate their use, if you were to look up the term 'young people's housing' in ASSIA, for the year 1994, you would find the following items listed:

    > Rickford, F., (1994), 'Home at last', *Community Care*, 1009, 24th March, 16-17.
    >
    > Knibbs, S., (1994), 'Host from care', *Community Care*, 1028, 10th August, 16-17.
    >
    > Pickvance, C., and Pickvance, K., (1994), 'Towards a strategic approach to housing behaviour: a study in the South East of England', *Sociology*, 18, 3, 657-77.

5. There are other 'bibliographical instruments' such as the *British National Bibliography* (BNB), which provides information and an index of all books printed in a particular year. These annual listings are compiled by the British Library in London from all the publications deposited with them given their Copyright status (See Chapter 10 for further details of Copyright Libraries).

6. Academic theses relevant to your area of interest may be held in the library and there are indexes of theses such as the *ASLIB Index to Theses*. Theses may be particularly useful if you are researching for a higher degree as they will give you a feel for the format, style, and expected standard of work.

Much of this bibliographical information is now available in electronic format, either on-line through BIDS or via CD-Roms. BIDS is an interactive abstract which again employs keywords. To access BIDS you need to have an account. Most university libraries are linked and students can get access. Outwith the university sector access varies. The two most useful CD-Roms for housing searches are Sociofile and Geobase. This makes life easier in some respects: keyword searches are very fast and most databases contain abstracts that allow you to get some idea of the relevance of the book or article to your research. That said, it can be frustrating to find that a particular book or article identified using the new technology is not readily available through the library system.

Finally, mention should be made of the specialist library facilities offered by the Planning Exchange. Their library is dedicated to planning, housing and environmental issues. For subscribing members, in the main local authority planning departments and research sections within the chief executive's and housing departments, they produce a weekly abstract of material received by their library, broken down by topic. These topic listings are consolidated on a monthly basis into a listing. Members request items and these are posted out. As a subscription organisation this service is beyond the reach of individuals but it could be accessed through either employers or placement organisations.

Other Sources of Information

Remember that in surveying the literature, consideration should be given to statistical material, as well as to written texts. When working your way into the mass of official statistics it is essential to consult the *Guide to Official Statistics* (Central Statistics Office, 1996). This guide is about to be published on a CD-Rom version. Ask for assistance when first exploring this very specialised area. Digests of official statistics such as *Social Trends*, produced annually and *Economic Trends*, which is published monthly, are good starting points. *Regional Trends*, also produced annually, is a very helpful source for regional comparisons. Each government department produces its own annual abstract of statistics and with computerisation it is sometimes possible to get more detailed statistical analysis carried out, for example, on local unemployment records.

There is also the internet, which supports both e-mail and the World Wide Web. If you have access to the web you can search for your particular interest using keywords. The information facilities on the web are more developed in America, given the investment made in relation to the internet by the United States Government. Having said that, American material is not generally that applicable to either the British or European context. There is no point in giving specific details of these facilities, as they change all the time. If you can access the web, then 'surf' and see what you can find. If you are familiar with the techniques involved in electronic data searches then the web should present few difficulties. Whether it will produce the information you require is quite another matter. Given the continuing and rapid advances in information technology this facility will become more significant in the years to come, so it is worth starting to learn (Baxter, 1995). Also be aware that this medium has the potential to be highly distractive should you let it become so.

While the scale and complexity of the web can work against its usefulness, e-mail has been the recent big advance in information technology and this too has clear housing research applications. e-mail listings are a facility which allows you to receive any information posted on e-mail on a particular topic. Within the British context this facility is provided by Mailbase, which is located at the University of Newcastle. To access this facility you type MAILBASE@MAILBASE.AC.UK from your e-mail link and ask to receive the inventory of listings. Having selected the topics you wish to receive information on, you open a subscription. All material passing to this Mailbase listing will then automatically be copied to your e-mail address. Similar facilities are available through the web, and in certain instances on-line discussion groups on various topics have been created. Posting a message to an appropriate Mailbase listing could be a useful means of exploring the parameters of a particular research topic. Such a message would have to include an outline of the project and a request for any comments or suggestions. These facilities are constantly developing and it is clear that their research applications will expand greatly over the next few years. (See Chapter 13 on Information Technology for more details).

As noted above, books and journal articles that are not readily available locally can usually be obtained through the British Library's Inter-Library Loan service. To get a copy of a book or photocopy of a journal article through Inter-Library Loan can take a few weeks, and your library may charge for using the service. A scheme currently being piloted is designed to allow the automatic downloading of articles, which can then be printed off at your library. Books, given their size, are still posted out, but with the advances in technology that could change before too long.

Planning the Search

With such a wide array of sources to choose from it is essential that you plan your search carefully; it is all too easy to waste valuable time browsing the library shelves for material that turns out to be of little or no relevance to your research topic. Conducting a literature search is not an exact science, but the following steps should help:

- Be focused – start by making sure you have a clear sense of what it is you are looking for. A well thought out research question(s) will provide the necessary focus.
- Define your terms – what are the keywords that best describe your research area? For example, if you are researching 'the private rented sector', the keywords might include private, rented, rental, landlord and housing. Most systems only allow three keywords so you have to employ different combinations to see what is available. In most search facilities there are 'or' and 'and' facilities. The 'or' command broadens the search so that you can find as much as possible on your topic. Once that has been achieved, you want to narrow the field so the 'and' facility is employed. It may also be important to define the limits of your search in terms of geographical areas (e.g. UK only, Europe, USA), time scale (1985 to present), language, and so on.
- Ask for help – if you are not familiar with the library, or have not used certain of its up-to-date facilities, ask for help in identifying and using the most appropriate search facilities whether a general or specific catalogue or via a CD-Rom.
- Use what you find to access more – find and read the relevant books and journal articles (using Inter-Library Loan if necessary). Citations in these publications will provide a link to other related and useful material.

Taking Notes

Finding literature is a time consuming business, even using the information technology now available. The importance of taking good notes as you progress cannot, therefore, be stressed too much: having to go through the search again because you have forgotten the source of some important information, or had only scribbled a note on the back of your hand, is not only a waste of time, it is also extremely frustrating and quite unnecessary. Always make good notes on the source of any reference. Many hours can be wasted trying to find a book or article on the basis of an inadequate initial reference.

Once you have found the book or article it pays dividends to develop the habit of taking good notes and proper reference details right from the outset. How you choose to keep your notes and in how much detail is to some extent a matter of personal choice. The following information is the minimum necessary for research purposes:

1. The author(s) surname and initial or first name. Note too whether the named author is an editor, rather than the sole author of the book. When referencing an edited collection, the author of the individual chapter has to be acknowledged as well as the editor.

2. The date of publication. If the work is a second or subsequent edition you should note the date of original publication.

3. The title of the book or article.

4. The place of publication and publisher's name.

5. For a journal article, note the name of the journal, volume and issue number, and the page numbers of the article. Take care if you abbreviate the name of a journal. Use only accepted abbreviations and not your own idiosyncratic shorthand because you could get mixed up between similarly titled journals.

6. The International Standard Book Number (ISBN) or the International Standard Serial Number (ISSN) in the case of journals are unique reference numbers. They are therefore useful if you plan to get the book or article through Inter-Library Loan.

7. If the item was found in your local library you might want to record the specific catalogue reference – the Dewey decimal reference – so it can be easily located in the future. If you are using a number of libraries, it is also worth noting the actual library where the item was found .

8. A brief comment or abstract of the contents of a book, chapter, or article might be useful as a reminder of why the item was considered noteworthy in the first place.

Presented below are typical examples of notes made on a book, an edited collection, a research report and a journal article.

Figure 5.1: An Example of Notes on a Book

Sim, D., (1994), *British Housing Design*. Harlow: Longman/Chartered Institute of Housing. (ISBN 0-582-10248-0)

The book examines the different design models for public housing which have evolved throughout the twentieth century. The first four chapters trace the history of design policies up to the early 1970s. It explores the relationship between design, politics and reform agendas. Consideration is given to back-to- backs, the Garden Cities Movement, Arts and Crafts and Modernism as expressed through high rise. The book's main theme is the contemporary challenges in house design. Within this context it then provides an insight into the various factors which housing managers currently have to consider in providing appropriate housing for different user groups. The theme centres on the need to develop good quality and responsive housing based on meeting real and specific needs through active user participation. In this way it challenges the continuation of paternalistic design processes. While the current debates on defensible space, environmental and community architecture are helpful the text could have had provided a few case studies to illustrate the key points. Also while it covers the British context well, some of the recent developments in England via Estate Action could have had more comprehensive coverage.

Figure 5.2: An Example of Notes on an Edited Collection

Blackwell, J., and Kennedy, S., (eds), (1988), *Focus on Homelessness. A New Look at Housing Policy*. Dublin: Columba Press.

Chapter 1, by Michael Bannon, looks at planning and social segregation in Dublin; Chapter 5, by John Sweeney, focuses on the Ballymun Estate; Chapter 7, by the West Tallaght Resource Centre, looks at the problems of suburban Tallaght; Chapter 8, by Paddy Morrissey, looks at policy in relation to marginal groups; Chapter 9, by Pat McDonnell, examines the role of the planning authority (especially regeneration); Chapter 10, by Aidan O'Sullivan, looks at allocations to homeless families in Dublin; Chapter 13, by Bernard Thompson, summarises problems and policy issues in the social rented sector; Chapter 16, by Philip Geoghegan, looks at housing design; and finally, John Blackwell, in Chapter 19, asks if there needs to be a change in housing policy to address the needs of the homeless more effectively. These specific chapters provide a useful insight into contemporary Irish housing.

Figure 5.3: An Example of Notes on a Report

Anderson, I., and Quilgars, D., (1995), *Foyers For Young People: Evaluation of a Pilot Initiative*. York: Centre for Housing Policy, University of York. (ISBN 1-874797-67-6)

The report examines the appropriateness of developing the French Foyers concept within England. Foyers are housing projects which aim to tackle the housing, employment and development needs of young people. Chapter 1 considers the concept of foyers and traces the introduction of this idea from France. Chapter 2 sets out the details of a pilot initiative in England, and Chapter 3 examines the support services provided in the pilot foyers. Chapter 4 considers the views of the young people who stayed in the foyers. Chapter 5 explores the issues associated with capital and revenue financing to new projects. It also looks at the operational issues in new foyers. The perspective of potential employers is discussed in Chapter 6. The final Chapter presents the conclusions and recommendations arising from the study. The conclusion is that this approach has a certain momentum and therefore the policy agenda should be to refine and improve upon current practice.

Figure 5.4: An Example of Notes on an Article in a Journal

Robertson, D. (1992), 'Scottish home improvement policy, 1945 – 1975: Coming to terms with the tenement', *Urban Studies*, 29, 7, 1115-1136. (ISSN 0042-0980)

> The article traces the development of home improvement policy in Scotland, illustrating how the traditional housing form for a long time hindered, then eventually distinctively shaped this policy. It notes that tenement housing was a constraint on the promotion of home improvement policy due to a variety of technical and administrative factors. Political prejudice against landlords and the social attitudes about tenements was shown to be a more crucial consideration. There is much detail about the policy-making process within a Scottish context. Provides an interesting insight into the complexities of policy implementation.

Traditionally, researchers would have recorded this information on some type of card index. Increasingly, however, computer databases have replaced the card index. Most on-line bibliographical sources allow the user to download items from a search onto a disk and from there the information can be copied to your personal database. Take care, though, for this deceptively simple operation can easily lead to you developing a massive database of information much of which you will never have time to read. Try to seek out the key texts and articles, rather than constructing a large, comprehensive and unwieldy bibliography. Be clear about what you need and try not to become seduced by the technology.

References

It might be useful to select the referencing system you intend to adopt in your final report before you begin taking notes. Figures 5.1 to 5.4 above have used the Harvard system. Originally developed in America it now has almost universal application. Another, the British referencing system, was developed by the British Standards Institution (BS 5605) (BSI, 1978). Information on the various referencing systems should be available from your local library. Your organisation, or institution may have a preferred 'house style' of referencing, in which case that is the one you should adopt. The important point to remember, no matter the style of referencing you adopt, is to be both thorough and consistent. To get a clear idea of how the Harvard referencing system functions in relation to the range of published output consult the bibliography at the end of this book.

Literature Reviews

In writing up a research study, and especially when producing a housing project, you will be expected to produce a critical review of the literature. This literature review should serve two purposes. Firstly, it provides the context, the background to the current research: it should give the reader an insight into the state of knowledge on the chosen research area. If possible it should also identify any gaps in current knowledge that the research proposes to fill. Secondly, it should show that the writer can locate the relevant literature, summarise it and consider its relevance to their research project. A literature review should not be a reiteration of all the items found as a result of the literature search. Nor should it be simply a catalogue of *"books and articles I have read."* Rather it should demonstrate a critical awareness of the literature within the subject area, through careful consideration of relevant work.

The precise details of the literature review, illustrating the depth and breadth of coverage, will depend on the nature of the project. You would not expect as much from a brief internal research report, for example, as you would from an academic thesis. Nevertheless, all literature reviews require three things of you, the writer:

1. That you are selective in your presentation of the literature. You will have to leave out some things, perhaps many things, which you have found from your searches. This may be frustrating, but it is a discipline that must be learned.

2. That you only identify themes or features in the literature that are relevant and of particular interest.

3. That you discuss the range of relevant literature, not simply that which supports your position. A good literature review should compare and contrast different aspects of the literature.

The success of the literature review, however, is in the reading. Reading for research is not like reading for fun. That is not to say it cannot be enjoyable, simply that it demands that you read widely, that you read carefully, and that you read with a purpose. Delamont (1992) identifies three types of reading with a purpose: reading on and around your topic; reading for contrast; and reading to develop analytical or theoretical concepts. The important point is that you need to read and when writing this material up, for the literature review, it has to be critical, while maintaining a sense of scepticism and curiosity.

Reading Critically

Being critical, however, is often easier said than done and it is all too common to find:

> *"... the uncritical review, the furniture sale catalogue, in which everything merits a one paragraph entry no matter how skilfully it has been conducted. Bloggs (1975) found this, Smith (1976) found that, Jones (1977) found the other; Bloggs, Smith and Jones (1978) found happiness in heaven."*
> (Haywood and Wragg, 1978, 38)

One way to develop this critical habit in both your reading and subsequent writing, is to scrutinise published research work and ask the same sort of questions of it as you would be expected to have answered in designing your own research project. Such an 'evaluation' should include topics such as:

1. Research Question – what is the research question hypothesis and is it a valid and relevant question?

2. Literature Review – is the review relevant and up-to-date; are the links between theory, earlier findings, and the study being reported clearly and explicitly?

3. Sample – who are the research subjects, how were they selected and are there aspects of selection that might limit the wider applicability of the results?

4. Data Collection – how was the data collected and what steps (if any) were taken to ensure reliability and validity?

5. Presentation of Findings – was the data analysed appropriately and were the findings clear and concise?

6. Conclusions – do the conclusions follow logically from the analyses and does the data actually warrant these conclusions?

7. Ethics – does the research meet accepted standards of ethical practice?

All research is dependent on reading to a greater or lesser extent and it is, therefore, important that you read critically, widely and with a clear purpose.

Further Reading

Bell, J., (1993), *Doing Your Research Project – A Guide for First Time Researchers in Education and Social Sciences*, (Second Edition), Milton Keynes: Open University Press.

Delamont, S., (1992), *Fieldwork in Educational Settings: Methods Pitfalls and Perspectives*, London: Falmer.

Vaughan, J., (1982), 'Searching the Literature: Additional sources of information and how to keep up to date', in Hartnett, A. (ed) *The Social Sciences in Educational Studies: A selective guide to the literature*. London: Heinemann.

British Standards Institution, (1978), *Citing Publications by Bibliographical References* (BS 5605). London: British Standards Institution.

CHAPTER 6:
Measurement

Objectives of the Chapter

This chapter is designed to ensure that the reader:

- understands the basic issues associated with measurement;

- understands the various approaches to measurement commonly used in housing research; and

- appreciates the issues associated with validity and reliability in relation to measurement.

Introduction

Measurement is the process by which theoretical concepts are given a tangible, measurable form – operationalised – to use the technical jargon. While certain issues or topics prove easy to measure, many topics within the social sciences present more complex problems. The familiar concepts of weight or height present few measurement problems. Weight is represented worldwide by kilograms and grams. That said, there are still large parts of the globe that still prefer to use stones, pounds and ounces. Converting from one to the other can create measurement difficulties. The same is true for height or length. These measurement problems can be resolved easily through agreed conversion tables.

But what if you cannot get an agreement on how you should best measure a particular item? For example, how do you measure poverty, or social class or house conditions? Measuring performance also throws up complexities. Each of these items can be measured, but there may be little agreement as to the appropriateness of the measure. It is not uncommon for a range of different measures to be employed to illustrate one of these specific concepts.

Different countries also tend to employ different measures to explain specific issues. The basic housing condition standard in Sweden, as defined by space standards and amenities, would produce a measure within Britain reflecting a very high standard. A comparison of basic standards would, therefore, produce a meaningless result. However, if the basis of measurement was reworked for comparative purposes, something more meaningful would result. The importance of measurement is that it provides a bridge between the abstract world of theory and the observed world of either people, objects, or events that the researcher wants to explore and explain. Without measurement the social and physical world would only be explicable in terms of theory.

This chapter provides a basic overview of measurement issues within social science research. The main themes to be explored are units of analysis, actual levels of measurement and the concepts of validity and reliability. Each of these broad themes has implications for any subsequent statistical analysis. They also throw up issues that require to be considered in relation to the links between measurement, theory and analysis. The chapter also touches upon the long-standing debate, within social research, over the merits and demerits of qualitative and quantitative measures.

Measurement and Meaning

Measurement is one means of representing theoretical concepts. They are classification systems that approximate to the real world, but they are not in themselves the real world. The measurement is not the concept, if for no other reason than that most concepts in social research are multi-dimensional. The concept of social class, for example, cannot be reduced to a single measure. It is a concept that involves any number of dimensions such as occupation, income, wealth, status and educational attainment. As no single measure can encompass this diversity, researchers when measuring social class will use two or more dimensions to generate an approximation of social class. This provides a measure of the concept, but it is not an encapsulation of the concept itself.

All this might seem a little esoteric, but it is nevertheless an important point to remember. It is all too easy to get caught up with measurement and forget that it is only a means to an end – to understand and explain the social world – and not an end in itself. A.A. Milne, the author of *Winnie the Pooh* provides a humorous illustration of this point when he wrote about Pooh Bear coming downstairs,

> *"... bump, bump, bump, on the back of his head behind Christopher Robin. It is, as far as he knows, the only way of coming downstairs, but sometimes he thinks that there really is another way, if only he could stop bumping for a moment and think of it."*
>
> (Milne, 1926, 12)

It would be an easy matter to develop a measure to record the number of times Pooh's head bumps on the stairs, but would such a measure help explain why he is descending the stairs in this unorthodox way?

Quantitative versus Qualitative Measures

This brings us neatly to a debate that has exercised social researchers for decades; the debate on the relative merits of quantitative and qualitative measurement. The details of the debate need not detain us, but it is worthwhile making one or two points at this stage. Put simply, the quantitative side of the debate argues for the pre-eminence of a 'scientific approach' which produces quantifiable results and generalisable conclusions. From this perspective qualitative measures, such as participant observation, tend to be viewed as unscientific, too vague and value-laden, to be credible. Those who favoured qualitative measures, on the other hand, counter that social reality is too complex to be reduced to mere empirical 'facts'. For them the techniques of quantitative research can only reduce social reality to numeric categories which destroy their essential meaning.

Representing the debate as a dichotomy between qualitative and quantitative measures does, however, tend to polarise opinion. Quantitative researchers are encouraged to ignore the potential insights afforded by qualitative measures and vice versa. In reality there is but one dimension and different styles of measurement differ not in kind, but in either the degree or level of measurement. Qualitative and quantitative researchers have very different, often antagonistic views about the nature of the research process. Yet, these differences do not necessarily dictate the measures or methods of data collection that are used. Dey (1993) uses a T'ai-chi Tu diagram to illustrate the dynamic balance between qualitative and quantitative data.

Diagram 6.1: The Dynamic Balance Between Qualitative and Quantitative Data

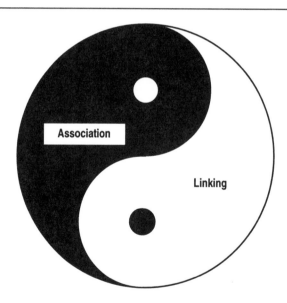

"The diagram reflects the mutual dependence of both types of data. It indicates that meanings cannot be ignored when we are dealing with numbers, and numbers cannot be ignored when we are dealing with meanings. Each complements the other, though at lower levels of measurement questions of meaning are uppermost, while at higher levels of measurement, questions of number loom largest."

(Dey, 1993, Page 28)

Units of Analysis

The unit of analysis concept is critical to any understanding of measurement. Put simply, the unit of analysis is the person, event, or social structure that is being measured in the research. If you were interviewing, for example, young single people about their experiences of homelessness, the unit of analysis would be the individual men and women interviewed. If, on the other hand, your interest was in the provision being made for these young single homeless people, the focus of the study and the unit of analysis might be the local authority housing department or hostel accommodation. It is not unusual, however, to find more than one unit of analysis in a single study. A study of single homelessness, to continue with this example, might have at least two units of analysis; the individuals who are homeless and the organisation(s) that provide housing and welfare services dedicated to their needs. The unit of analysis is critical when it comes to deciding upon the actual level of measurement to be employed in a particular study.

Levels of Measurement

There are four levels of measurement: nominal, ordinal, interval and ratio. The level of measurement achieved determines the types of statistical procedures that can be employed to analyse the collected data. Measurement at its simplest operates at the nominal level. With nominal measurement it is only possible to differentiate broad categories such as sex or marital status. Where the concepts being measured are defined more clearly, it may be possible to make finer distinctions whether at the ordinal, interval, or ratio levels of measurement.

Nominal

Nominal level measurement involves naming, or labelling, a quality. The object, as with everyday language, has to have the capacity to be categorised – whether these are objects, persons, attributes, or behaviours – in order to distinguish between them. For the measure to be effective, however, the nominal categories must be mutually exclusive and exhaustive. What this means is that an observation should fit one, and only one, category. The appropriate nominal category should then be available for each and every observation. When you join an organisation, for example, whether it is as a member of a sports club, or as an employee in a housing organisation, you will usually be given an identification number. This is a nominal category that distinguishes you from all other members of the organisation. The categorisation here is exclusive, because the number is unique to you. It is also exhaustive, because every member has a number. Beyond this the number itself has no meaning: it is simply a label and does not signify that someone having a higher or lower number is any more or less important.

As there is no order, or degree element to categories constructed at the nominal level of measurement, this imposes certain limitations on the analysis and subsequent interpretation of the data. The main limitation concerns the use of measures of central tendency, or averages. There are three such 'averages':

1. the mean   –   the arithmetic average derived from adding together a series of scores and dividing by the number of observations;

2. the median   –   the middle value of a set of scores;

3. the mode   –   the most frequently occurring values or scores.

As you cannot add, subtract, multiply, or divide nominal scores, the mode is the only appropriate measure of central tendency for nominal data. To show this, suppose you had conducted a study of housing tenure and had found the following distribution of tenure among the 500 persons surveyed:

Table 6.1: House Tenure League

Type of Tenure	Code	No. in Category
Owner occupied	1	150
Local authority	2	100
Private rented (furnished)	3	80
Private rented (unfurnished)	4	75
Housing association	5	85
Other	6	10

The code, (1) owner occupied, (2) local authority, and so on, is simply a label which represents each discrete category – no order or degree is implied. Consequently, calculating the mean or the median produces a meaningless number. The mean, for example, is calculated by adding together the scores in each category and dividing by the total number of observations. In this case, $[(1 \times 150) + (2 \times 100) + (3 \times 80) + (4 \times 75) + (585) + (6 \times 10)] / 500 = 2.75$. This makes no sense. Nor is the median any more helpful. There are 500 observations and, therefore, the median or middle value must lie between the 250th and the 251st score, in this case between '2' and '3' giving a median of 2.5. The mode, on the other hand, tells you about the most frequently occurring score, the common form of housing tenure. In this case the mode is 1; hence, owner occupation is the most common type of tenure in this survey.

Ordinal

There are of course many situations in which the researcher would want to go beyond such a simple classification in order to measure with more discrimination. One way to do this would be to attempt to order, or rank responses in some way. Ordinal measurements do just this. They allow the researcher to make a judgement that one item is ranked above or below another. What it does not do, however, is to make statements about how much above or below. For instance, suppose your salary was in Category 4 in Table 6.2. That would place you in the top eight per cent of all employees, in terms of salary, within the organisation. The researcher would know from this that you were better off than most of your colleagues. However, without more precise knowledge the ranking does not allow them to say how much better off you are than the other 90 per cent of your colleagues, or how you are doing relative to similar staff within other organisations.

Table 6.2: The Salary League

Salary Scale	Category Code	No. in Category
Below £10,000	1	200
£10-20,000	2	250
£20-30,000	3	175
Over £30,000	6	50

Ordinal level data is an improvement on nominal level data, but it still has some limitations. Again these limitations are most obvious in terms of the statistics that can be derived from the information. Calculating the mean for ordinal data such as appears in Table 6.2 would be just as meaningless as it was for nominal level data. You could, of course, use the mode, which in this case would be 2. It is more usual, however, to use the median as the basis for statistical comparisons with using ordinal data.

Interval

Interval level measures have all the properties of ordinal measures, and, in addition, have equal intervals between the scores. This equal spacing means that you can make judgements about the degree of difference. Temperature is perhaps the best known example of an interval scale. If the temperature in a house is 40°C, then we can say that it is twice as warm as a house in which the temperature is only 20°C. The same applies to income. If you have an income of £30,000 a year, then you earn twice as much as a colleague earning £15,000.

There are potentially some problems in interpreting interval level data because of the involvement of an arbitrary anchor point. The anchor points on the centigrade scale, for example, are the temperatures at which water freezes and boils, 0 and 100 degrees respectively. In practice, however, there are few limitations on the types of analysis that are appropriate to interval level data. If it is possible and/or practicable it is best to design measures that produce the highest level possible because you can always step down levels – from interval to ordinal to nominal – but not vice versa.

Ratio

There is one further level of measurement, namely ratio, which combines all the attributes of the interval level with an absolute zero point. The Kelvin Scale of temperature uses an absolute value of zero, which represents the total absence of heat. Unfortunately, there are few if any meaningful examples of ratio levels of measurement in the social sciences. Income might seem to be an obvious exception, with zero representing a total absence of money. In practice, however, income is usually used as an indicator of socio-economic status. In this case it is not a ratio level measure since having no money does not mean that you have no socio-economic status.

Validity and Reliability

Whatever the level of measurement being used in a study, it is important that the measurement should yield reliable and valid results. Validity refers to how well an item measures what it is supposed to measure. Reliability is concerned with the consistency of the measurement; will the test or method yield similar results in similar situations?

Table 6.3, showing the readings from three electricity meters, is designed to illustrate the significance of these points. Meter C runs erratically; sometimes it reads over and at other times it reads under. Such a meter is clearly useless. It is not valid because it does not measure what it is supposed to, namely the amount of electricity used. Moreover, the meter is not reliable since it does not measure consistently. Meter A, on the other hand, is both reliable and valid; it measures what it is intended to measure and it does so accurately. But what about meter B, which always measures exactly one hundred units over? The reading is clearly not valid, since the measure of power use is consistently wrong. Yet it is reliable because it measures consistently. If a test is reliable, it does not mean that it is valid. For a test to be valid, however, it must also be reliable.

Table 6.3: Validity and Reliability

Correct Reading	Meter A Reliable and Valid	Meter B Reliable but not Valid	Meter C Not reliable or Valid
58000	58000	58005	58160
58500	58500	58505	58800
59000	59000	59005	58905
59500	59500	59505	59123

Unfortunately, in many research situations the issues of validity and reliability are not so clear-cut. It can be difficult to judge if test or survey items are directly relevant to the research question. There are however many tests that can provide an insight into validity.

Testing Validity

There are three basic techniques for assessing validity: face, criterion-related, and construct validity. Choosing which technique to use will be influenced by the nature of the particular research project and the availability of resources. If you are planning a small scale study, for example, it is unlikely that you will have the resources to go beyond a consideration of face validity.

Face Validity

Face validity is a subjective method that makes use of opinion and judgement as the sole means of determining validity. At it simplest, face validity may involve no more than the researcher reflecting on whether the test measures what it was intended to measure. A more sophisticated method would perhaps involve assessments by a panel of judges expert in the field. This would provide a stronger form of face validity, but it is still a limited test of validity since it is dependent upon the quality of the judges. Selecting an expert in housing management to comment on the measurement approach for a house condition survey may not be helpful. Yet, they may help greatly in developing performance measures for rent collection and rent arrears work. Face validity, while hard to defend on scientific grounds, can be a useful starting point. After all, if you cannot demonstrate face validity, it is unlikely that other methods of assessing validity will be convincing.

Criterion-Related Validity

A more powerful tool, criterion-related validity, makes use of statistical measures such as correlation coefficients to assess validity. There are two common types of criterion-related validity; concurrent validity, and predictive validity. Both types are similar, in that they use criterion measures and statistical correlation as a means of assessing validity. The correlation validity coefficient ranges from 0 to +1 and the closer to +1 it gets, the stronger the criterion-related validity.

Concurrent Validity
Concurrent validity relies on authoritative measures, rather than authoritative individuals (or experts) to assess validity. Quite simply it involves comparing a new measure with an existing and valid measure. For example, if you had some questions that are intended to measure the self-esteem of young single homeless persons, you could also ask questions from a published, standardised test. If your items were valid, you would expect respondents' scores on your items to be statistically correlated to the published criterion; the scores achieved using the pre-existing test.

Predictive Validity
If a test is valid it should be possible to predict future outcomes on the basis of the test. The best known examples of predictive validity are those used to predict academic performance in higher education. Suppose you had a test which you believed could predict, within certain statistical limits, a particular student's performance on a professional housing course. Using the new test at the start of the course you would predict the outcome – the class of award – then await the actual outcome, at the end of the course, when the two results could be compared. Predictive validity, in the form of a correlation coefficient between subjects' predicted award classification and their actual classification (the criterion), establishes a correlation coefficient. As with concurrent validity, the closer the coefficient value to +1, the more valid the test.

Criterion-related validity is a valuable tool, but one that needs to be used with care. The difficulty with this form of assessing validity is that it relies heavily upon the quality of the criterion measure. How can you be sure that the criteria, the pre-existing test or the outcomes measures, against which the new test is being assessed are in fact valid. Suppose, for example, you were to find a high degree of concurrent validity between your items on self-esteem and those produced by a standardised test. This might be an indication that both tests are equally good, but it could also suggest that they are both poor measures. Similarly, a strong correlation on predictive validity may be flawed by faulty outcome measures.

Construct Validity

Construct validity is the most complex approach to validity and involves comparing new measures with pre-existing valid measures. In this sense it is similar to concurrent validity. The difference, however, is that construct validity attempts to correlate validity with different methods of measurement and with measures of different concepts.

In the previously mentioned study of young single homeless people, a questionnaire was to be used to measure self-esteem. A correlation between the new instrument and an existing questionnaire, however, might be related to the type of instrument being used (both are questionnaires). If, on the other hand, your questionnaire correlated with an existing questionnaire and another method, such as an interview, you could be more confident of the validity of the new measure.

The extent to which a measure does not correlate with measures of a different concept is also considered in assessing construct validity. Suppose the new measure of self-esteem were contrasted with a questionnaire about the effectiveness of allocation procedures. A high correlation between the two measures would not be expected because they are measuring different concepts.

Construct validity is a powerful means of assessing validity. It is also a complicated one that usually involves the use of multivariate factor analysis and, as such, is perhaps best left to those who have the necessary resources and expertise.

Assessing Reliability

Validity is about the ability of an item or test to measure what it is supposed to measure. Reliability is concerned with the extent to which a measure is consistent. As was mentioned earlier, however, the reliability of a measure says nothing about its validity – a measure can be reliably invalid. There are many ways of assessing reliability, most of which involve statistical correlation. The most common techniques are: inter-rater, test-retest, split-half, alternate forms, item-total reliability.

Inter-Rater Reliability

As the name suggests, inter-rater reliability involves more than one person making judgements on a measure. For instance, if you have several surveyors involved in a local house condition survey, they might be asked to make a judgement on the external condition of property using a ten-point scale. If each surveyor scores the same properties, inter-rater reliability would be assessed by correlating the scores from various surveyors. A high correlation between the surveyors would suggest that the measurement was reliable.

Test-Retest Reliability

The test-retest approach simply involves repeating a measure after some time has elapsed. In theory at least, if the measure is reliable, subjects should achieve the same scores on both occasions. Another way of assessing the reliability of your house condition surveyors, for example, would be to have them repeat a property survey some time after the first inspection. All things being equal, they should produce the same score for the same property on both occasions. There are problems, however, with the test-retest approach. Observed differences between the test and the retest might be the result of an actual change in the respondents, or the situation, rather than an indication that the measure is unreliable. In the case of the house condition survey, for example, the practice which surveyors will have gained in using the measurement during the test phase might have an impact on the subsequent retest measures. Alternatively, the property may have deteriorated markedly between the two surveys.

Split-Half Reliability

The split-half reliability approach is a variation on the test-retest method. Essentially what you do is develop twice as many items as needed to measure the concept, administer the instrument using all the items, then split them into two equivalent halves – by odd and even-numbered items – and correlate the halves. The idea is that, if the test is reliable, the scores between the two versions should be strongly correlated. As before, the higher the correlation, the greater the reliability. The difficulty, of course, is in assuming versions of the measure are readily comparable in content and difficulty.

Alternate Forms Reliability

This approach is the same as the split-half method, except that two completely separate, but equivalent, versions of the same measure are compared. One method is to give the same group of respondents different versions of the measure at different times. In this way they are tested twice, once with each equivalent measure. Alternatively, the same measure might be administered to different groups of respondents. In either case, a correlation coefficient is calculated from the scores to assess the alternate forms of reliability for the measure.

The success of the alternate forms approach relies on the true equivalency of the two versions. Developing such items can be a difficult and time-consuming business. Add to this the need for two separate administrations of the measure and clearly to use the alternate forms approach demands access to considerable resources.

Item-Total Reliability

Item-total reliability assesses the internal consistency of a measure by correlating the score on one item in a measure with the total score on all the other items. If each item on a measure is reliable, then you can be more confident of the reliability of the measurement in total. If a measure contains many items, calculating the correlations for item-total reliability can be a time-consuming exercise, even when using of a computer.

Although these approaches to assessing reliability can be used either with achievement or attitudinal measures, they are more usually applied to the former. Attitudinal measures are harder to assess, since attitude is generally much less consistent than aptitude. That does not mean, of course, that it is not just as important to try to establish the reliability and indeed the validity of attitudinal measures.

Linkages

Measurement is only valid in the light of theory. Without clearly defined concepts there is no point in attempting to define valid measures. The important point about measurement is that its function is to provide a link between theoretical concepts and social reality. Theory should guide your research, but it is measurement that enables you to test out your propositions and theories.

In choosing to conduct a study aimed at addressing the question: *"What are the factors associated with homelessness among single young people?"* you would first carry out a literature search on the various theories and explanations that might help answer this research question. This literature review would throw up structural and individual explanations for youth homelessness. The structural explanations might focus on the growth in youth unemployment and changes in the welfare system, especially for those under 18. Individual explanations would focus on individual circumstances and the life experiences of these young people to date. From the literature you might find that the concept of social networks seemed especially relevant, given it has both an individual and structural component. The theory of social networks is complex, but the basic hypothesis would be that the stronger the individual's social network, the less likelihood of homelessness.

To take this concept further you would need to work out a means of measuring social networks. That might involve assessing the importance of family, kinship, and friendship ties as well as membership of formal organisations. A good measure would be expected to reveal the presence or absence of a given entity, such as a family bond in a particular situation. It might also suggest a measure of degree, such as how strong are the bonds with family. Homelessness studies present major problems for measurement given that the subject is both dynamic and often hidden.

Measurement, then, is not merely a technical exercise, it is an integral part of the research process. Thinking about measurement issues early on in the study, can often help you focus more clearly on the important concepts. This in turn will help you to design a more rigorous research study.

Further Reading

Blalock, H., (1984), *Social Statistics*, (Second Edition). London: McGraw-Hill.

Bryman, A., (1989), *Research Methods and Organisation Studies*. London: Routledge.

Dey, I., (1993), *Qualitative Data Analysis: A User Friendly Guide for Social Scientists*. London: Routledge.

Moser, C. and Kalton, G., (1983), *Survey Methods in Social Investigation*, (Second Edition). London: Heinemann.

CHAPTER 7:
Sampling

Objectives of the Chapter

This chapter is designed to ensure that the reader:

- understands the appropriate use of sampling;

- knows and understands the various types of sampling techniques commonly used in housing research; and

- can construct an appropriate sampling frame to address a research topic of interest.

Introduction

In an ideal world a research project would survey the whole population. This would only be feasible where the group you wanted to study was reasonably small in number, or where the study had unlimited access to resources. Unfortunately, these conditions rarely exist; hence the need to select a sample. Suppose you wanted to explain why certain tenants had opted to buy their council house, while others had not. Clearly it would be impractical to interview all those who currently reside in what were originally council houses. So to get round this logistical problem a sample of this population would be used. At its simplest then, a sample is a compromise between obtaining complete information and accommodating the reality of available time and resources to carry out the research. Yet, sampling can offer the researcher far more than this.

Moser and Kalton (1983) suggest a number of advantages which sampling has over an enumeration of the whole population. The main advantage of sampling is that it is cheaper to conduct, because fewer people are required to collect and analyse the data. Sampling also saves time, since it is quicker to analyse and process. It also makes for greater accuracy, as sampling size allows checks to be made on the design and implementation of the data collection instrument. The small number of staff involved also makes it possible for the researcher to train the interviewers properly and to check on their accuracy in conducting interviews. This issue was touched upon in the previous chapter in relation to the reliability and validity of measurement. Sampling also makes it possible to collect and deal with more elaborate information about individual cases, albeit in a smaller number.

Two terms need to be clarified at this point. Firstly, when a sample is drawn it is not necessarily people who are the unit of analysis, or entity being sampled. Given the need for both local and national house-condition surveys, for example, the actual property itself is a common unit of analysis. Secondly, the term 'population' refers to a discrete group of units of analysis, and not to the population in the conventional sense. For example, in a survey of tenants opting to exercise 'Tenants' Choice' the unit of analysis might be the tenant, or the head of household, or the household collectively. The population being all tenants who were offered this choice over a given period. The actual population in question is, therefore, defined by the researcher. The important point is that the sample should be representative of the larger group, namely, the researcher's defined population. If you have properly selected your sample then your findings from the sample survey should be representative of the entire population. If the sample is not representative, the results may be unrepresentative of this wider population. In the case above, clearly the person holding the tenancy might seem to be the most appropriate in any examination of 'Tenants' Choice'. The other two categories might produce a different result.

One classic example of sampling failure comes from a public opinion poll conducted for the *Literary Digest* during the 1936 United States' Presidential Election campaign. This survey used car registration records to identify a sample of voters – remember this was 1936 and car ownership was far more limited than it is today. They then telephoned the selected car owners thus further reducing the representativeness of the sample, given that telephones were also very much the preserve of the wealthy. The result predicted a landslide victory for the Republican Alf Landon over the Democratic contender Franklin D. Roosevelt. History records that Roosevelt comfortably won the day!

Similar problems still arise today. The growth of 'telephone polling' at election times ably illustrates the point: although most people now have access to a telephone, there is still not universal coverage. Those who do not have a phone in their house may represent a distinct group within society. At the same time, a considerable number of those who own phones are ex-directory and again this may be more common practice for certain groups within society. One further complication is that the researcher can never be sure who they are speaking to, therefore another distortion is introduced. As a result, telephone polls can be unreliable and may misrepresent voting patterns.

Other examples are provided by the ubiquitous market researcher seen sampling people's views on a range of issues outside the local shopping centre. Such passers-by are clearly not typical of the entire population; rather they simply happen to be available, at that time and place. Such a sample probably under-represents those people in full-time employment, those at school or in higher education, or those who shop elsewhere. Television 'phone-in surveys' are another example of an unrepresentative sample, since they typically attract only those who watch daytime television and can be bothered to respond. Such groups are unlikely to be representative of the entire population.

Types of Sampling

To avoid the more obvious problems of unrepresentativeness, a range of sampling techniques have been developed. There are two broad categories of sampling techniques; random (or probability) sampling and non-random (non-probability) sampling. Within these broad categories there are a range of approaches. Table 7.1 summarises the main advantages and disadvantages of some of the more common approaches to sampling.

Random Sampling

The best way to achieve an unbiased sample is to use some form of random or probability sampling. A random sample is one in which every unit of the population has a known, independent and equal chance of being selected. The National Lottery numbers, for example, are selected at random by placing numbered balls of equal size and shape into a machine which rotates them. Each time the machine spins, each ball has an independent and equal chance of being selected. As the balls are removed from the machine, after each selection, the odds will change, but the remaining balls still have an equal, albeit different chance, of being selected.

Simple Random Sampling
A simple random sample assigns a number to every item within a sampling frame and then selects a specified number of items, as a sample, at random. The sampling frame is simply a list of all the items in a population. It could be the electoral register for a particular area, a list of all households on a housing association waiting list, a list of all local authority housing departments, an employer's payroll, or whatever. Suppose, therefore, you wanted to draw a sample of 100 tenants, to be interviewed about their attitude to the quality of housing service delivered by a local authority housing department which has 5,000 tenancies. One way to do it would be to give each tenant a unique number and then use a table of random numbers (or computer generated random numbers) to select the sample.

This procedure can, however, be rather tedious and time consuming. Further, its value is dependent upon the accuracy of the sampling frame. Using the telephone directory, for example, as mentioned earlier, excludes all those who don't have a telephone or who have an ex-directory number. The Post Office address list might be a better choice of sampling frame, given its more comprehensive coverage.

Systematic Random Sampling
One alternative to the laborious method of numbering all the units within a sampling frame is to use systematic random sampling. The technique is similar to simple random sampling, but instead of numbering all the items within the sampling frame you select every nth case from a randomly chosen starting point, to generate your sample. For example, taking your list of 5,000 tenants you would calculate the sampling interval (n) which is required to produce your sample of 100 tenants. This is achieved by dividing the population size by the sample size – in this case 5,000 is divided by 100 to give a sampling interval of 50. You then select a random starting point between 1 and 50, using a table of random numbers, and then pick every 50th case thereafter until you have generated the required sample.

Problems can arise with this approach where there is some non-random order to the sampling frame. When conducting a house condition survey in Scotland, for example, where four storey tenement housing is prevalent, if you choose to select every eighth house to sample you could end up with all the selected properties being at the same floor level. Surveying only ground floor or top floor flats, for example, would clearly bias the survey results. The sample might also be systematically biased where the sampling interval corresponds to a particular characteristic of the population. In a survey of client satisfaction, for example, it might be decided that every fifth tenant who comes into the local housing office should be interviewed. Before adopting this approach, however, it would be as well to think carefully about any possibility of patterns occurring in the population – do different kinds of clients come into the office on different days, or at different times of the day? This might present problems when the data is analysed and interpreted.

Where there is a problem with the sampling frame, the solution might be to randomise the frame before selecting the sample. With a very large sampling frame such as a telephone directory or an electoral register this would clearly be impractical, but as a general rule you should randomise the sampling frame wherever possible.

Stratified Random Sampling

The basic principle behind random sampling is that because the sample is drawn by chance, it is likely to be reasonably representative of the population. In using the simple approaches outlined above, there is always the possibility of over-representing one category. For example, the sample could select more women than men. The stratified sampling approach attempts to improve representativeness by drawing separate samples from different strata of a population, using a characteristic that is thought to be important. If you are conducting a local house condition survey you might first stratify the sample to ensure both owner occupied and council housing was properly represented. If owner occupation represented 65 per cent of the local housing stock you would want to ensure the sample achieved the same representation.

Stratified sampling can also be employed to boost the representation of a particular group, to ensure you have adequately covered their position or interests. A common problem in many local house condition surveys is that given the small size of the private rented sector it is often difficult to say much about the physical condition of housing stock. To get round this problem, you could employ a stratified sample to boost the size of the private rented sector sample. You would then be more confident about the results generated. In house condition surveys, where this practice is common, specific rules have been laid down for applying this approach (see Scottish Homes, 1993).

The important point is that there needs to be some rationale for stratifying the population. In other words, you should have some reason, perhaps based on previous research knowledge or theory, for grouping the sample by tenure, as opposed to adopting some other variable such as construction date, or house type.

Cluster or Multi-stage Sampling

Cluster sampling is useful when there is no readily available sampling frame, where one would be difficult to construct, or where the population is so geographically dispersed that a simple random sample would be beyond the resources of the project. This approach to sampling can be carried out in stages; first you select the clusters, then you sub-sample within clusters. A random sample of 100 households scattered across a small town would not yield more than a handful of responses in each area or street. However, if you selected four or five areas at random, and within each area four or five streets, and from these four or five households to interview, you would have a cluster sample which would provide more detailed information about the range of views across the town.

In many cases, cluster sampling will be a more convenient option than a simple random sample approach. There is, however, a price to pay for such convenience. Cluster samples tend to have more sampling error than simple random samples. This is because they involve more steps and error is incurred at each step of any sample design. Thus, all things being equal, two steps produce more errors than a one step approach.

Non-Random Sampling

Random sampling may be difficult or inappropriate in some research situations. When surveying 'rough sleepers' for example, it is clearly impractical to conduct a random sample, as you would have no idea as to the characteristics of the population. Random sampling may also be inappropriate when conducting qualitative research – where the generation of either figures or statistics is less important than exploring specific views and experiences. Non-random samples are often easier and cheaper to achieve, but with such sampling methods variability and bias cannot be measured or controlled. This can be a serious problem and certainly one which should be considered before using a non-random sample strategy.

Quota Sampling

As with any sampling technique, quota sampling starts from the premise, firstly, that the sample should be drawn from across the population and, secondly, that the main characteristic(s) of the sample should match the incidence of that characteristic(s) within the population. The actual procedure starts by dividing the population into an exhaustive number of mutually exclusive groups or 'strata', such as age, sex, occupation, or house tenure preference. The distribution of these characteristics within the population may be found in Census data, or it may have to be estimated from other sources. Each interviewer is then given a group, and told the number to be interviewed. For example, they may be told to obtain 50 men and 50 women for the sample, 50 owner occupiers and 50 tenants, and so on. The numbers to be drawn from each sub-group are proportionate to their actual (or estimated) prevalence within the total population. How the individual respondents are chosen is left to the interviewers, just so long as their quotas are filled.

Such lack of control over the selection of respondents can undermine this approach, given its potential as a source of bias. Steps can be taken to improve quota sampling, but even with these improvements it still falls far short of random sampling in guaranteeing a representative sample of the population. Moreover the improvements tend to undermine the main advantages of quota sampling. Quota sampling is comparatively cheap and easy to use. There is no need for a comprehensive sampling frame, and no need to call back if a particular respondent is not available; you simply replace them with someone else who 'fits the bill'. That is why, despite the problems of bias, it continues to be popular particularly with those conducting market research and political opinion surveys.

Purposive Sampling
In some situations you might want to focus your research on a small geographic area, or on a relatively small number of people. In such cases you might purposively select your sample. The ubiquitous 'exit poll', is perhaps the most obvious example of purposive sampling. What exit polls do is to interview people as they leave the polling station and ask them how they voted. Typically, additional information is also collected, covering such topics as age and the nature of current employment. This allows the 'pollsters' to generate a socio-economic profile of the voters. This information is not only used to predict the outcome of that particular election campaign, but can then be employed to target similar groups at the next election, in an attempt to predict that result through tracing any noticeable shifts in political allegiance. Alternatively, by knowing how all the parliamentary constituencies voted last time, you might choose to target those constituencies which best reflect the national pattern. You could then purposively select those constituencies for polling prior to the next general election, as a means of predicting its outcome. Such an approach could be employed, for example, to conduct a survey into customer perceptions of the housing service.

Snowball or Reputational Sampling
Snowball sampling involves purposely selecting one respondent as a starting point and then asking them to recommend other suitable respondents. Suppose you wanted to interview those who had been influential in determining national housing policy over the last 25 years. It is difficult to identify all the relevant actors, but you happen to know one person who is considered to be an influential decision maker. You would start the process by interviewing them, and then ask for a recommendation as to who you should interview next. By repeating this approach over time an appropriate number of subjects will be interviewed. The value of snowball sampling is as a means of identifying interviewees whose characteristics are not obvious from any other source.

There is also some benefit in using this approach as it is a means of overcoming resistance to participating in a survey. If the person to be interviewed has effectively been introduced or recommended there is a greater chance that they will participate. It is, therefore, a valuable tool when embarking on a study of individuals who may be wary of 'outsiders'. Examples of this would be the housing needs of certain ethnic minorities, or people with special needs. Studying the housing experiences of women in a Womens' Aid Hostel would undoubtedly require such an approach. Generating a random sample of such groups is hindered by the fact that no easily accessible or accurate record exists for particular sub groups of the population. The problem, of course is that the sample is based on personal contacts and reputation: it is entirely possible that in making their recommendations respondents might, consciously or unconsciously, ignore other important actors and that bias might be introduced.

Making Choices

The most commonly asked questions about sampling must be (i) which is the best sampling method to use, and (ii) how large should the sample be? There is no straightforward answer to either question. The decision on which method to use will be influenced by a variety of considerations – the research goals, the nature and size of the population and, not least, the resources available to carry out the research.

Naturally, you will want to adopt the best approach, the one which you are confident will produce the most representative sample and the fewest errors. Yet, the practical nature of the decisions which often have to be made mean that the sampling method used is a compromise between the desirable and the possible.

As for sample size, the basic point to remember is that accuracy increases with size. Suppose the research was considering the income of tenants in a small sheltered housing complex. There are 50 tenants whose incomes range from £5,000-£50,000 per annum, with the mean income for the population being (say) £18,000. If just five tenants were sampled at random you might well get a figure significantly higher or lower than the true mean; just by the luck of the draw. If, on the other hand, you were to survey 40 tenants the anomalies would tend to be ironed-out. Consequently, the estimated mean would be closer to the true mean for the population. In other words, the larger the sample size, the closer the sample estimate will be to the true figure for the population. Also, the larger and more varied the population, the larger the sample will have to be.

Statistical Sampling

As a general rule many researchers would suggest that where statistical analysis is being contemplated the sample size should be not less than 30. You can of course use statistical techniques to determine the appropriate sample size. The object here is to be able to make generalisations about a population within a known and acceptable margin of error. There should be no significant difference between the sample and the population on any important characteristics. To determinine sample size by statistical means, two important considerations need to be addressed; namely sampling error and your confidence in the representativeness of the sample.

Sampling Error
It is unlikely that the characteristics of any sample will be identical to those of the population from which it is drawn. Small differences will always exist, but the aim here is to make sure that these differences are as small as possible and certainly within a few percentage points of the mean.

Confidence Level
Confidence in the representativeness of the sample is expressed in terms of the probability of error. Typically, confidence levels of between 95-99 per cent are chosen. If you chose a level of 95 per cent, for example, you are saying that you are confident that the sample and the population characteristics will be the same 95 per cent of the time, but that there is a five per cent chance that they will be different.

Formulae for determining sample size are available in many research methods text books (see for example Fowler, 1988; Nachmias and Nachmias, 1996). These formulae make use of statistical procedures which are beyond the scope of this book. However anyone with a basic understanding of statistics will have no difficulty in determining sample sizes using such a formula.

Suppose you wanted to extend the household income survey mentioned above to the whole tenant population (say 10,000 homes) the sample size could be determined following the formula given in Nachmias and Nachmias (1996: 198-199). This formula is derived from the equation for standard error thus:

$$SE = s/\sqrt{n}$$

where

SE	=	standard error
n	=	sample size
s	=	standard deviation

Inverting the formula the calculation would then look like this:

$$n = s^2/(SE)^2$$

This leaves parts of the calculation unknown, namely the standard deviation, which is the amount of variation around the mean, and the standard error. As it is impossible to know accurately these figures without collecting the data, some estimate has to be made. This might be achieved by using a pilot study or by making use of the results of previous studies, for example a local or national income survey. In this case if a random sample is to be drawn from a population of 10,000 households we might settle for an $SE = 0.16$ and $s^2 = 0.20$ as Nachmias and Nachmias (1996) do in their example. The sample size would be:

$$n = 0.20 / 0.00026 = 769$$

If this estimated sample size is too great a proportion of the population, a correction can be used. In this case the final sample size is calculated by:

$$n' = n/1+(n/N)$$

where N = population size (in this case 10,000)

$$n' = 769/1+769 / (10,000) = 714$$

A random sample of 714 cases should be representative of the population, given the limits that have been set. In practice, however, decisions on sample size are usually more complex, particularly where more than one variable is being considered. Resource constraints have to be taken into account, as was noted earlier, so you often have to settle for whatever degree of accuracy is practicable. Statistical formulae such as that used here may provide a useful guide to appropriate sample size but they still need to be treated with care as there always remains an element of guesswork, particularly in estimating standard deviation and standard error.

One other factor to be taken into account when deciding on sample size is non-response. If, as above, you want a sample of 714 tenants to complete a postal questionnaire, but you estimated that 20-25 per cent would not reply, you would select a sample of 900 tenants in order to improve the chances of reaching that target. Again this illustrates the degree of subjectivity that is required when conducting this type of exercise. Unfortunately, there is no simple statistical formula that can provide the ideal sample size.

Table 7.1: Sampling Techniques

Type of Sampling	Characteristics	Advantages	Disadvantages
RANDOM SAMPLING			
Simple random	Assign each unit in the population a unique number then select sample using random numbers.	Easy to analyse; requires minimal prior knowledge of population; free of possible classification errors.	Does not make full use of any knowledge of population characteristics; larger errors for same sample size than stratified random sampling.
Systematic random	Choose a random starting point within the sampling interval (n) then select every nth unit for inclusion in the sample. The natural order of the population is employed.	Easy to draw and check; where population is ordered with respect to relevant characteristic, gives stratification effect which reduces variability.	Estimates of error likely to be high where there is a stratification effect; if sampling interval is related to periodic ordering of the population, there may be an increase in variability.
Stratified random	Identify strata in the population by certain characteristics (e.g. age, sex) and then select at random from each stratum.	Assures representativeness with respect to the property which forms the basis of the classifying units and, therefore, reduces variability; decreases chance of failing to include members of population because of classification process; characteristics of each stratum can be estimated, and hence comparison can be made.	Requires accurate information on proportion of population in each stratum, otherwise increases error; if stratified lists are unavailable, may be costly to construct with possibility of faulty classification and, hence, increased variability.
Multi-stage cluster	Randomly select hierarchical groups (clusters) from the sampling frame. Select the sample at random from these clusters.	Can save time and cost if clusters are defined by geographic area; requires lists only for units in selected clusters; characteristics of the cluster as well as those of the population can be estimated; can be used for subsequent samples because it is the cluster and not the individual unit that is selected and, therefore, substitution of units may be permissible.	Larger errors for comparable sample than with other probability samples; requires the ability to assign each unit of the population to a unique cluster, inability to do this may result in duplication or omission of units.
NON-RANDOM SAMPLING			
Quota	Classify the population in terms of relevant characteristics, determine the desired proportion of sample in each strata, and then decide on quotas for fieldworkers.	Sampling and conducting fieldwork is efficient and relatively cheap, since units can be selected to be close to each other.	Introduces bias with fieldworker's classification of respondents and non-random selection within classes.
Purposive	Target individual units on the basis of pre-existing information (e.g. 'Exit Polls').	(As above)	(As above)
Snowball	Purposely select starting point and then ask respondents to nominate other suitable subjects.	(As above)	(As above)

Further Reading

Blalock, H., (1984), *Social Statistics*, (Second Edition). London: McGraw-Hill.

Bryman, A., and Cramer, C., (1990), *Quantitative Data Analysis for Social Scientists*. London: Routledge.

Fowler, F., (1988), *Survey Research Methods.* Newbury Park CA: Sage.

Moser, C., and Kalton, G., (1983), *Survey Methods in Social Investigation*, (Second Edition). London: Heinemann.

Nachmias, C., and Nachmias, D., (1996), *Research Methods in the Social Sciences* (Fifth Edition). London: Arnold.

Rowntree, D., (1981), *Statistics Without Tears*, London: Penguin.

CHAPTER 8:
Questionnaires

Objectives of the Chapter

This chapter is designed to ensure that the reader:

- understands the appropriate use of questionnaires;

- can construct a questionnaire to address a topic of interest;

- knows and understands the various types of questions commonly used in questionnaires; and

- is able to consider the steps necessary to administer a questionnaire survey successfully.

Introduction

Questionnaires and interviews are the main tools employed in housing research. The distinction between them is that a questionnaire is a structured interview which requires the respondent to answer a pre-determined set of questions. Interviews are typically less structured, and allow for a wider ranging exploration of a particular topic. While this chapter focuses upon questionnaires, Chapter 9 considers the use of interviews.

Questionnaires are perhaps the best known of all available research instruments. Within housing, both tenant surveys and social surveys are widely used as a means to gather structured and representative information, as was noted in Chapter 1. This material can provide an insight into how current services are operating, or perceived to be operating, and is, therefore, critical to organisational monitoring. Such questionnaires can also provide information for policy planning exercises. With the recent spate of stock transfers from the public sector to the so-called 'independent' sector, a tenant survey would be a useful means whereby new landlords could get clear insights into the social make-up of their tenants. While each of these tasks has a direct operational and strategic output, the information generated can also be employed in public relations.

The objective of the survey will largely determine the questions to be asked. Everyone is familiar with the questionnaire, from an opinion pollster on the street with a clipboard, to the glossy magazine survey which is invariably entitled *"Does your sex life shape up?"*, or even by the angst created, every ten years, when attempting to fill in the Census. The reasons for the ubiquity of questionnaires are not hard to find. They can offer a quick, relatively cost-effective and efficient means of gathering a broad range of information, directly from people about their feelings, attitudes, beliefs and personal circumstances, as well as their social and economic situation. It should be noted, however, that the quality of information derived from such questionnaires is dependent upon the nature of the questions asked, the type and actual size of survey, and the care taken in its execution. While they are a well used research tool, questionnaires need to be treated with caution; great care must be taken at every stage of their design, if they are to yield truly meaningful and useful information.

This chapter will consider some of the main issues involved in questionnaire design, highlighting the strengths and weaknesses of this data-collection method. Once the questionnaire has been designed and administered, the data collected has to be analysed and interpreted. These aspects of the research process are covered in Chapter 14.

Types of Questionnaire

Having decided on the basic objectives of the survey, consideration needs to be given to the most appropriate type of questionnaire to be employed. There are three basic questionnaire methods: the postal survey, the face-to-face interview and the telephone survey. The final choice will be influenced by a number of considerations such as the nature of the topics to be explored, the type of respondent, available resources, (essentially time and finance) and considerations about data accuracy.

Postal surveys are relatively cheap, can accommodate a large sample size more readily, but often produce low response rates. Such low response rates can undermine the reliability of the sample, as those who reply may not be representative of the population. It may be the case that only a particular type of person responds to the questionnaire. Another problem with this type of survey is that it is not particularly suited to complex questions. Obviously, a question that requires monitoring is outwith the bounds of this type of survey. On the plus side, the anonymity offered by questionnaires can be very useful when dealing with sensitive issues. The specific issue of response rates is touched upon later in the chapter.

Face-to-face surveys are more expensive to conduct, given the labour and travel costs involved. Face-to-face interviews can offer support, and can help clarify any misunderstandings that arise from the questions. As a result, they can be used to tackle more complex questions. However, without careful training, interviewers can introduce their own bias and can either consciously or unconsciously steer the respondent in a particular direction.

Telephone surveys, while not as expensive as face-to-face interviews, still require trained interviewers and the expense of telephone charges. Obviously, they exclude those without a telephone, or who are ex-directory. As was noted in the previous chapter, this can introduce a marked bias in the results, as the inaccuracy of by-election predictions based on such poll evidence often shows. While the short and well focused telephone survey can deliver a high response rate, the best results tend to come from a pre-contact, as opposed to a 'cold calling' approach, particularly where such an interview method – especially to a person's home – would be viewed as intrusive. The main disadvantages are that such interviews have to be short, no longer than twenty minutes, and that it is not always possible to identify who exactly you are speaking to.

Where possible, when using any questionnaire method, a covering letter should be sent to all selected respondents which explains the purpose of the research. This letter should also stress why their participation is important, outline any permissions that may need to be obtained, such as from employers, and indicate what use will be made of the subsequent results. In the case of a face-to-face survey, the letter should clearly indicate when exactly the survey will be taking place. With postal surveys, a deadline should be set for the return of the completed questionnaire. Two weeks is seen as about the right length of time, but state a precise date. It is also usual to guarantee confidentiality or anonymity, but be sure that you have the systems in place to honour such a guarantee. Don't promise what you cannot deliver, especially in relation to anonymity. The letter should, therefore, be brief and friendly, but businesslike in tone. In other instances it may be more appropriate to get an article about the survey published in the local newspaper, or to have a special newsletter distributed to the selected residents. It is also worth briefing all those who might be contacted by those affected by the survey, especially the relevant housing department staff and the local police. In this way any rumours about the survey can be dispelled at an early stage, before they gain momentum.

Asking Questions

Initial thoughts about the purpose of the survey act as a guide to which questions should be asked. If you were using a questionnaire to assist in the planning of adequate housing provision for the elderly, within a particular locality, over the next ten years, questions about household age and make-up would be critical, as would those on income levels and benefit dependence. The nature of the population's current housing might also have a bearing, as would future housing preferences, in respect of sheltered housing.

A point worth bearing in mind is that, in most cases, you will only have one chance to put your questions. The questions (often referred to as items) must, therefore, reflect the aims of the study. It is often too easy to include additional questions which, although of general interest, are not germane to the task in hand. Questions must also be constructed in a way that ensures clear and unambiguous interpretation. Respondents must understand clearly what they are being asked.

> *"A good questionnaire has to be designed specifically to suit the study's aims and the nature of its respondents. It needs ... to be clear, unambiguous and uniformly workable. Its design must minimise potential errors from respondents, interviewers and coders. And, since people's participation in surveys is voluntary, a questionnaire has to help in engaging their interest, encouraging their co-operation, and eliciting answers as close as possible to the truth."*

(Honville and Jowell *et al*, 1987, 27)

Table 8.1: Examples of Survey Types

Survey Type	Use made of survey
Tenant Surveys	Satisfaction or perception of service delivery or policies. Tenants' attitudes or preferences towards new or proposed alterations in services. Potential entitlement to social security benefits/other entitlements.
Target Population Surveys	Assessing whether the policy is reaching and meeting the requirements of the target population (such as Right to Buy, Rent to Mortgage (RTM), Scottish Homes Grants for Renting or Owner Occupation (GRO) purchasers). Experiences and attitudes towards a particular aspect of the housing market and/or particular policy direction (e.g. DoE private renters' survey in England; Scottish Office roofless).
General Population Surveys	Profile of households in population at large (Census). Housing careers and future housing intentions (Consumer Attitude Survey). Opinion surveys (BMRB Omnibus Survey).
Survey of Experts	Generate feedback on the operation of a particular policy. Canvass views on new areas of policy development.

Time spent thinking about the wording of questions, at this stage, will avoid a lot of hard work and frustration, when the time comes to analyse the collected data. As noted earlier, the method adopted for questionnaire delivery has a bearing on the type of questions that can be asked. Postal questionnaires do not lend themselves to sophisticated questions, as you will have no control over the completion of the questionnaire. Questionnaires carried out by interviewers have their own problems, but with proper training interviewers can elucidate information on more complex topics. A useful rule is that at all times you need to ask yourself why am I asking that particular question? Does it add information which might be relevant to this study? If the answer is no, then omit the question.

Care and attention should be paid both to the use of language and to the wording of items. Think carefully about the audience and construct the questionnaire using language that is as simple as possible, yet still conveys the meaning of the question. Similarly do not ask questions which fall beyond the respondent's knowledge or ability to answer. Asking tenants their views on 'void levels' or 'open space management' would normally produce a blank response. Further, a housing officer may be reasonably expected to know about the operation of the allocation policy, but may not be conversant with the procedures by which the allocations policy is amended or revised. If specific information is required you may need to identify more clearly the members of staff to be surveyed. Another approach is to give advance notice of the topic areas to be covered, so that the respondent can look up and become familiar with the necessary information.

How you make sense of a response is the critical consideration in this context. If you fail to define clearly and precisely what you mean, the differences between respondents may reflect differences of interpretation, rather than differences in experience. Always ensure, therefore, that a question does not contain any words, expressions, or technical terms that might be confusing, or have a different meaning for different respondents. Consider, for example, the following question taken from an appraisal questionnaire on a new housing development:

Q.1
Do you find your house satisfactory?
YES   ❑
NO   ❑
Don't Know   ❑

The answer generated here would be meaningless. It is also crucial to avoid prejudicial language and that which has unconscious sexist or racist assumptions. Just how easily questionnaire designers fall into this trap is illustrated by the following question from a survey:

Q.2
Do you agree or disagree with the following statements?
It is generally better to have a man at the head of a department composed of both men and women employees ... It is acceptable for women to hold important political offices in State and National Governments.
(Eichler, 1988, 43-44)

This question asks respondents to measure women against an assumed norm, namely, that men head departments. In this case respondents could only agree or disagree with the statements. They could not, for example, express a preference for a woman head of department. Similarly, asking a person for their Christian name can also be considered offensive by members of other religious groups. A more appropriate convention is to ask for their first name(s).

Also be careful when asking questions which rely upon memory; people are often better at remembering what has happened to them, rather than when. For example:

Q.3
If you have moved home please provide the month and year of your last move.

❑❑ month.   19❑❑ year.

Is the level of detail demanded by this question necessary for your purposes? If not, it might be better to provide respondents with a list of options to tick. This alternative approach would ask:

Q.4
If you have you moved home, was your last move:
[Tick the appropriate box]
In last twelve months   ❑

In last five years ☐
In last ten years ☐
More than ten years ago ☐

In this way you might ensure that all the main options are covered. Any list of options should be exhaustive, in that all possible answers are covered. This is often achieved by introducing an 'Other' category, perhaps with an additional 'Please specify' request.

It is also important to ensure that each item contains just one question. Do not ask double-barrelled questions where the respondent's answer could fit more than one category. For example:

Q.5
Do you think the Council should cut spending on planned maintenance, or make savings on staffing costs in housing management?

Leading questions should never be employed. For example, it might be difficult to answer 'no' to a question couched in the following terms:

Q.6
Do you disapprove of the proposals for probationary tenancies?
Yes ☐
No ☐
Don't know ☐

Whereas:

Q.7
Which phrase is closest to your views of the proposal for probationary tenancies?
They are a much needed tool to reduce anti-social behaviour ☐
They will not achieve anything that cannot be achieved already ☐
They represent an infringement on the civil rights of tenants ☐

Researchers often construct questions in a way which invites the respondent to agree with their personal views or prejudices. Such leading questions encourage biased replies and negate the whole research exercise. Questions must, therefore, be designed in such a way that the respondent does not feel that their answer is incorrect, or that the response will meet with disapproval, or that the question is intrinsically biased. The exception to this rule is when the researcher specifically wants to test the strength of their respondent's views on a particular set of statements. In such instances, use is made of a *Likert* scale question, a technique which will be discussed later in the chapter. The issue of bias, while being touched on in this chapter, will be given fuller attention in the following chapter when consideration is given to interview techniques.

If the questionnaire has to glean information on sensitive issues it is important to make sure you get the information you need, and need the information you get. Four useful questions to consider, in relation to asking sensitive questions are:

- Do I need to ask the question at all?
- What level of detail do I require?
- How should I word the question?
- Where should the question be positioned within the questionnaire?

Many researchers prefer to place potentially sensitive issues near the end of the questionnaire, so that, should the respondent decline to answer any more questions, you at least have all the information from the earlier sections. Bear in mind that the introduction of a sensitive question may terminate the interview. Another avenue is to develop a more appropriate or acceptable way of asking the question. Potentially sensitive issues are often diffused by asking respondents to tick categories or place themselves within bands. When asked about income, for example, a respondent might be happier to indicate a broad income band rather than state their actual gross salary. If you fail to get the information you need, or choose to drop certain questions, bear in mind there may well be other sources of data which could shed light on the your topic of interest. Generalised income information for particular groups within the population could be generated from the national Family Household Survey. Unemployment levels within particular neighbourhoods may be available from the local Department of Social Security.

Question Types

When selecting question types there are a number of choices to make. Do you, for example, write the question as a statement? To glean information on the quality of the housing management service do you pose the statement: *"Housing staff are usually helpful when dealing with enquiries"*, and then ask the respondent to·select from a response menu? Or do you set a question, such as: *"How helpful are housing staff when dealing with your enquiries?"*. In this case you would record the individual response. Statements tend to be seen as less threatening, since they are usually phrased in a general, non-personal way. This might be helpful when dealing with sensitive issues, in that respondents are asked to react to somebody else's idea, rather than answer a direct question about their own views. The approach adopted will depend upon the sort of information you want to glean. Using both styles, in the same questionnaire, can be a good way of breaking the monotony created by relying solely upon questions or statements. Changing the rhythm of a questionnaire is a useful tool, especially in the case of surveys that take some time to complete.

Open-ended or Closed Items

Questionnaire items written in an open-ended format, such as in Q.8 below, allow respondents to answer questions, or respond to statements, in their own words:

Q.8
How helpful are housing staff when dealing with your enquiries?

Write Response...

The advantage of this open-ended format is that it allows for greater freedom of expression: the respondent can say what they feel without being encumbered by the researcher's idea of what are appropriate response categories. Limiting response categories can act as a source of bias, which can be avoided by using open-ended items. The respondent can expand and/or qualify their answers as they feel necessary. By adopting this method of question construction, an insight can be gained into why people believe what they do.

The difficulties with this open-ended format come when you are trying to analyse and interpret the data. Their very flexibility can make coding – preparing the data for computer analysis – difficult and time consuming. Further, because respondents answer using their own words, responses have to be interpreted and classified. This too can give rise to misinterpretation and misclassification.

Most questionnaires rely more heavily upon the alternative 'closed', or 'forced choice', format. In this instance, the respondent is faced with a number of alternative answers to the question or statement posed, and is asked to select the response that comes closest to how they feel. For example, Q.8 above could be presented in a closed format:

Q.9
How helpful are housing staff when dealing with your enquiries?

Very helpful	❑
Helpful	❑
Neither helpful or unhelpful	❑
Unhelpful	❑
Very unhelpful	❑
No opinion	❑

Closed items are quicker to answer and easier to code than their open-ended alternatives. They are also more reliable, given all respondents are asked to react to the same set of options. The respondents also do not have to be articulate. On the other hand, they can give a misleading impression by forcing respondents to choose from a limited range of options. There is no opportunity for respondents to qualify their responses.

Closed format items come in a variety of guises, with the most common categories being: the single answer list, the multiple answer list, category rank order, numeric, grid, *Likert* type and semantic differential.

Single Answer List

As the name suggests, a single answer list involves the respondent choosing one answer from a given list of options. The response categories, as in all types of closed item, must be mutually exclusive; that is, the respondent's answer should fit one and only one category. They also require to be exhaustive, in that the available categories should cover all the possible options. The usual way to ensure that closed-ended items are exhaustive is to provide a catch all category such as 'Other' or 'Don't know'. A typical single answer list item would be:

Q.10
What type of dwelling do you live in?
[Please tick the appropriate box]

Detached	❑
Semi-detached	❑
Terraced	❑
Tenement flat	❑
Other flat	❑
Maisonette	❑
Converted house	❑
Other *(please specify)*	❑ ....

A supplementary question is often used to get additional information from those who select the 'Other'category. The example, 'please specify', invites the respondent to write in details which can be coded at a later date.

Multiple Response

In some cases a question might invite more than one response. If you wanted to build a profile of household affluence within a particular area (and that owning labour-saving devices was felt to be an appropriate indicator), you might opt for a multiple response format such as:

Q.11
Which of the following household appliances do you own?
[Please tick one or more box(es) as appropriate]

Dishwasher	❑
Microwave oven	❑
Tumble drier	❑
Vacuum cleaner	❑
Washing machine	❑
Food processor	❑

Category

When personal information is needed in a survey, as noted above, it is often better to provide categories of responses because these appear less personal and specific. Information about age and income is commonly elicited using categories or bands, for example:

Q.12
What is your age?
[Please tick the appropriate box]

Under 16	❑
16-20	❑
21-25	❑
26-30	❑
31-35	❑
36-40	❑
Over 40	❑

Q.13
Into which of these categories did your gross annual income for last year fall?
[Please tick the appropriate box]

Below	£10,000	❑
£10,000 – £15,000		❑
£15,001 – £20,000		❑
£20,001 – £25,000		❑
£25,001 – £30,000		❑
Over	£30,000	❑

The disadvantage is that such banding may obscure the information you really require. Income information for rent policy exercises would, more often than not, need to be of a finer grain than that provided by an income banding question. As is obvious from both Q.12 and 13 it is important to ensure your banding categories do not overlap.

Rank Order

The rank order response format is similar to the multiple response question, but in this case respondents are asked not only to make a choice, but to provide relative judgements by putting their preferences in rank order. Suppose, for example, a new building programme was being planned and several sites were available to develop. It may be useful to find out which areas of the town potential tenants would prefer to live in. To gather such information, use could be made of a rank order item, such as:

Q.14
Please indicate, in rank order, the five areas in which you would prefer to rent a new house. Your top preference should be ranked 1; 2 denotes your second choice, and so on, while the place you would least like to live is recorded using the number 5.

Broomhill	❑
Eastgate Estate	❑
Foleys Farm	❑
Greenwood Gardens	❑
Princes Park	❑
Other *(please specify)*	❑ ....

It is important not to ask people to make too many ranking decisions. When asked to express more than about five preferences, the task becomes too difficult and respondents may start to allocate ranks on an arbitrary basis.

Quantity

If the required response is a numeric value, giving the amount of some characteristic such as age, number of bedrooms, number of children, or travel to work time/distance, it can be expressed either as a quantity, or numeric response. This reduces the need for lists. Data categories can then be determined at a later stage when the pattern of responses is considered. For example:

Q.15
What is the approximate distance (in kilometres) from your home to you workplace?
[Please enter your answer in the boxes provided]

□□Km.

Grid

Grid response formats can be used where it is both possible, and appropriate, to ask a series of related questions at the same time. Householders might be asked about the condition of internal repair within their property using a grid or table, such as:

Q.16
How would you assess the condition (state of repair) of the following aspects of your home?

CONDITION	Ceilings	Walls	Floors	Doors	Paintwork
Very good	□	□	□	□	□
Good	□	□	□	□	□
Minor repairs needed	□	□	□	□	□
Major repairs needed	□	□	□	□	□

Likert Scale

The *Likert* scale is a method to test the strength of attitudes to a given set of statements on a particular topic. Respondents are asked to indicate on a scale, the strength of their agreement or disagreement with each statement. The statements should be equally divided between those which indicate a positive attitude towards the issue and those which reflect a negative attitude. Unlike other questionnaire items, the statements used in *Likert* type scales are intended to solicit attitude scores and can, therefore, be biased. The following example attempts to explore attitudes towards CCT in housing management services:

Q.17
The introduction of CCT into housing management will improve the quality of service delivered to tenants.
[Please consider the above statement carefully and then tick the box which comes closest to your opinion.]

Strongly Agree	□
Agree	□
Undecided	□
Disagree	□
Disagree Strongly	□

Semantic Differential

Here again the respondents are asked to react to a series of concepts or statements. In the case of the semantic differential, however, the extremes of the scale are labelled with opposing adjectives, such as good or bad, rich or poor. Respondents indicate the strength of their feeling on a scale between these two extremes. A seven point scale is generally used, but other ranges of numbers might be more applicable.

Q.18
How would you describe your job as a housing officer?
[The following adjectives represent extreme views. Please consider each set of adjectives carefully and then place a circle around the number which comes closest to how you feel about your job.]

Satisfying	1	2	3	4	5	6	7	Unsatisfying
Interesting	1	2	3	4	5	6	7	Boring
Demanding	1	2	3	4	5	6	7	Undemanding
Responsible	1	2	3	4	5	6	7	Menial
Varied	1	2	3	4	5	6	7	Repetitive

Layout and Design

The layout adopted in any questionnaire is an important consideration. Not only should the document look professional, but good layout is also an essential element for the smooth execution of any questionnaire. Questionnaires should be typed or printed. People will be put off by a poorly presented questionnaire and access to word processing and Desk Top Publishing (DTP) should ensure a better quality of design is achieved.

While there are no hard and fast rules about questionnaire design there are a number of points that should be considered. Firstly, it is important to leave plenty of white space around each question. Questionnaires should never look cramped, as this may confuse either respondent or surveyor. Secondly, any instructions to the respondent, or surveyor, should be clear, especially when use is made of contingency questions. Use should, therefore, be made of different typefaces, or **bolding** to distinguish questions from instructions (for instance, normal type face for questions, *italics* for surveyor instructions). Thirdly, if computer analysis is to be used, the right hand column should be left solely for coding purposes. Actual response boxes should be towards the right-hand side of the page, as this helps the respondent in completing the questionnaire, and helps with any subsequent coding of results. A clear separation, on the right hand side of the page between response and coding boxes is, therefore, required as in Q.19 below. Often the coding section of the page is shaded, or printed in a different colour. To get a better feel for layout and design issues look at a range of questionnaires, such as the Census and any previous surveys conducted by your organisation.

Q.19
How would you describe your job as a housing officer?
[The following adjectives represent extreme views. Please consider each set of adjectives carefully and then place a circle around the number which comes closest to how you feel about your job.]

									CODE
Satisfying	1	2	3	4	5	6	7	Unsatisfying	❑
Interesting	1	2	3	4	5	6	7	Boring	❑
Demanding	1	2	3	4	5	6	7	Undemanding	❑
Responsible	1	2	3	4	5	6	7	Menial	❑
Varied	1	2	3	4	5	6	7	Repetitive	❑

Questionnaire design is not merely an issue of visual design, in layout terms, but also involves the ordering of questions. A useful convention is to start with closed questions leaving any open items until later. The initial questions set the tone for the questionnaire. Begin with straightforward questions, those that are non-controversial and easy to answer. Questions of a sensitive or personal nature should generally be left until nearer the end. In that way the respondents have had a chance to get the feel of the questionnaire, and may be more willing to answer the more difficult questions later. If they choose not to, at least you will have gleaned some relevant information, which you might not have had if you antagonised the respondent early on in the questionnaire. It is also a useful practice to end with an open question, such as those which ask for further comments. This gives respondents an opportunity to bring in their own experiences or points of view.

With the advent of lap-top computers there is now the possibility of designing and conducting a questionnaire survey directly onto the computer. This design approach can ease the difficulty of confronting a respondent with a large complex questionnaire, for its actual size is hidden. Questionnaire software packages can also automatically miss the pages that are irrelevant, given a previous response to a particular question, thus reducing the time taken to conduct the questionnaire. This approach also has the advantage of minimising data preparation exercises, at a later stage, and thus enhancing accuracy.

Having completed the design exercise, take some time to look over the completed questionnaire and ask yourself how would you feel about answering such a document. In essence, is it well presented, does it contain a logical structure, and are all the questions necessary? It is also useful, at this stage, to check again whether your desired cross-tabulated questions are still logical and possible. Often the editing and refining task inadvertently cuts out some of the initial ambitions you had for the survey.

Piloting the Questionnaire

Before the design process can be completed the questionnaire must be tested to determine if it does the job it was designed to do. Does it in fact provide the information needed? This process of piloting is particularly important where self-administered questionnaires are being used, given so much depends upon the clarity of language, and the instructions to the respondents. Piloting should reveal ambiguities and/or difficulties with either the questions or instructions. It will also give you an indication of just how long it takes to complete the questionnaire. Try as far as possible to duplicate the environment in which the survey is to take place. This means, for example, that the questionnaire should be tested on a small group of people who are typical of those who will receive the final version. If a particular survey focuses on housing considerations within a particular neighbourhood, the pilot should be tried on a small group within a similar neighbourhood.

The pilot should focus on all aspects of the questionnaire design. Was the covering letter clear and informative? In relation to overall appearance, was the layout and presentation acceptable? Were the questions clear, and were there any which were misunderstood or duplicated? Were the lists provided too long, and could they be pruned back? Are the accompanying instructions clearly understandable and were they followed correctly? Finally, how long did it take to complete, and can this be shortened?

Having carried out a pilot exercise it is important that you take on board the results and revise the questionnaire. Ignoring what appear to be small problems at this stage, because it presents too much hassle to revise the question, could result in major difficulties when the survey is used out in the field.

Administering the Survey

Probably the most important issue, in relation to administering any questionnaire survey, is that you have a means of identifying individual surveys. If you are using a number of interviewers to carry out the work you will also need a unique identifier for them as well. Such codes allow you to cross-check easily and quickly on the survey's progress. If the coded surveys show up a particularly poor response rate in a specific locality, remedial action can be taken quickly. By having both a survey and an interviewer number you can, if necessary, take action to address issues of interviewer bias that may arise should one individual be found to be misinterpreting or mis-coding certain results. Within house condition surveys such identification codes are used to quickly locate the specific survey form that relates to a specific property. This allows for regular cross-checks to be conducted to ensure that surveyors are assessing each property in a uniform manner. This issue of validity was discussed in some detail in Chapter 6. If errors are found, the properties assessed by the offending surveyor can be isolated and re-surveyed or if it is a consistent fault then a re-coding exercise may be needed to rectify the situation. Unique identifiers are also critical if you intend to attach additional information, from other records, onto the questionnaire result. This is common practice when conducting a related physical and social survey for a specific neighbourhood.

In relation to good fieldwork practice, where possible allocate the individual questionnaires on a random basis when the survey is being undertaken by a group of interviewers and there is potential for survey bias. By adopting such an approach you effectively equalise out the potential effects of bias.

It is also worth establishing an on-going quality control system to check whether the initial enthusiasm of surveyors is maintained throughout. Too often, once the survey is into its second week interviewers adopt practices which speed up the survey, but in doing so they undermine the quality of answers provided. There is also a greater tendency for them to steer respondents in a particular direction because they get used to a pattern of responses. If you only collect the completed questionnaires at the end of survey such biases may not be apparent.

As a means of overcoming some of these bias difficulties, right from day one, it is essential that the interviewers are adequately briefed, and are given enough training to ensure they are conversant and comfortable with the survey. If you can get them to feel fully involved and committed to the research, and they appreciate the critical role they play in elucidating answers to key questions, then the quality of the finished survey will benefit greatly.

It is also good practice to ensure that all interviewers carry an identification card, with their photograph, as this will overcome a certain level of distrust. Informing the local police about the survey is a further help in overcoming potential distrust. As mentioned earlier, informing those who are to be surveyed either by letter or via a newsletter is also helpful in this regard.

Response Rate

Given the care taken in designing, piloting and administering the questionnaire it is natural that the researcher wants to receive as many replies as possible. Yet, not everyone will complete the questionnaire. Non-response can be a serious problem, especially in the case of postal questionnaires. The possibility that those who chose not to reply, are different from those who do, can seriously exacerbate this problem. What then is a good response rate? The general rule would be, *"... the more the merrier"*, but it really comes down to a question of how many replies would be needed for the results to be credible. If there were 20 households in a block of flats, being surveyed as part of a housing condition exercise, receiving only 10 replies might not be viewed as being a particularly good result. If, on the other hand, 1000 replies were received from a sample of 2000 households you might feel that such a response was satisfactory. While in both cases the response rate was 50 per cent, there would be greater confidence in reporting the views of 1000 out of a potential 2000 households, than those received by the 10 out of the possible 20.

How then do you improve the response rate? In the case of postal surveys the initial inclusion of a stamped, self-addressed envelope, is a useful aid to encouraging a response. Alternatively, if the geographical coverage for such a survey is small, the questionnaire could be delivered by hand, thus allowing the opportunity to introduce the survey, and make arrangements to pick it up at a convenient time. Such an approach is employed by the Census. In the case of most postal surveys, once the specified date has been exceeded a reminder, or follow-up, is sent to those who have not returned the questionnaire. The reminder should be brief and to the point, and it often helps to enclose another copy of the questionnaire. Sometimes a second or even third reminder may have to be sent, but there is a diminishing return to such an exercise, as costs increase while responses decline.

In the case of face-to-face interviews response rates can be improved by ensuring adequate training of the interviewers. Calling at the most convenient time is also crucial. Calling on a winter's evening does not produce a good response, particularly with elderly residents. Calling on Sunday mornings, or during public or trade holidays also produces a poor response. In this context, it is also important to have in place a clear call-back procedure. Again there is an issue of diminishing returns, in that the more return calls, the higher the cost, yet responses are invariably more difficult to generate.

If you plan to operate a follow-up system it is necessary to have some means of identifying the respondents. Questionnaires can be numbered, for example, so that non-respondents can be identified and reminders sent. However, if you have guaranteed respondents anonymity then, of course, you cannot follow-up non-respondents. Decide at the planning stage if a follow-up is to be used, or if anonymity is so important that you are prepared to accept a lower response rate. Consideration might also be given to other methods of encouraging people to respond such as offering incentives. Incentives can range from copies of the final report to money, or the chance to win a prize such as a portable television. You need to consider whether you have the resources to offer such incentives and whether they are appropriate to the research group being studied. For example, would it be appropriate to offer a television set to homeless people?

Questionnaires: Strengths and Weaknesses

As a means of collecting certain sorts of information, questionnaires have a great deal to recommend them. Questionnaires are:

- an efficient means of collecting information from large numbers of people and/or over a wide geographical area;
- relatively inexpensive, especially where they can be administered without the direct support of an interviewer/researcher;
- convenient for respondents who can work at their own pace;
- able to offer a degree of anonymity that is not possible with other research methods;
- if designed in a standardised and structured way, able to improve the reliability of the information collected; and
- easy to analyse using computer-based statistical packages.

As with all research methods, however, there is also a downside. Questionnaires are:

- essentially superficial, in that they elicit answers that are descriptive, rather than explanatory, since there is no capacity to probe or explore the provided answers;
- not particularly flexible in terms of questions and response categories;
- likely to yield poor response rates, especially in the case of postal surveys;
- very time consuming, in terms of development, design, execution and analysis; and
- also unpredictable, in that while a questionnaire may be targeted to a particular person there can be no guarantee that they will have answered the questions and that they did so unaided.

Table 8.2: Questionnaire Flow Diagram

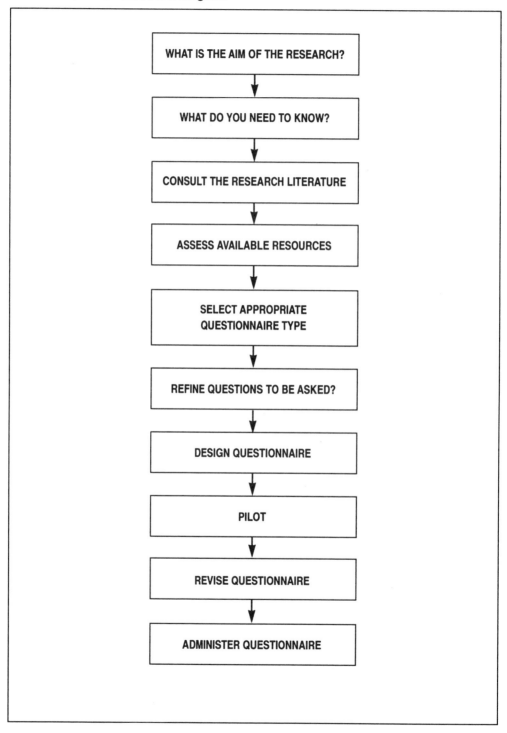

WHAT IS THE AIM OF THE RESEARCH?

WHAT DO YOU NEED TO KNOW?

CONSULT THE RESEARCH LITERATURE

ASSESS AVAILABLE RESOURCES

SELECT APPROPRIATE
QUESTIONNAIRE TYPE

REFINE QUESTIONS TO BE ASKED?

DESIGN QUESTIONNAIRE

PILOT

REVISE QUESTIONNAIRE

ADMINISTER QUESTIONNAIRE

Further Reading

Dillman, D., (1978), *Mail and Telephone Surveys: The Total Design Method*. New York: Wiley.

Hakim, C., (1987), *Research Design: Strategies and Choices in the Design of Social Research*. London: Allen and Unwin.

Moser, C., and Kalton, G., (1974), *Survey Methods in Social Investigation*. Heinemann: London.

Munn. P., and Drever, E., (1990), *Using Questionnaires in Small Scale Research*. Edinburgh: SCRE.

Newall, R., (1993), 'Questionnaires', in Gilbert, N., (ed), *Researching Social Life*. London: Sage.

Oppenheim, A., (1992), *Questionnaire Design, Interviewing and Attitude Measurement*. London: Pinter.

Prescott-Clarke, P., Atkins, J., Clemens, S., (1993), *Tenant Feedback: A Step-by-Step Guide to Tenant Satisfaction Surveys*. London: HMSO.

Procter, M., (1993), 'Measuring Attitude', in Gilbert, N., (ed), *Researching Social Life*. London: Sage.

de Vaus, D., (1993), *Surveys in Social Research*, (Third Edition). London: UCL Press.

CHAPTER 9:
Interviewing: Principles and Methods

Objectives of the Chapter

This chapter is designed to ensure that the reader:

- understands the appropriate use of interviews;

- can construct an interview appropriate to the topic of interest;

- knows and understands the various types of interview techniques commonly used in housing research; and

- is able to consider the steps necessary to conduct an interview successfully.

Introduction

Interviews have much in common with questionnaires. Careful planning and considered wordings are just as necessary to achieving a successful outcome. The difference is that interviews are always held on a face-to-face basis but questionnaires, while at times making use of this approach, are not confined to it, as was discussed in Chapter 8. It is also the case that most face-to-face questionnaires could not be described as an interview, in that the discussion is confined to answering the pre-set range of questions. Further, while questionnaires are good for gathering facts, as was noted in the previous chapter, they are less useful if you want to try to explore the attitudes and feelings which lie behind the often bland statements of fact. What exactly are the thought processes and intentions which underlie such facts or opinions? Questionnaires, particularly the postal variety where there is no face-to-face contact, are also limited as important non-verbal cues are lost: a facial expression, a shrug of the shoulders, or an intonation in the voice can make a real difference to how a particular answer might be interpreted. A skilful interview can yield a wealth of information, thus providing the study with both depth and colour, which can be missed through employing a questionnaire. Consider the question of housing neighbourhood preferences, for example:

Q.1
Please indicate, in rank order, the areas in which you would prefer to rent a new house. Your first preference should be ranked 1; 2 denotes your second choice, and so on with the least favoured area being indicated by the number 5 or 6.

Broomhill	❑
Eastgate Estate	❑
Foleys Farm	❑
Greenwood Gardens	❑
Princes Park	❑
Other *(please specify)*	❑ ....

This question is fine, as far as it goes, but it doesn't provide an opportunity to explore the attitudes which inform the respondents' preferences. If that is what you want to focus on, then consideration should be given to using some sort of interview instead of, or even perhaps as well as, a questionnaire. The alternative is ask people to respond to some pre-conceived notion of why they might want to live in one area, rather than another. Such structuring inevitably shapes the pattern of responses to fit the researcher's, rather than the respondents' views of the world. The advantage of the interview is that the respondents are free to express themselves in their own way, in their own words. The researcher, through using an interview, provides a framework – more or less loosely constructed – within which the respondent can answer the various questions. Further, it allows an opportunity to go on to discuss the various issues which they feel are relevant to the topic under consideration. It is this flexibility which distinguishes an interview from the typical questionnaire. Interviewers have the opportunity to probe the responses, thus creating the opportunity to explore the feelings and beliefs which help shape the respondents' attitudes. This assumes, of course, that the information you want to glean is meaningful, knowable and able to be made explicit. Interviews are also useful when addressing sensitive issues, or for exploring the possible parameters of a previously unresearched area. Interviews in the latter case can be helpful in framing the questions for a larger scale survey, perhaps using a questionnaire.

Given the interview's capacity to generate large quantities of material it is important to ensure that it is well thought through prior to being used in the field. As with questionnaires, therefore, it is crucial to consider fully the wording of individual questions and their ordering, although the interview format does create the opportunity to clarify any ambiguities, or conflicting definitions, should the need arise. This chapter begins by discussing the various types of interview, detailing the basic approaches to interviewing method. Later sections focus on interview techniques, the critical problem of bias, and how to record information. Certain logistical issues, which need to be considered before opting to pursue the interview as a research method, are also discussed. The chapter concludes by considering the advantages and disadvantages of this particular research method.

Types of Interview

Having decided to use interviews as a means to collect data, you then have to decide which is the most appropriate type for your purposes. There is a clear continuum in relation to interviewing; at one end the highly-structured interview, at the other the open unstructured interview. Between these two extremes there is a range of semi-structured options. For a more comprehensive discussion of interview types see May (1993), Spradley (1979) and Fielding (1993).

The Structured Interview

The structured interview is designed to be a standardised research instrument. The basic principle is that each respondent is taken through the same sequence of events; they are all asked the same questions in the same order. This procedure is intended to limit any variation in the way questions are asked and, therefore, minimises the possibility of bias being introduced. By adopting this approach you limit the possibility that a series of different interviews held with different people would focus on a differing set of questions.

The advantages of adopting this structured format lie in the ease of analysis and replicability. The downside is that much of the colour, spontaneity and flexibility, which is the hallmark of the interview method, is lost. In essence it mirrors the questionnaire format. Some probing of responses is possible (see below), but this tends to be limited by the pre-conceptions of the researcher, rather than those of the respondent. That said, for those who are new to conducting interviews, the more structured approach provides additional security. A typical question from a tightly structured interview would mirror a questionnaire, for example:

> **Q.2**
> **What phrase best describes your views of probationary tenancies?**
> They are a much needed tool to reduce anti-social behaviour ☐
> They will not achieve anything that cannot be achieved already ☐
> They represent an infringement on the civil rights of tenants ☐
> Other ☐

The Unstructured Interview

Unstructured or informal interviews depend on establishing a rapport between the interviewer and respondent, so that the interaction produces a natural flow of conversation. Indeed the respondent may be left with the impression that the interview was simply an interesting and stimulating conversation. However, from the interviewer's perspective this was a conversation with a very clear purpose. The interview questions posed were generated from the flow of the discussion, with the clear intention of creating an open atmosphere which encouraged the respondent to answer with considerable latitude. Unstructured interviews also give the interviewer great flexibility in that they can, at any time, alter their line of questioning in response to the differing situations that can emerge from individual responses. In relation to Question 2 above, within an unstructured interview session the respondents would be asked for their views on probationary tenancies, and the interviewer would explore each of their responses. They might also be asked their views about other responses, as a means of understanding the range of opinions on this particular topic.

Informal interview techniques are typically used in participant observation or ethnographic research. They may also be employed in the early stages of a research project to provide the necessary background material, which is then used to help inform a specific questionnaire item, or to develop a more structured interview schedule. When thinking about the research instruments to be used for a particular study it may be helpful to first explore the topic by conducting a set of interviews with people directly involved in the subject area.

All interviews are designed to elicit information. Getting the required information using the unstructured format demands considerable skill. The term unstructured interview should never be misconstrued to imply that the method represents a soft option. As with any interview or questionnaire they require careful planning and execution. The interviewer must be confident with the subject area and be capable of pursing a particular line of questioning, while still keeping to the topic in view. Interviewers, therefore, have to possess considerable personal skills and a sound knowledge of the topic in question. Another problem associated with employing this technique is the fact that unstructured interviews have a tendency to be both time consuming, and are open to the charge of bias, due to what is called 'interviewer response effect'. The problem of bias is, of course, common to all interview methods and will be considered more fully later. That said, bias is especially relevant when unstructured interviews are being used. Data management, analysis and interpretation can also be a problem. The very flexibility which allows the interviewer to accommodate not only different people, but also different situations, means that the resulting data may be very difficult to analyse and interpret for patterns and trends, given its diversity, quantity and inevitable differences in focus and emphasis.

The Semi-structured Interview

Most interview methods take a compromise position between these two extremes. The semi-structured, or guided interview, allows the respondent to talk about those aspects of the topic which are relevant to them. It does so within a loose framework which is intended to ensure that all the issues thought to be important by the researcher are adequately covered. In essence, it's a compromise which draws from both the checklist of the structured interview and the flexibility of the unstructured format. As a consequence, it makes the analysis of data more manageable, while retaining the opportunity to be flexible and open in certain areas of questioning. An interview schedule is used to guide and to focus the interview session, but this should not be viewed as a script. The semi-structured interview requires that the interviewer uses their skill and judgement to adapt the wording of the questions, as well as the question sequencing, to the demands of each individual interview situation. The schedule should help keep the interview focused and provide a degree of continuity across a set of related interviews. It should not do so, however, at the cost of interrupting the flow of the conversation. An example of an interview schedule, for training evaluation purposes, is reproduced below. The target group, in this instance, was the housing staff who had responsibility for organising and managing placements for trainees.

Figure 9.1: Interview Guide for Training Evaluation (Placements)

1. **What has the trainee achieved during the placement period?**
   [PROBE: Tasks accomplished; specific duties and responsibilities]

2. **How did the trainee perform in relation to non-task related functions?**
   [PROBE: Attitude towards work; interpersonal skills]

3. **What benefits do you see the trainee gaining from practice placements experience?**
   [PROBE: Strengths, weaknesses; best and worst aspects; internal organisational issues; areas which could change]

4. **What problems have you had to address when hosting placements within the organisations?**
   [PROBE: Internal management co-ordination problems; feelings of resentment by other staff; unique personnel management problems]

Group Interviews

Interviews are normally assumed to be a face-to-face interaction between two people; the interviewer and the interviewee. Group interviews, however, offer another potentially valuable source of information, and can provide data not only about the research topic per se, but also about the group norms and any associated dynamics which may have a relevance to the particular set of issues under investigation. Group interviews can, therefore, provide a distinct and different insight into an issue, one that may not have been revealed by individual interviews. How people react in groups and how the actions and opinions of individuals are affected by the way the group interacts, may be highly relevant to researching certain issues within the housing field. The dynamics of organisations in relation to accepted practice within housing management is one case in point. Group interviews can also provide a means of exploring a topic where the group members bring with them a range of experiences. As a consequence, group interviews can be useful in helpful to define the parameters for evaluating an existing programme.

Group interviews also have the added advantage of offering a relatively low-cost means of increasing the sample size in a qualitative study through the mechanism of focus groups. Focus groups are commonly employed within the commercial sector to provide feedback on product development and proposed marketing strategies. As Krueger points out:

> *"Focus groups are typically composed of six to ten people, but the size can range from as few as four to as many as twelve. The size is conditioned by two factors: it must be small enough for everyone to have an opportunity to share insights and yet large enough to provide diversity of perceptions."*
>
> (Krueger, 1994, 17)

Interviewing groups of people, of course, brings its own problems. Group interviews can be difficult to control with the resultant data or information being hard to record and analyse. An interview schedule, or checklist, is therefore essential to keeping the group focused on the research topic. Above all, conducting successful group interviews demands that the interviewer possess considerable skills in facilitating and moderating group discussions. Any interviewer, no matter which type of interview they are conducting, should gain both practice and skills in asking the questions. They need to know when and how best to probe the responses. It also takes time to learn how to guide the interview session so that it starts to flow more like a conversation. There are, as a consequence, a number of significant training issues involved in using this type of exercise.

Table 9.1 overleaf provides a summary of the main characteristics of each of the four basic types of interview method. It is important to remember, however, that these do not represent a definitive list of the available options. You might decide, for example, that you want to use an interview strategy which makes use of a number of types: starting off on a structured format to collect more limited details and then moving to a semi-structured or unstructured format when exploring particular issues in greater depth. Which interview style you choose to employ depends on the particular needs of the your research study. Unstructured interviews might be useful for preliminary work, but it is probably better to impose some sort of structure later on, otherwise you may quickly find yourself drowning in a sea of information, with no time left to properly analyse and interpret the material. Worse still, you might end up having no clear idea of how to make sense of the collected data.

Interview Techniques

How do you conduct an interview? There is no simple answer to that question. The best interviews tend to occur when conducted in a comfortable, relaxed manner. This not only implies that the location for the interview should be familiar to the respondent, but that the interview session should not be perceived to be threatening. Respondents are also more likely to confide in you if they feel fully involved in the research process. It is, therefore, crucial to try to ensure that they feel valued for what they have to contribute, and are not just being viewed by the interviewer as an information source. Finally, it is important that they feel confident that what they have to say will be treated both seriously and confidentially.

How the ideal situation is best achieved depends upon the specific situation, but there are some general points which should be borne in mind when conducting any interview:

Provide a short introduction

Start by introducing yourself and explaining the purpose of the interview session. Briefly explain to the respondent why they have been chosen for interview and assure them of the confidential nature of the interview (if this is appropriate).

Try to impress upon the respondent the importance both of the research and of their active participation. People are more likely to co-operate if they feel that the subject is both important and relevant to them.

Tell the interviewee how long the interview will last; and ensure that you keep to the agreed time. The introduction should always be brief and to the point.

Table 9.1: Summary of the Main Characteristics of the Four Basic Interview Types

TYPE OF INTERVIEW	CHARACTERISTICS	ADVANTAGES	DISADVANTAGES
Structured	Structured schedule specifies, in advance; the nature of the topics and the issues to be covered; the exact sequence as well as the wording of questions. All respondents are asked essentially the same questions in the same order.	Interviewees answer the same questions, thus increasing the comparability of responses. Simplifies the organisation and analysis of data Reduces bias.	Limited flexibility and standardised wording can appear mechanical and may inhibit responses. Some questions might be irrelevant to or inappropriate for certain respondents. The structure can build in a bias right from the start.
Unstructured	Questions emerge out of the natural flow of the interview; there is no attempt to determine the sequence or exact wording of questions.	Flexibility. An interviewer can respond to both the individual and the situation. Interviewees are free to express themselves in their own words. When used with care information can be obtained on sensitive and/or personal issues.	As data is less structured, comparison across interviews is made more difficult. Data management, analysis and interpretation can be difficult. The quality of the collected data relies heavily upon the skill of the interviewer.
Semi-structured	Scheduled outlines gives notice of the general topics and issues to be covered. The interviewer is then free to ask about other issues – which emerge during the course of the interview – or probe responses as and when appropriate.	Retains some of the openness and informality of the unstructured approach, while allowing for comparisons to be made across the 'core questions'.	As the interviewer selects which issues to follow up this may increase the possibility of bias and limit the potential comparability of interviews.
Group interviews	Provides data not only about the research topic *per se*, but also about group norms and any associated dynamics.	Useful tool when trying to set down the parameters of a study.	Can be difficult to control and therefore should not be conducted by a novice researcher. There are also limitations for comparing the data.

An introduction to an interview on tenant satisfaction, for example, might look like this:

> *"My name is Douglas Robertson and I work for the Housing Department. I am conducting interviews with tenants to find out how they feel about the housing services provided by the Council. Your name was one of those selected at random for inclusion in this study. If I can get a good idea of what tenants think about the current service provided by the housing department then, hopefully, this might help to improve its quality in the future. It is important, therefore, that we get the views from as wide a cross-section of tenants as possible. We should, therefore, be grateful if you would agree to take part in this survey by answering a few questions. The interview will take about 15 minutes. All of the answers you give will be treated in complete confidence, and your name will not be used without your permission."*

As with questionnaires it is often good practice to post a written introduction, by letter, where the interview is dealing with a potentially sensitive area of work, or where the population has limited experience of interviews.

Interview one-to-one

Except in the case of group interviews, it is best to conduct all interviews with just yourself and the interviewee present. That is, however, not always possible especially when conducting interviews in people's homes. The presence of other people can be distracting and inhibiting for the interviewee. It is also a potential source of bias. Imagine, for example, being interviewed about job satisfaction with your line manager present in the interview room. No employee would feel comfortable with this situation and any responses would be affected.

Be sensitive

It is important to be sensitive to how the interview may be affecting the interviewee. It is obviously important to get the wording right before starting the interview, but it may help to rephrase some questions, or to change the ordering of questions in response to the individual needs of the interviewee. Similarly, if the respondent has difficulty in understanding or hearing the questions, you will have to speak more slowly or loudly.

Listen

The main aim of an interview is to get the respondent's point of view. The interviewer's job is to facilitate this, and not to present their own view. The more the interviewer talks, the less the respondent does. At the very least this will affect the quality of the data and may bias the findings by leading the respondent to agree with the values and/or opinions of the interviewer.

Avoid interruptions

Try to arrange a time and place for the interview where you are not likely to be interrupted. If the interview is taking place in your office make sure that all phone calls are re-directed, or disconnect the phone, and ensure that colleagues know not to interrupt during the interview session. If the session takes place in the interviewee's place of work try to ensure the same conditions. Obviously if the interview takes place in someone's home avoiding interruptions can be more difficult.

Use Visual aids

Visual aids can be helpful in trying to clarify ideas or questions. The most commonly used aid is the flash card. For example, respondents are shown a card which has a range of gross salary bands printed on it and are asked to select the category which they fall into. Another visual aid which might be used in a survey of attitudes towards a particular design proposal for a new housing development could involve showing the respondents a number of alternative layouts and ask them to give their reactions to each. Care should be used in designing visual aids because what you perceive as easy to understand drawings or diagrams may produce a blank response from an untrained eye. This issue is also touched upon in Chapter 15 when discussing the use and misuse of visual aids in research presentations.

By adhering to the above points the interview session should convey the impression of being well thought through and professionally carried out. Creating the right impression is crucial, especially when carrying out the less structured interview sessions. If the proper introduction and procedure is not employed the interviewee could start to think that the session has not been clearly thought through and is a waste of their time.

The Causes of Bias

All interviews are subjective and therefore run the risk of bias. The most obvious source of trouble emanates from the interview schedule itself. As was noted in the preceding chapter on questionnaires, ambiguous wording and poor structure can result in unreliable, or biased data. Other factors at play during the course of an interview can also lead to bias creeping in. The interviewer, for example, may well have strongly held opinions on the topic being considered and these may, intentionally or unintentionally, be introduced thus influencing the respondent. As with questionnaires, the use of particular words or phrases can create a particular reaction, as can non-verbal expressions of approval or disapproval.

An interview is in essence a social interaction and to be successful it requires a certain rapport between interview and interviewee. This rapport, however, can also lead to bias. Borg (1981) sums up the main causes of what he calls the 'response effect':

> *"Eagerness of the respondent to please the interviewer, a vague antagonism that sometimes arises between interviewer and respondent, or the tendency of the interviewer to seek out answers that support his preconceived notions are but a few of the factors that may contribute to biasing of data obtained from the interview."*

(Borg, 1981, 87)

How can you eliminate such bias? The short answer is that you can never totally eliminate the possibility of bias. What you can do, however, is be alert to the possibility of bias and be prepared to deal with it. The issue of bias was touched upon in Chapter 2, where the notion of 'value free' research, was discussed. Recognise that you will have views on the research topic. Be alert throughout the interview for any signs that you might inadvertently be leading the respondent to agree with these views by the way in which you ask the questions, or by your manner when recording the response. It is also important to recognise that gender, race, age and social status will introduce a bias into any interview situation. If possible, use more than one interviewer on the project, since it is easier to pick up such bias, than when only one interviewer has been employed. As was mentioned in the previous chapter it is also good practice to randomise the interviews to be undertaken by a group of interviewers so that any bias can be dissipated.

Recording and Verification

The data produced through conducting interviews are essentially words – quotations which reveal what interviewees think, feel, or do in the specific situations which they have been asked to talk about. The goal of interviewing is to try to understand these experiences. Recording the actual words used by interviewees is, therefore, critical to the success of the project. The views of the interviewees cannot be represented accurately, using verbatim quotations, unless you have carefully recorded their words in the first place.

Exactly how you record the interview will depend upon a variety of factors. If you are using a highly structured format, one which requires the circling or ticking of categories from a checklist, for example, then recording is a straightforward exercise. In the case of the less structured interviews, however, some means of recording responses is needed. One way is to take brief notes as the interview progresses, perhaps using the interview schedule as a guide, and then expand upon these notes shortly after the interview has been concluded. It is possible, with practice, to produce an accurate record of the interview in this way.

Taking lengthy verbatim notes of what is being said, however, can disrupt the flow of the interview. If the respondent agrees, another approach is to tape record the interview. Tape recording offers a cross-check on the accuracy of your notes, helps clarify any uncertainty, and guarantees that any quotations used in the final report will be verbatim. It does not eliminate the need for note taking. Notes are useful in understanding the context in which certain responses were generated, and as such are an invaluable aid to the subsequent analysis and interpretation of the interview data. Using a tape recorder does, however, allow the interviewer to be more aware of the needs of the interviewee. They need not focus unduly on trying to take a set of comprehensive notes and can, therefore, pick up the various signals that can add colour to the study. Clearly the logistics of recording a focus group interview are technically more complex.

If you have sufficient time and/or secretarial resources it is best to make a full transcript of the interviews and use this as the basis for subsequent analysis – perhaps making use of certain qualitative analysis software packages which are now available on the market (see Chapter 11 for details). You should, however, be very clear about the amount of work such an approach involves and consider, at the planning and design stage, whether or not such detailed analysis is worth all the effort. Another consideration is that with the new digital tape recorders, which are now coming onto the market, used in conjunction with your notes of the interview, you can quickly locate and number the relevant excerpts from the interview. These can then be accessed and transcribed within the appropriate subject blocks. This would reduce the time involved, and improve the reliability of subsequent qualitative analysis.

Special Circumstances

Interviews can provide very high quality information, but at a price. Interviews are labour-intensive, in terms of design, implementation and analysis. As a rule of thumb, an hour-long interview might take seven hours to transcribe, and even longer to analyse and interpret in detail. Add to this problems associated with arranging interview appointments, dealing with call-offs, postponements, return visits, and the necessary travel time to and from interviews. Working full-time, you might expect to complete no more than four hour-long interviews on a good day, although this is considered optimistic by some seasoned researchers.

Given that research resources are always tight, the eventual sample size for a study might have to be quite small. Certainly interviews can never approximate to the coverage possible by employing a postal questionnaire. Such small sizes can present problems in relation to representativeness, especially if you come up against a significant level of non-responses. Again this possibility should be clearly thought through at the planning stage and contingency plans made.

Interviews: Strengths and Weaknesses

As a means of collecting certain sorts of information, interviews have a great deal to recommend them. Interviews are:

- a useful means of eliciting answers that are explanatory rather than descriptive, given the capacity to probe or explore the responses;
- flexible in terms of questions and the ordering of questions;
- convenient for the interviewee as they can work at their own pace; and
- a useful means to compare different responses if designed in a structured way.

As with all research methods, however, there is also a downside. Interviews are:

- not an efficient or cost-effective means of collecting information from large numbers of people;
- very time-consuming in terms of development, design, execution and analysis;
- relatively expensive, given the time involved in carrying out such work and the fact that a skilled interviewer/researcher is required;
- unable to offer the same degree of anonymity that is possible with questionnaires; and
- difficult to analyse particularly where no clear structure has been employed.

Further Reading

Fielding, N., (1993), 'Qualitative interviewing', in Gilbert, N., (ed), *Research Social Life*. London: Sage.

May, T., (1993), *Social Research: Issues, Methods and Process*. Buckingham: Open University Press.

Oppenheim, A., (1992), *Questionnaire Design, Interviewing and Attitude Measurement*. London: Pinter.

CHAPTER 10:
Documentary Studies

Objectives of the Chapter

This chapter is designed to ensure that the reader:

- appreciates the various types of documentary studies that can be employed in conducting housing research; and

- understands both the value and practical difficulties involved in using documentary studies.

Introduction

Almost all housing research projects involve examining and analysing a range of documentary material. The term 'document' refers to a broad range of written sources, encompassing official reports, internal management reports, and the full range of file records, or archival material. It can also include non-written material such as film, video, slides, photographs and tape recordings. The procedures and skills involved in executing documentary studies closely replicate those detailed in Chapter 5, in relation to literature reviews. Documentary studies can often be part of the literature review exercise, for it is essential to have a clear appreciation of the range, content and quality of available documentary material. Such material provides both an insight into the proposed area of study and the necessary information to assist in the planning of the various requirements of a specific research project. As with a literature review it is crucial that the researcher never hurries into the field. Time spent seeking out and reviewing documents in the same way as books, journals and related relevant studies will reduce subsequent information problems. This approach also assists in refining the particular research questions which the study is intended to address. On occasions it also throws up some innovative and novel research questions which may not have been considered if the preliminary focus was solely on secondary sources.

While documentary work can be used to explore the parameters of a proposed study, as a method in itself it can generate material which can either supplement a study, setting a piece of research within its historic context, or alternatively be the sole means of conducting the research study. A useful example of the former is Forrest and Murie's (1986) historical examination of council house sales policy within Norwich. Another, Whitham's (1989) study of the development of the Rosyth naval settlement on the Forth Estuary prior to the First World War, provides an insight into the State's growing involvement in the direct provision of housing.

The critical facilities which are required to execute this type of work are those of the historian. Historic method involves the researcher in first locating the relevant material – questioning exactly where they are likely to find that type of information. Having located the material the next task is to select what is relevant. This involves a rigorous questioning of the document's specific purpose and then asking exactly why you are consulting it. The selection and evaluation of evidence is the corner stone of all research. The purpose of this chapter is to detail the various issues involved in adopting such an approach when examining documentary material.

Documentary Research

Documents can be divided into 'primary' and 'secondary' sources. Primary sources are those that came into existence in the period under research; contemporary written reports or material collected by those who witnessed or were engaged in the execution of a particular event. An example of such material would be the minutes of a local authority housing committee or those of a housing association management committee. They would also include any records that were generated about the various functions carried out by either housing organisation. Secondary sources are someone's interpretation of the event based on their consideration of these primary sources. Secondary sources were discussed in detail in Chapter 5. The pamphlet produced to celebrate the twenty-five year history of a Glasgow community-based housing association would be a typical example of secondary documentation. Such a document would draw on the minutes, reports and the recollections of both committee and staff. Use would also be made of photographic material. While such a pamphlet would probably lay great emphasis upon the promotion of local community empowerment, through the process of housing renewal, the primary material may not clearly articulate such a policy aim, at least in the association's formative years. Rather than this emphasis, another author might provide a slightly different interpretation, arguing that the community-based association provided a tangible example of resident participation within local planning. Alternatively, the author could choose to focus on another aspect entirely of the association's work, such as the technical and administrative achievements involved in improving tenemental housing stock. As an aid to locating either type of source material, reference is made of what is called 'tertiary' sources, namely abstracts and bibliographies (see Chapter 5 for further details).

Primary sources can be further divided into 'inadvertent' sources and 'deliberate' sources.

Inadvertent sources

This refers to material which is used by the researcher in a way which was not originally intended. These are typically the myriad of material produced by the process of public administration. Examples would be the minutes of various debates or meetings held by either local authority or housing associations. Some material may have a more operational focus such as the local authority's Housing Investment Plan (or the Housing Plan in Scotland). Guidance material produced by government also has much value, given the emphasis that it places upon certain practices. Management plans and business plans, in that they contain performance as well as planning information, are another valuable source. The full panoply of management information, from tenancy files, house sales records, maintenance record cards, allocation records and notes, plus the range of correspondence, whether letters, tenant newsletters, or press clippings provides an insight into the day-to-day workings of specific organisations.

As these documents are produced for practical purposes, the researcher might not always appreciate the usefulness or significance of what, at first glance, may seem rather mundane material. Yet, when planning the study, if the content of such material is known and appreciated then the quality of the resulting work could be greatly enhanced. That is not to say such material is not, in itself, problematic. Given the ephemeral nature of so much of management material it rarely survives a whole. It is also possible that reports have been constructed in such a way as to make a particular point, and this can result in misconceptions arising. For example, information on performance is likely to be constructed with a specific purpose in mind.

It is also the case that records are written without thought for subsequent classification and analysis. As a result, the terms used in forms tend to be vague: difficult to classify and compare. In a study of housing allocations based on medical criteria, it was found that the records held by general practitioners proved especially hard to classify (Smith *et al*, 1991). More often than not, records reflect more about the recorder than the particular topic in question. In Booth's (1889) pioneering work on the living conditions of London's poor, use was made of School Attendance Officers' official case reports. Aware of the personal biases that could influence such material, Booth held interviews with the officers about each individual case in order to address that bias and come to his own views about the living conditions of truants (Englander and O'Day, 1995).

Deliberate sources

This refers to those documents that have been produced with the intention of influencing future researchers. These include autobiographies or memoirs, diaries or letters intended for later publication, as well as various documents of self justification. So while inadvertent sources, at least initially, appear to be straightforward, deliberate sources are always treated with more caution.

Richard Crossman, Labour's Minister for Housing and Local Government under Harold Wilson's first Administration of 1964-66, produced perhaps the best known diary of that period. Such a document has the explicit aim of preserving particular evidence for the future. There is, as a result, a tendency for the evidence provided in this way to be either incomplete or inaccurate. Information which might not show the author in the best light may be amended or ignored. That said, such deliberate sources can also provide a unique insight into how decisions were made, often illustrating the various considerations and tensions that had to be accommodated in making a particular decision. Such colour is often missing from the official report, for the purpose of such a document is to illustrate consensus in decision making. Despite the insight these deliberate sources can provide, it is vital not to ignore their intention of trying to get over a particular point.

Witting and Unwitting Evidence

Both types of document also provide what is referred to as witting and unwitting evidence. Witting evidence is the information which the author of the document wanted to impart, whereas unwitting, or 'hidden' evidence, is everything else that can be gleaned from the document (Marwick, 1977). Studying the speeches made by government housing ministers, about the role and function of council housing would illustrate certain stated aspects of their housing policy at the time. In the 1980s, 'extending choice' and 'giving people greater responsibility for their housing decisions' would be very much to the fore. The unwitting material would reveal much about the Government's faith in market solutions and their desire to stimulate greater consumerism in relation to the delivery of the full range of council services. It might also disclose an acceptance of residualisation and a welfare role for council housing, given the public expenditure savings such privatisation would bring. All documents contain unwitting evidence. The challenge for the researcher is to be able to identify its existence and assess its actual significance. Again analysis and interpretation are the critical skills required of the researcher.

Practical Issues in Documentary Research

Historic Housing Studies

History is not what happened in the past, rather it is what we can know, and therefore interpret, about what happened the past. History is constrained by the information that can be obtained and by how an individual chooses to interpret that information. In order to be able to interpret documents you have to be aware of the context in which the document was produced, and that requires obtaining a broad, as well as a specific knowledge, of both the topic and period under consideration. This can only be achieved through reading a broad range of secondary and primary sources. Without such background knowledge and understanding the significance of specific documents could easily be overlooked. At the same time, there is the danger that with such knowledge and understanding you may opt to over-emphasise the significance of material held in a document to justify your particular interpretation of events. Historical study is, as a consequence of these two parameters, in a constant state of flux. Our understanding of past events is constantly being reassessed through either the reinterpretation of existing documents, or through the discovery of new ones. The fact that our understanding of the past is influenced by understanding of the present, also ensures that historical events are always being revisited and therefore reinterpreted.

Historical studies of housing *per se* are not that common (Holmans, 1987). Historians have tended to treat housing in a very general way, using it as one means of illustrating general living conditions at a particular point in time. There are but a few housing history classics, such as Burnett (1986), Merrett (1979 and 1982) and Swennarton (1981). Biographies on key figures in the development of housing are also rare, with Darley's (1990) work on Octavia Hill being an exception. There is also a dearth of local housing histories. One area that breaks this general rule is Clydeside, but the focus of much work here has been on the 1915 Rent Strike which resulted in the introduction of rent restrictions legislation (Damer, 1982; Melling, 1982). Planning literature on the 'Garden City' movement also has some useful insights into local housing history issues (Hague, 1984). The lack of national and local studies could well mean that much conventional wisdom about the reasons for the development of certain housing policies could be challenged. One obvious example is provided by the assumption that council house sales was solely the preserve of Conservative political thought. The reality is that the Labour Party, under the first Wilson Government, had worked through the idea of either giving, or selling council houses to their tenants as a means of providing the working class with a capital stake in society. For the author of this policy, Joe Haines, such a move represented true socialism (Haines, 1992). Given the policy development focus of so much current housing research, there is a strong tendency to avoid trying to set any study within its historical context. That said, given this dearth of historic housing studies, this could provide a rich seam for the housing researchers of the future.

Document Searches and Selection

Document searches need to be as comprehensive as possible. As noted earlier, it is extremely helpful when drawing up the research design to have a reasonable knowledge of what documentary material is available. Assumptions about access and/or the contents of documents can often undermine the initial aspirations of a research project. Much of the documentary material used in housing studies emanates from national governmental archives in London, Edinburgh, Cardiff and Belfast. The information held relates to the government departments which are based in these localities. Given the territorial, rather than functional basis, of the Scottish, Welsh and Northern Ireland Offices, these archives hold comprehensive policy-based material. Given the legal distinctiveness of Scotland, and the requirement on many occasions to enact separate legislation covering similar policy initiatives, the Scottish Office tends to have a more comprehensive policy archive than its Welsh or Northern Irish counterpart. There are also national archives such as the British Library in London, where collections of papers by eminent individuals, and other documentary material are often left to the nation.

The problem with national governmental archives is that they tend to record the views of the Government of the day – reflecting their perspective on events. Work on the local implementation policy is beginning to illustrate that while national government may have promoted a particular policy for specific reasons, it does not necessarily follow that it was implemented in different local areas for the same reasons (Robertson and Bailey, 1996). To gain an understanding of the interplay between national and local policy objectives, as well as ambitions, it would be necessary to consult both national and local archives. By doing so a better appreciation of the policy formulation and implementation processes would be gained.

Such document searches have been made easier by the recent development of local archives. While archives previously covered either national records or those relating to the creation of large urban settlements, smaller rural localities were rarely well-served. Local archives resulted from the creation of larger local government administrative units (1974 in England and Wales and 1975 in Scotland).

There is, however, no really comprehensive archive. National and local archives contain many gaps. Only by using both can some of these gaps be filled. With the advances in information technology, locating material within this extended archival coverage has greatly improved. It has also improved the quality of the catalogue records held, given the standardisation requirements of many database and cataloguing systems. Occasionally specialist books have been published which provide a guide to using specific archives. Public housing researchers in London can benefit from the recent publication of such a guide (Cox, 1994). Regional archives are not so well funded and you will invariably find some material which has never been properly catalogued.

What is actually held in any archive tends to be haphazard. It all depends on what has been deposited by local government officials; what has turned up in lawyers' offices; or even what has been retrieved from skips on the way to the municipal tip. Chance plays a certain role in determining what ends up being deposited in an archive. University archives tend to be no less eclectic, holding both the papers of eminent academics of the past and those of once renowned local public figures.

While archive searches provide one avenue, the most widely used starting point for many documentary studies is the local history section of the public library. The Glasgow Room of Glasgow's Mitchell Library is well-renowned, as is the Edinburgh Room in Edinburgh's Central Library and Liverpool's Picton Library. Mention should also be made of the four Copyright Deposit Libraries – The British Library in London, The National Library of Scotland in Edinburgh, The National Library of Wales, in Aberystwyth and the National Library in Dublin – which by law require a copy of everything published to be deposited with them. It has to be said, however, that the individual collections are not uniform. Finally, to get yourself started on a documentary study, a trawl of second-hand book shops and their current categories or the indexes in certain relevant old books, can often provide an initial stimulus.

Clearly, you could spend many hours, days or months digging out material. As time is money, you need to adopt a strategy which allows you to explore what's available and from that make a selection. Given what has been said above, this can only ever be a bit 'hit-and-miss'. If you have some familiarity with the different categories of evidence this will help you decide what is fundamental and what is less important, thus controlling your selection. The danger is that digging out material becomes a substitute to getting on with appraising the selected material. You will have to use your own judgement in deciding whether you have got what's required. Perhaps the most crucial decision in the selection process is ensuring you achieve some corroboration of the selected material. Always try and ensure that the key findings from one source can be corroborated from other sources. That is not to say the points being made should be identical, rather that the pattern of events appears consistent.

Official Records as Research Sources

Official records refer to the full panoply of government papers. While *Hansard*, green papers, white papers and acts represent the official published outputs of government, there is substantially more information to be obtained from reports, files notes, press releases, briefing materials and minutes of meetings. The usefulness of these official records is, however, constrained by issues of access and confidentiality. Further, as was noted above, what is archived can produce an incomplete record. It is often hard to find out from a catalogue exactly what is held within a particular topic file. Such official records can contain a diversity of material, much of which is of limited value. Taking the time to read the handwritten comments, often found in the margins of these reports can provide an illustration of official attitudes to certain ideas and initiatives. In reading through this type of documentation be aware that civil servants are often asked to prepare proposition papers which may, or may not, fully acknowledge the other side of any argument. It is also common for material to be left out of the file on grounds of confidentiality. Not all public documents are readily accessible, with many being either termed 'closed' or 'restricted'. Official papers, those which refer to Cabinet discussions and decisions typically operate to a 30 year rule – that is access is denied to the public for a period of 30 years. For example, January 1996 was the first opportunity that the public had to access the 1966 cabinet papers. Only then could Crossman's interpretation of events, as detailed by his diaries, be reassessed and perhaps reappraised. It is also questionable whether the material made available provides a total record. Civil servants or ministers can request concealments in respect of specific documents or topics. It is also the case that any researcher working on these papers has to sign the Official Secrets Act, which can limit what they can report. As a consequence, it is almost impossible to know whether what is being presented is a comprehensive record of what is held.

Concealments and restricted access is supposed to address concerns about security and confidentiality. Certain documents could contain information that is of a personal nature – certain criticism or observations could be considered hurtful to the people concerned, or to their relatives. Hence, the general operation of the 30 year rule. This issue is not that dissimilar to the issues of confidentiality raised in the previous chapter. It is also worth stating that the UK Government is somewhat obsessed with secrecy, and that all tiers of Government feel uncomfortable with the concept of open access to all public information. Although there have been some moves to promote more open government, at both a local authority and housing association level, it would be hard to argue that this has resulted in greater openness. Rather, minutes of meeting and associated background reports have tended to become more terse and difficult to follow. Minutes, as noted earlier, tend to record decisions rather than report on the discussion that took place prior to that decision being taken.

It is also important to be aware of the presumption that lies behind the presentation of specific statistics. The old adage that there are, *"lies, damned lies and statistics,"* is extremely apt. Statistical information presented one way reveals a particular pattern. Yet, quite another interpretation can be constructed had the data been presented in another format. To get some insight into this it is worth reading the commentaries that accompany Census statistics. The changing conceptions about work and employment through time are clearly illustrated in this way, as is the changing status of different types of employment (Hakim, 1980). It is these interpretational norms that have determined the way the statistical information has been presented. Change the perspective and quite a different picture can be created. Again to be alert to this issue you need to understand the policy context in which the statistics have been prepared. As with all documentary work it is critical to question the motives of the source. What was the specific purpose of a particular document, or set of statistics? Can it be interpreted in a different way? In order to fully appreciate the limitations of documentary research it is worth detailing the standard historical method which is employed in pursuing this type of work.

Documentary Research: Adopting a Critical Approach

As will be clear by now the major difficulty in respect of documentary work relates to bias. People are selective in what they choose to record and, more importantly, what they choose to leave out. It is, therefore, important to be alert to the possibility of bias due to such selectiveness and manipulation. Documents should never be viewed as neutral artifacts. Consequently, they must be treated with great care and a fair measure of scepticism (Platt, 1981). Those who adopt a more critical approach to documentary sources would go further and argue that the principal objective of documentary analysis is to explore the hidden or unwitting meanings that may be present within the book or document. As with literature reviews, critical awareness of the source and the context in which the document was produced is all important.

> *"What counts as reasonable fact in a casual conversation, in a courtroom, a scientific laboratory, a news interview, a police interrogation, a medical consultation or a social security office? What is the nature of social organisation within which these facts find support? To what vicissitudes, exigencies and considerations are the formation of these facts responsive?"*
>
> (Heritage, 1984, 94)

In order to pursue this approach it is necessary to adopt both an external and internal criticism of the document in question.

External Criticism

External criticism of a primary source is a means to try and avoid misrepresenting, or being misled, by the information provided in the document. Through this approach of questioning the status of the documentary source, you are trying to assess whether it is both genuine and authentic. External criticism of a written text would include such questions as:

- Was the supposed author of the document known to be contemporary with the document?
- Is there any collaboration supporting their authorship? Is the document consistent with other information known about the author?
- Is the document typical of the author's style?
- Is the style consistent with other documents produced in the same period?

Internal Criticism

Having established the document is genuine, internal criticism attempts to establish the credibility of the document's actual contents. Internal criticism would consider questions such as:

- What is the nature of the document? Is it a letter, a policy statement, or the minutes of a meeting? How many copies would have been made?
- How did the document come into existence? When, where, and for what purpose was it produced?
- What does it actually say, and in what sort of language?
- How long after the event was this record made?

- Did the source of the information actually witness the event? If so, is the author a reliable observer?
- Was the primary witness, the source of the information, able to tell the truth?
- Was the primary witness willing to tell the truth?
- Is the document complete? Or has it been altered or edited in any way?
- Is there any external corroboration of the events described?

While many of these questions will have no relevance to the specific documents you are studying, they should not distract from the main objective which is to assess whether the contents of the document reflect facts or biases. As noted throughout this chapter the author of a particular document will rarely set down the assumptions and beliefs which underpin their particular point of view. By drawing out such biases, and then understanding where they come from, the study will be greatly enhanced through making a considered and critical review of the available material.

Much of the discussion in relation to this research method would appear to be common sense. Yet, too often the basic common sense outlined here is ignored. Documentary work should not be regarded as a 'filler', a means of padding out a few pages with essentially boring background material. By adopting a rigorous and critical approach to documentary work there is much to be gained. Only through gaining experience of this type of work will you develop better critical awareness skills and a true appreciation of the value this approach has to all research work.

Further Reading

Bell, J., (1993), *Doing Your Research Project – A Guide for First-Time Researchers in Education and Social Science*. Buckingham: Open University Press.

Hakim, C., (1983), 'Research based on administrative records', *Sociological Review*. 31, 3, 489-519.

Marwick, A., (1977), *Introduction to History*, (Units 3, 4 and 5 of A101, Arts Foundation Course). Buckingham: Open University.

Platt, J., (1981), 'Evidence and proof in documentary research', *Sociological Review*. 29, 1, 31-66.

CHAPTER 11:
Observational Methods

Objectives of the Chapter

This chapter is designed to ensure that the reader:

- understands the basics of structured and participant observation;

- appreciates the various issues associated with recording and interpreting observational data; and

- is able to appreciate the various steps involved in conducting successful observational studies.

Introduction

Observation may seem to be amongst the easiest, most natural of research methods: it is after all something that we do, to a lesser or greater degree, all the time. The reality of course is rather different. It takes careful thought, rigorous planning and lots of patience to use observational methods successfully. The investment, however, can be very worthwhile since observational techniques can give access to aspects of behaviour that may be difficult to get in another way. You can interview housing officers about how they relate to clients, for example, or you may send out a postal questionnaire to canvass clients about how they see the relationship; but can you be certain that the views expressed reflect what actually happens in the housing office? Without being there, directly observing events as they happen, it is impossible to be sure.

Observational methods have a long history in social science research in general, although they are not so widely used within housing research. This chapter, therefore, examines the role that observation might play in housing research. You will learn something about the direct observation of everyday life using both structured observation and participant observation. The advantages and disadvantages of intruding into the behaviours or events being observed will also be discussed.

The Observer Effect

It might be argued that even where you can directly observe events you cannot be totally confident of your interpretation of the meaning of those events. Your presence as an observer may affect the situation you are trying to study; people may behave differently if they realise that they are being observed. This observer effect may be even more marked if you are observing your colleagues in a work setting; if you are in some sense a participant in the events being observed. Familiarity may not breed contempt, but it can affect your objectivity and the behaviour of those being studied. One obvious way to minimise the observer effect would be to distance yourself from the group being observed; to adopt an approach that allows you systematically to record events without taking any active part in them. At one extreme you might view events covertly using a one-way mirror or closed circuit television. On the other hand, it might be argued that such detachment makes it impossible to relate to the events and to understand the meaning of the behaviour of those involved. If you adopt this perspective, you might eschew structured observation in favour of a more qualitative form of participant observation.

Participant observation is an approach in which the researcher enters into, and becomes part of, the events being studied. The researcher, experiences the events as those involved do, in Lacey's phrase they learn, *"to live in and understand the new world."* Lacey's study of the experience of the staff and students of Hightown Grammar provides a good example of participant observation (Lacey, 1971). The study demanded a great deal of commitment in terms of time and effort but it resulted in an interesting and informative picture of life in a comprehensive school. Similar studies have been done in other organisations including the military and the police, so why not in housing departments?

Whichever style of observation you adopt, the more quantitative structured approach or the qualitative participant observation model, you must bear in mind that your job is to observe and to record, to analyse and to interpret events. Remember you are an observer first and a participant only second (if at all); and that is not always an easy task.

Structured Observation

Structured or systematic observation is a process in which you first decide what it is you want to study. You then develop some form of framework for recording, coding and making your observations, before finally analysing and interpreting the results. Let us consider the questions to be addressed at each stage:

1. **What do you want to observe?**
   The answer to this question will of course depend on your interests and on the research question(s) that inform the study. Perhaps the most important point to realise at the outset is that you cannot observe everything. It may seem a rather obvious point but you must be clear about what it is you are looking for before you begin. If you are not clear you are likely to find yourself swamped with so many images and potentially interesting observations that you may well end-up recording nothing.

2. **How do you record the observations?**
   Once you have decided what to look at, the next step is to devise a framework, typically some form of checklist, for recording the observations. Suppose you are researching the organisation of a housing co-operative. One aspect of the study might involve an observation of committee meetings. The recording framework might be a simple matrix in which each member of the committee is identified by a number and the activities/behaviours you want to record are coded, say one to twelve, as in Table 11.1 below. Recording of observations can then be made at predetermined intervals (say every two-three minutes). At the end of each time interval you observe what is happening and record the appropriate code against the relevant member of the committee. If during the first period of observation the Chair of the committee (A) is giving information to the group you would record six in the appropriate cell. Similarly, when a committee member (C) asks for information during the third observation period a nine is recorded in that cell. Where a committee member does not say anything during the period the cell is left blank.

The sort of time-point sampling technique shown in Table 11.1, provides a snapshot of the events being observed, in this case a committee meeting. It is not, however, a detailed account of the meeting; for example, the record won't tell you precisely how much time was spent in giving information. What you will get is a sense of how much time is spent on this or that activity. You might also be able to conclude that some members take a more active part in committee meetings than others (or that they simply talk more).

TABLE 11.1: Bales' Interactive Process Analysis System (Bales, 1970)

Committee Member	Observation Period							
	1	2	3	4	5	6	7	8
A (Chair)	6	4	–	5	6	6	8	6
B	3	4	7	12	3	4	3	3
C	2	2	9	5	5	6	–	2
D	–	3	4	5	7	7	–	7
F	11	1	7	7	11	3	3	3

Codes			
Positive Actions	1. Seems friendly	Questions	7. Asks for suggestions
	2. Dramatises		8. Asks for opinion
	3. Agrees		9. Asks for information
Answers	4. Gives suggestion	Negative Actions	10. Disagrees
	5. Gives opinion		11. Shows tension
	6. Gives information		12. Seems unfriendly

Depending on the nature of what it is you want to observe, you may not have to design your own recording and coding frame. If you are interested in interaction, for example, there are a great many systems available 'off the peg' which you might use. Perhaps the best known of these is Bales' Interactive Process Analysis (IPA) system; the categories in Table 11.1 are taken from Bales (1970). Bales' IPA system is based on analytical categories that reflect verbal, non-verbal and extra linguistic interactions among groups. As you will see from the Table each behaviour has a corresponding number. This is simply for coding purposes and no rank order is implied. The phrase 'seems friendly' is *not* quantitatively better than 'seems unfriendly'.

Coding in this structured way involves you in both recording and interpreting the meaning of an event and associated behaviour at the same time. Clearly this can be difficult since you have to decide not only that a behaviour has occurred but also to attach a meaning to it; what criteria would you use to decide that, for example, a particular behaviour was 'unfriendly' rather than indicative of 'tension'? This problem becomes more acute where a number of researchers/observers are being used. In such cases you must agree on the interpretation of behaviours at the outset, otherwise the recording and coding of the events may be invalidated.

The Naturalistic Paradigm

Not all researchers are happy with the structured, rather quantitative approach to observation outlined above. They would prefer the more naturalistic approach offered by qualitative research. As noted previously in Chapter 6, qualitative research is based on epistemological assumptions – assumptions about the nature of knowledge – that are in opposition to the those of quantitative research. Put simply, quantitative research tends to the assumption that knowledge is concrete, tangible and objective: social 'facts' are akin to facts in the natural sciences. In qualitative research, on the other hand, social reality is more ambiguous and subjective. As was mentioned earlier, which side of the debate you fall on does not inevitably determine the sorts of research methods you will use. Nevertheless, how you answer the questions, what can we know, and what is the best way to know it, will influence your research design. If you subscribe to a subjective viewpoint your research design is more likely to be influenced by the naturalistic paradigm which argues that people, events and behaviours should be studied in as natural a way as possible. Matza (1969) argued that the quantitative tradition, which conceived of people as objects used:

> "... *methods that probe human behaviour without concerning themselves with the meaning of behaviour, [and] cannot be regarded as naturalist ... because they have molested in advance the phenomenon to be studied. Naturalism ... claims fidelity to the empirical world.*"
>
> (Matza, 1969, 8)

Hence, participant observation, in as much as it is concerned with events that were not created or maintained purely for research purposes, is an important tool of qualitative research.

Participant Observation

The first consideration in planning a study using such observational methods is to consider your own role as a researcher. The main question is, to what extent do you participate in, as opposed simply observe, the activities or events that are being studied? At the one extreme, you could be a 'complete observer'; a detached, objective recorder of events. An unobtrusive spectator, the complete observer, has no involvement with the subjects and no responsibility for the event being observed. At the other end of the continuum there is the 'complete participant', who is intimately involved as an integral part of the group and, therefore, involved in shaping the events which are being investigated. Those being observed are, however, unaware of the identity of either researcher.

Suppose you were interested in studying the day-to-day experiences of homeless people. One approach might be to interview a range of homeless people. While this would produce qualitative information, you may feel that it does not give data which accurately reflects the deprivations involved in this lifestyle, because those interviewed may have grown immune to certain aspects of their daily lives. To overcome this problem you might opt to become an observer; recording the day-to-day events, while remaining detached from the individuals concerned. Information gathered in this way would be limited, especially if your declared intention was to see the world as those who are homeless experience it. Another approach would be to become totally immersed in the world of the homeless, replicating what George Orwell did in the 1930s in researching his famous novel *Down and Out in Paris and London*. This novel clearly documents the difficulties inherent in adopting such an approach, not the least of which are the major ethical issues involved.

None of the options would be entirely satisfactory, yet each has its strong points. As a participant you might get nearer to the perspective of a homeless person because you are sharing the same situation. That said, living the life of a homeless person for a defined period is never going to give a full or true insight. It does, however, have the potential to produce better data than solely relying upon interviews. Adopting the role of a participant always runs the risk of 'going native' and losing sight of the research goals. By adopting the role of observer, on the other hand, such risk is avoided. Yet, while detachment ensures a degree of objectivity, you might never get close enough to the lifestyle and the values of homeless people to properly understand and, therefore, articulate their point of view.

The solution might be to combine the two approaches in one role, that of the 'participant observer'. This might involve being known as a researcher, which would give a different meaning to your participation. You would not be an insider, but neither would you be a complete outsider. The participant observer may still be playing a role, but that role need not interfere with the demands of the research. That said, giving the same attention to recording information as to playing the role may not prove to be so simple. And the problems are not always academic in nature, as Hobbs' (1988) study of working class relations with the police in East End of London illustrates. Hobbs' study necessitated a certain amount of 'socialising':

> *"... for the most part I spoke, acted, drank and generally behaved as though I was not doing research. Indeed, I often had to remind myself that I was not in a pub to enjoy myself, but to conduct an academic inquiry and repeatedly*

woke up the following morning with an incredible hangover facing the
dilemma of whether to throw it up or write it up."

(Hobbs, 1988, 6)

Finding a Setting

Sampling issues within participant observation studies are more concerned with
setting, than with the more usual issues of representativeness. The methods of
sampling, therefore, do not necessarily follow the basic rules, as set out in Chapter
7. In a study of homelessness, for example, random sampling may not be possible.
Suppose that you wanted to focus on the experiences of homeless women or young
people. In gaining access to such groups you might have to settle for an
opportunistic sample. That way you decide on the group of people you want to
study and then look for locations or settings where they are most likely to be found.
For a discussion of sampling issues in relation to studying homeless groups, see
Anderson, Kemp and Quilgars (1993).

As noted in Chapter 7, snowball sampling is a technique which is widely used in
identifying appropriate settings and individuals to study. The process often involves
the use of key informants, people who have expert knowledge of the area and/or
group you want to observe. These key informants can also help with problems of
access, which is clearly important to successful participant observation. If you want
to learn about how people manage and interpret their everyday lives, you will have
to develop some sort of rapport with them. In essence, they have to trust you.

How you negotiate access is often an important part of establishing such rapport. If
you wanted to conduct some observation within a housing department office, you
might think it better/more appropriate to negotiate access through senior
management. That would not, however, guarantee you the co-operation, far less the
trust, of others within the department. They might quite reasonably suspect that your
research was part of some management strategy for re-organisation, or worse. As
the researcher you would have to address these concerns. It would be as well to be
aware of the important features of the department, such as the levels of power and
decision-making, prior to developing an access strategy.

Negotiating access can be viewed simply as an administrative problem; a practical
difficulty to be overcome. It would, however, be more constructive, to think in
terms of what might be learned from the experience. The process of gaining access
is part and parcel of the research activity and may reveal a great deal about the
nature of the organisation or group being studied.

Taking Notes

Having found your setting, you now face the problem of how to record your
observations. Researchers now have a staggering array of techniques, from simple
checklists to tape recorders, camcorders and laptop computers, with which to record
the information gleaned from respondents. The recording equipment used in
participant observation studies, however, tends to be limited to pen and paper, or
perhaps a tape recorder if the setting allows. Memory is also important in certain

situations, especially when covert observation is being employed. It is, however, important to bear in mind that memory can be fallible for all sorts of reasons, as can be seen from the previously cited experience of Hobbs (1988).

How and when you record information will be influenced by the practicalities of the setting, but most participant observers keep some kind of fieldwork notes. Precisely how these notes are kept varies with the researcher. This description of taking field-notes in a study of educational practice is fairly typical:

> *"My field notes fell into three main categories. On large note cards I recorded material that was primarily observational in nature. Observations of classroom activities were recorded chronologically and classified under class name. Observations that were about particular students or Mrs Lewis were also kept chronologically, but were classified under the student's or teacher's name.*
>
> *On loose-leaf size paper I kept typed accounts of each interview. These accounts were about ten pages in length, single spaced and were classified under the student's, graduate's or teacher's name ..."*

(Valli, 1986, 227, quoted in Delamont, 1992, 61)

You might choose to record the information differently and, depending on the nature of your study, to record various sorts of information. The important consideration is that you are thorough and consistent; that you know what it is you want to observe and why, and that you make a note of everything that might be relevant. This should include all decisions made by you as the researcher and any insights that might be useful in interpreting the data. Lofland and Lofland (1984) and Wolcott (1981) offer a useful discussion on keeping field-notes.

Problems of Interpretation and Generalisability

There are a number of criticisms that can be made of participant observation and of qualitative methods in general. The two most important concern the problems of interpretation and generalisability.

Interpretation

While acknowledging the idea that looking at events through the eyes of those most directly involved is an integral and appealing aspect of qualitative methods, it is also highly problematic. To what extent is it really possible to see the 'real thing' – to view and interpret events from the point of view of others? Research information, however it is collected, will be mediated to some extent by the values held by the researcher. Where participant observation is concerned, this problem is exacerbated by the fact that the technique is dependent upon the observational and selection skills of the researcher. It is possible that the researcher will include or choose to exclude information because it does not fit with their preconceived notion of the situation, thus leaving the study open to a charge of bias. Similar problems can be caused by the researcher going native; over-identifying with their subjects to the extent that the needs of the study becomes secondary to those of the subjects. Delamont (1992) provides an interesting discussion of the problems of going native. It is, of course, possible that subjects will react to the very presence of a researcher and that this reactivity will change the situation in some way, no matter how carefully the researcher tries to be non-intrusive. This point was also touched upon in relation to interviews.

Generalisability

Observations are typically small scale and limited to one or two settings. This means that they are always vulnerable to the charge that the findings are too specific and, therefore, not generalisable; that they lack external validity. To some extent this problem can be addressed by combining methods – using triangulation – to view the event from a range of different vantage points. Many qualitative researchers, however, simply reject the notion of generalisability as being unacceptable or irrelevant, or both. Denzin, for example, notes that:

> *"The interpretivist rejects generalisation as a goal and never aims to draw randomly selected samples of human experience. For the interpretivist every instance of social interaction ... must be seen as carrying its own logic, sense of order, structure and meaning."*

(Denzin, 1983, 133-4)

Participant observation, in that it is part of the interpretivist tradition, undoubtedly is concerned in engaging with and trying to understand this 'sense of order, structure and meaning'. It should not be viewed as an easy option, nor is it without its critics. Yet as a research method, participant observation has the potential to offer new and interesting insights into many areas of social activity, and especially within housing.

Further Reading

Bales, R.F. (1970), *Personality and Interpersonal Behaviour*. London: Holt, Rinehart and Winston.

Delamont, S., (1992), *Fieldwork in Educational Settings: Methods Pitfalls and Perspectives*. London: Falmer.

Lofland, J. and Lofland, L., (1984), *Analysing Social Settings: A Guide to Qualitative Observation and Analysis*. Belmont, CA: Wadsworth.

CHAPTER 12:
Case Studies

Objectives of the Chapter

This chapter is designed to ensure that the reader:

- appreciates the various types of case studies that can be employed in conducting housing research;

- understands both the value and practical difficulties involved in using case studies; and

- is alert to the limitations of working with case studies.

Introduction

'Case study' is an umbrella term for a particular approach to research design and should not be mistaken for a research method. Rather, the range of research methods detailed in Chapters 5 to 11 can all be used in a case study. What case studies have in common is the decision to focus an inquiry around a single instance or instances (Adelman *et al*, 1977). Another definition, this time by Mitchell (1983), is that a case study is an idiosyncratic combination of elements or events. At its simplest, a case study is merely the unit for further systematic analysis or investigation, as defined by the researcher. This can be as basic as a description of one or two cases. At its most complex, however, a case study can be used to test experimental research within a natural setting, by controlling the influence of particular elements (Hakim, 1987). It is the means to provide a snapshot of an event, occurring at a particular time, in a particular place. Case studies therefore can act as either a spotlight or a microscope; their value depends on how well the study is focused (Hakim, 1987).

Case studies can be employed in a number of ways. They can be used as a follow-up to a questionnaire survey; as a means of providing colour for that survey. They can also precede a survey; acting as a sensitising operation, highlighting issues that may require more detailed investigation. As well as being illustrative, they can also act as a proxy for a specific approach, or type of organisation. Selected case studies can be used to illustrate the merits (or demerits) of a specific policy, or can focus on a unique project which is considered to be an example of 'best practice'. Case studies, therefore, offer the researcher a certain degree of creative flexibility, not only in the type of case study that can be employed, but also in the variety of research techniques that can be used to examine the selected case study.

Types of Case Studies

A case study can, therefore, focus on an individual, a group, an institution, a resource, an intervention or a geographic area. Outlined below are a number of examples which not only illustrate this diversity, but also outline the broad range of research methods which can be employed. The majority of these techniques have been detailed in the preceding chapters of this block.

Table 12.1: Case Study Types

Type	Description
Individual	Tracing the housing careers, or housing histories, of individual people. This approach has been used to illustrate the varied paths to homelessness experienced by those living on the streets.
Group	Interviews held with the directors of selected housing associations about the changes which the introduction of private finance has brought to their organisations. Another example would be interviewing ex-offenders about their experiences of housing on release from a penal institution.
Resource	Detailed examination is made of the role and impact of a particular facility. An example would be a case study examination of a hostel for women, or a family centre, or a project established to tackle anti-social tenants. Case studies, in this context, are used as a means of evaluating specific projects. Often such projects are one-offs, unique experiments which attempt to pioneer a particular method or approach.
Institution	This type could be used to examine the practices adopted by similar institutions when operating a particular piece of housing legislation. An example would be the practice of local authorities in respect of homeless legislation. Another would be an examination of private financiers' reactions to the quality and content of housing association business plans. Both these studies would involve the possible use of questionnaires, interviews and documentary analysis.
Intervention	This would focus on a specific policy mechanism, and then trace its effects upon different organisations and groups. The impact of the Right to Buy provides a good example, given the impacts are different whether you are a landlord or a tenant. Reactions to community care planning or assessments by social workers, local authority housing officers, housing association staff and the various voluntary bodies would be another case in point. Again questionnaires, interviews and documentary studies could be employed. There is also much scope for quantitative techniques, given the scale and financial implications of these two specific interventions.

Table 12.1: Case Study Types – contd.

Geographic	Often case studies are selected on a spatial basis to act as a proxy for a particular category of geographical area. Scottish Homes, in developing its Rural Housing Strategy, commissioned research which examined eight case studies which although all were rural, the peculiarities of the actual local housing market situation were thought to vary markedly. The case studies were selected specifically to illustrate this perceived variation. The geographic scale employed can vary widely. In studying variations in housing finance systems operating within Europe, perhaps three broad categorisations could be highlighted. To explore this further, three countries could be selected, each being seen as illustrative of one of the broad category. Case study examinations would focus on their particular fiscal and legislative arrangements. As the geographic scale of the case study widens, there tends to be a greater reliance upon quantitative data and analysis. The housing finance study could, however, be complemented with interview material. By interviewing key members of the housing policy communities, within each of the three case studies, a better understanding of the cultural and political mores that help shape particular national policies would be gleaned.

From the above examples it is clear that these categorisations are not mutually exclusive. Individual, group and institution could, in certain instances, be interchangeable. While this illustrates the flexibility of case studies, it also aptly illustrates that any categorisation is, at best, arbitrary.

An Evaluation of Case Study Approach

The case study may be employed, in part, because it provides a scale of research work which is appropriate for an individual researcher to tackle. It allows one aspect of an issue, or a particular initiative to be studied, in some depth. This is important, given the limits imposed on all research studies by both time and resources. That is not to say that case studies cannot be employed over long periods of time. It is its scale and, therefore, ambition that distinguishes them from the larger, more comprehensive surveys. As such it is often viewed as a logistical compromise. It is the adaptability and wide applicability of case studies that explains their popularity within housing research.

Any case study should have two objectives, one being focused on description while the other opts for explanation. In conducting any case study examination, you need to ensure they comprehensively detail the various parameters of the particular case under consideration. To achieve this goal, a variety of techniques are employed to delineate the focus of the research. The second objective, namely, expanding our knowledge and understanding of the issue or project, could help in the construction of wider concepts that have an applicability for other cases. In this way, case studies can be seen to provide a means to contribute to, and engage with, wider theories. At their best, case studies should be descriptively valid and have a more general application. The problem here is that to be useful a number of research methods need to be employed within the case study. This therefore puts pressure on the researcher who may be proficient in only a few methods. By trying their hand at other methods, without adequate training, the potential value of the case study may be compromised. Case studies should not be viewed as an easy option, for they certainly are not.

Case studies also have the advantage of allowing the researcher the opportunity to appreciate what they are studying from the perspective of those being studied. There is never just one way of viewing the world, and case studies can facilitate a wider discourse. 'Official' interpretations of particular projects, policies or events can jar with those held by those who work on them, or those whose life experience has been touched by them. Being able to draw on this material improves our understanding of the various processes that are taking place, and thus can greatly improve the quality of the research. The challenge here is to write up the case study material in a manner which finds the middle ground between a mass of indigestible local, specific material and the key conclusions as determined by the researcher. Being able to tie-in carefully selected, robust and central items from the data, which explore the various questions and issues raised by the study, is a real skill (Hakim, 1987).

Case Study Selection

All case studies are unique. Each case study, no matter the type, will display certain common and unique features. Do the unique features not, therefore, act against it being seen as a proxy for those that share its common features? This, of course, pre-supposes that a case study should be seen to illustrate more than just itself. In some instances a case study is selected because it illustrates something that is quite unique. It may, for example, represent a specific point of view, or a particular approach. In other instances a case study is selected to illustrate the experience of operating within a specific environment.

The purpose for which the case study is to be put determines the way in which it is selected. The case study's purpose, in respect of the research question being pursued, directly influences its selection criteria. Researchers should always make explicit the reasons that lie behind the selection decision. This allows the reader to consider and challenge the basis of selection and may as a consequence lead them to accept or reject the research work. Case studies can be taken to be unique, or they can be illustrative of wider patterns, but a case study should not be described as being representative of a specific type. When writing any research study that has employed case studies you have to be careful not to fall into the trap of seeing the case study as being representative. Rather it should always be described as illustrative of a particular instance, and any discussion should focus primarily upon what the case study itself revealed. Great care must be taken when trying to extrapolate the case study findings into the wider context. That is not to say it cannot be done, but rather care needs to be taken when making links between the case study evidence and the perceived wider pattern. In a study of local authority housing management practice, for example, a rural case study was selected. If that rural local authority had a well-run housing department which had expended much time and effort in improving its administrative systems, could this be taken to be indicative of the situation in all rural authorities? Clearly not, but had the case study been selected on the basis that it illustrated a well-managed rural authority it could provide an example of best practice issues as they relate to all housing departments.

A related criticism is that the case study, in common with all research work, is inherently incomplete. In making this point, Schuller (1988) sees the virtue of case study work being the fact that, contrary to first impressions, it must confront and make explicit that incompleteness. A case study can be distinguished from the anecdote, on the one hand, or simple narrative on the other, by the fact that it is not randomly selected, and that it does have some potential for explaining events or circumstances beyond itself.

Another criticism is that, given the researcher selects the area for study, decides upon what data to collect and determines which material should be presented in the final report, it is difficult to cross-check the information generated. Case studies can, either consciously or unconsciously, lead to distortion and bias. This, of course, is not a problem unique to case study research. To avoid this criticism you have to be explicit about the approach adopted, explain why certain decisions were taken in the course of the study and be clear about their implications.

Policy Evaluation

Within social science, case studies are used to allow a fine-tuned exploration of a complex set of interrelationships. Case studies, within the housing context, have proved particularly useful as a means of monitoring and evaluating policy initiatives or developments. Case studies are commonly used in evaluation studies to allow an examination to be made of a particular process of change. For such evaluative studies to be of value, it is important that they should generate information from before and after the introduction of the intervention under examination. Further, relevant contextual material is also important. What did the intervention mean to the lives of the various participants? The focus of such work is often on the outcomes and processes of developmental action within a particular context. As case studies tend to be narrow in focus, they can lead to an increased understanding of the specific context and the various processes which have been at work.

Comparative Capacity

By using case studies as a means to engage in comparative analysis the approach moves beyond the notion of the case being solely illustrative. When data from similar situations are compared, common themes and patterns can be identified, hypotheses generated and theory developed. The examination of themes and patterns is common in all uses of case study, but is especially important where the research design demands comparative analysis of the cases. There are, however, limitations to the comparative capacity of case studies. Again this comes from the problem of the specific being used to highlight a general pattern. In cross-national comparisons the effects of national policy environments can limit the capacity to generalise. That said, it may be that the same issues arise, but what is different is the way they are addressed. Comparisons within the one national context are generally more useful, but care has to be taken in how you express the links between the separate case studies and what you feel this reveals about the wider pattern. Harloe and Martens (1984) provide a useful discussion of the practical problems associated with international comparative housing research.

Type, Quality and Range of Data

While observation and interviews are the most commonly used approaches within case studies, no method is excluded. Both qualitative and quantitative approaches are often combined to generate the information required to illustrate the range of points or issues. It is not uncommon in housing research for a comprehensive survey to be followed by selected interviews. Case studies can often involve detailed documentary studies, given such material is often essential in setting the context for the case under consideration. In relation to quantitative analysis it is also common for case studies to be subject to detailed statistical analysis using data generated from the Census. In looking at the impact of the Right to Buy on a particular neighbourhood, or in assessing the impact of a recent improvement project on a specific locality, the capacity to generate both past and present socio-economic information has clear advantages. Such studies would also try to access information on changing house prices and mortgage availability. In relation to data collection within the case study context, nothing is ruled out and nothing is ruled in.

Good case studies depend upon accessing the best information available (Bromley, 1986). Emphasis needs to be placed on the words 'best' and 'available'. The preceding chapters within this block should help you appreciate what is meant by these terms. These chapters should have also made it clear that what is best is not always available. Again time and resources usually result in compromise. The crucial point is that at all times quality should be the key objective in respect to data.

Case studies are often criticised as being 'soft subjectivity'. Yet, it is clear from above that adopting a case study approach is no soft option. It has its own rigour and should be judged in its own terms. To get around such criticisms it is important to ensure a range of data sources are employed – to ensure that triangulation is achieved. It is important to get different perspectives on any event or phenomena. This is achieved by employing several methods. Information gathered from several participants associated with the case is also crucial. Finally, as noted previously, it is often advisable, where possible, to try and use more than one researcher to gather information on the case. Clearly, when conducting a small scale project this may not be feasible, but it is worth considering when conducting or commissioning a larger scale study. A successful case study *"... will provide the reader with a three-dimensional picture and will illustrate relationships, micro-political issues and patterns of influence in a particular context."* (Bell, 1993, 9)

Case Studies: Some Practical Issues

As noted throughout this chapter case studies, in common with most research techniques, represent a logistical compromise. For example, time and money may whittle the large scale survey down to a compromise position of eight case studies. This final selection is in itself a compromise, in that each of the eight must try to cover a range of issues which the larger survey would have touched upon. Having selected and justified this selection, the use of a case study method can throw up a few practical issues.

When selecting any case, you will have an impact upon it, as was discussed in the previous chapter. For example, in the study of housing management practice the imminent arrival of a researcher may result in the 'brushing-up' of the administrative systems which are to be examined. Those involved in executing the day-to-day work may undergo individual or organised training to ensure that they are up to scratch. The researcher will always have an influence upon those being studied. While there is little that can be done about this, you need to be aware of it. Good interviewing technique can, on occasions, highlight inconsistencies and discrepancies in practices, thus breaking down such preparation. That said, the only way to get round this is to ensure you employ a range of data sources so that you can cross-check, thus highlighting any discrepancies that arise.

At the same time there are other practical problems associated with this approach to research (for further details see Schuller, 1988). Outlined below are four standard experiences of conducting case studies:

1. You go in and get nothing. Access issues were not thought through properly, or previous assumptions or guarantees come to nothing.

2. You go in but can only get so far, because it proves to be a lot harder and more time-consuming to access the data. The planned approach proves unworkable so a more complex one has to be instigated. This may create tensions with others involved in the case study.

3. You go in and get the material, but it is sensitive and easily attributable to one specific case and is therefore hard to use. An example of this is where income data from a case study highlights the fact that a number of tenants are engaged in defrauding the Benefits Agency.

4. You go in and get so much information it is not easy to manage. As a result it proves hard to keep a clear focus on the research topic at hand. The case study has thrown up a host of new ideas and this makes you re-think the basic assumptions of the study.

Again these issues are not unique to case study research, but are equally applicable within any research context. It is important to be aware of these potential problems, and try to plan out the research method to avoid the pitfalls. Yet, all the meticulous research planning in the world will not be capable of predicting the problems that can, and do arise in conducting case study work.

Advantages of Case Study:

- it allows for in-depth focusing on shifting relationships;

- it can capture complexities;

- it allows a focus on the local understandings and a sense of participation in the case; and

- it can produce readable data that brings research to life and is true to the concerns and meanings under scrutiny.

Disadvantages of Case Study:

- it can be an unwarranted intrusion into the affairs of others;

- it is bound by situation and time;

- it requires carefully collected, high quality data which takes time to collect; and

- the researcher can become so immersed in the case that subsequent data analysis can become difficult.

As has been outlined above, the purpose of adopting a case study approach should be more than just providing the means to add colour to a study. A case study, if properly conducted, is much more than just a story about, or a description of, a particular event or state. It should also be capable of providing more than just a means of generating generalisations. To take a case study beyond these limited outcomes, as with all research, evidence has to be collected in a systematic manner. Only through the methodical planning of data collection can you hope, at a later stage, to reveal relationships between the variables.

Further Reading

Adelman, C., (*et al*), (1977), 'Re-thinking case study: notes from the second Cambridge Conference', *Cambridge Journal of Education*, 6, 139-50.

Bromley, D., (1986), *The Case Study Method in Psychology and Related Disciplines*. New York: Wiley.

Hakim, C., (1987), *Research Design: Strategies and Choices in the Design of Social Research*, (Contemporary Social Research 13). London: Allen Unwin.

Mitchell, C., (1983), 'Case and situation analysis', *Sociological Review*, 31, 2, 187-211.

Schuller, T., (1988), 'Pot-holes, caves and lotusland: some observations on case study research', in Burgess, R., (ed), *Studies in Qualitative Methodology*, (Volume 1), London: JAI Press.

CHAPTER 13:
Information Technology and Housing Research

Objectives of the Chapter

This chapter is designed to ensure that the reader:

- appreciates the various applications which information technology offers housing research;

- understands the limitations, and potential problems that can arise from using information technology; and

- understands the importance of planning for the requirements of information technology right at the start of the project.

Introduction

"He coveted the files, staplers, erasers, coloured inks and gadgets whose functions remained a teasing mystery, thinking that if only he could afford to equip himself with all this apparatus his thesis would write itself: he would be automated."

(Lodge, 1981, 70)

If you substitute new technology for the paraphernalia of the 1960s stationery shop, anyone who has ever been involved in writing either a research report or dissertation will both understand and identify with Adam Appleby's desire for automation. What Adam was looking for was the means to organise and speed up the research process and, increasingly, that is exactly what the recent advances in information technology would appear to offer. Software packages are now available to help with almost every aspect of the research process – literature searches, research instrument design, data collection, data management and analysis, as well as writing up and presentation. The one notable exception is the complex task of thinking: that is one task you still have to do for yourself.

This chapter will provide an insight into the world of computers and information technology (IT), focusing on the various ways in which computers can make the tasks of the researcher that much easier. On the plus side the chapter illustrates how information technology offers new opportunities for collecting and manipulating information, which in the past would have been considered too complex and/or too time-consuming. In doing so, information technology can help in the construction of new insights into age-old problems. On the down side, IT can also give rise to a range of new problems. In this regard, the chapter concludes with a brief 'health warning' about the use and abuse of IT.

This chapter provides an overview. It does not seek to provide the detailed information which is required when deciding upon what software or hardware, if any, would best suit your specific research needs. That is something that you will have to decide upon for yourself, after careful examination of the available options. In particular, consult the CTI Centre for the Built Environment based at the University of Cardiff for a review of current software and resources. More information on the various applications can be found in the Further Reading section of this chapter.

Using Computers in Research

Research, in essence, is knowing what you want to ask, and of whom, and then knowing what you want to do with the findings. Once you have sorted out these conceptual and theoretical issues the research process can be speeded-up and enhanced by the sensible application of IT. How best to make use of this technology depends upon the nature of the research project, the type of analysis to be employed, the resources available to you, and of course your own level of competence. Thinking about the role and function of IT within your specific research task, right from the start, is good practice. Trying to find your way around a software application, with the deadline for the research project rapidly looming, is unfortunately, all too common. For most researchers, some basic keyboard skills are now essential, even if their application is limited to little more that basic wordprocessing or accessing information from library catalogues. The skills required to operate other packages often require a great deal more training, and therefore time to acquire these skills has to be built into any research proposal. Understanding the scope and limitations of the various IT applications is also useful for those involved in commissioning and managing commissioned research.

Literature Searches

The application of IT in literature searches was explored in some detail within Chapter 5, so there is little point repeating it here. The important point is that in using the range of literature search systems you need to be clear about which aspects of your topic you wish to explore. As these systems all operate by the use of keywords, it is crucial that a good deal of thought goes into defining the parameters of the topic, prior to embarking upon a computer search.

Databases such as *FileMakerPro* on Apple Mac or *DBaseIV* on IBM compatible PCs can also be a useful way of managing your personal information needs, such as constructing bibliographical notes or holding references with notes. Information once stored in this fashion can be easily retrieved, instantly updated and interrogated using keywords, in the same way as library catalogue searches. Having read through a range of relevant references, by carefully using a range of keywords you can quickly assemble this material in an order which best suits your purposes. For those who are active researchers, or who have an information function to perform within their organisation, such systems can make what was once a time-consuming and laborious task relatively straightforward. Cawkell (1991) provides a useful introduction to the various applications of personal information systems.

Wordprocessing

The wordprocessing package is now a ubiquitous research tool. Specifically designed to produce and revise text, the wordprocessor has obvious uses in a variety of research tasks such as making and editing field notes, transcribing interview material, as well as writing up and revising the final report. Wordprocessors can also be a useful tool when designing data collection instruments and can even be used as a means of conducting basic qualitative analysis through the word-search facility.

The advantages of any wordprocessing package are its ease of use, the ability to make corrections (whether for spelling or grammar) with the minimum of fuss, and the capacity to re-order text through the use of its 'cut and paste' facilities. This does not of course absolve the writer from the need to proofread all written work, given that spelling-checkers can only identify misspelt words. As such they cannot detect words which, though spelt correctly, are wrongly used: two, too and to are all perfectly acceptable so far as a spelling-check is concerned, but that may be too much for the reader. Some wordproccessing packages also have grammar-checkers which work on similar principles. While these can sharpen up your writing style by breaking up lengthy sentences and can pick up basic grammatical faults, they are an aid rather than a substitute for good writing.

Wordprocessing skills are not too difficult to pick up. Most packages have 'teach yourself' courses as part of the basic software package. Further basic wordprocessing courses are available in most parts of the country. Once the basics are grasped, it is down to use and practice to expand your knowledge and skills. To progress on from two-finger typing, use should be made of typing 'tutor' programmes which are available on disc. While wordprocessing packages can help with most basic aspects of research, other types of applications have been developed to address the more specific tasks.

Layout and Design

While basic wordprocessing packages can be used for designing most research instruments, questionnaires, interview guides, or observation schedules, desktop publishing software such as Adobe *PageMaker* can add that 'professional touch'. However, developing a competent skills level using such packages requires both time and a certain degree of design expertise. An appreciation of what will work and what does not, in relation to design, is something that requires training. Other specialist software is now available which allows you to set up a questionnaire, enter the data and analyse the results all within the one package. These packages require no use of paper, but do need careful management to minimise any potential for data loss, given you have no hard copy. One example is *QuestionMark* which can be used on either Apple Mac or on a PC, while another is *Survey System* which is PC dedicated.

Collecting and Recording Information

This is one aspect of research where more traditional collecting and recording methods are much in evidence. Interviews, for example, may be transcribed using a computer, but the initial recording of the data will usually be in note form, or via audiotape (see Chapter 9). Nevertheless, laptop computers are being used to record data directly in the field and some software packages now make it possible to run tests in-situ.

Once the information has been collected, however, the task of getting it into a manageable format is greatly helped by the use of IT. Data from questionnaires, for example, can be keyed directly into a format which the analysis package can handle. If you have the necessary funds, it is worth considering employing a commercial firm to carry out what can be a time-consuming chore. Bear in mind that data entry needs to be accurate and cost-cutting here can result in many hours being expended trying to remedy non-random errors. Through time this task may become that much easier by the use of machine readable instruments or optical scanners. At present, however, the technology is far form being a substitute to hand operated data entry through the use of typing.

Storing and Accessing Information

In the past storing research data involved holding large amounts of paper records in loose folders or bulky filing cabinets. Today a computer disk can store more information than that held in an average sized book, while the hard disk drive on even the most modest of desktop computers is now capable of storing the equivalent of millions of pages of data. Further, whereas once computers held only numbers or text, recent developments have meant that graphical material, photographs, audio and even video clips can now be stored and managed relatively easily using certain dedicated computer software packages.

If storage is easy, accessing the data is also straightforward. Files can be opened, closed, copied, created, deleted, or amended without difficulty. Information can be managed, organised and re-organised, which is especially useful for qualitative analysis. There is, however, a need to be systematic, and to ensure that backup copies of all data are made at regular intervals. It is all too easy to forget to backup material which can then be lost through a fault in either the hard drive or on the floppy disk. With the adoption of good housekeeping practices the problem of lost or misplaced data could be a thing of the past.

Analysing Data

Computer-based analysis tends to be associated with the production of statistics. In this regard spreadsheet packages such as *Lotus123* and *Excel* allow you to manipulate numbers, carry out a range of calculations, including basic statistics, and to present the results through either a variety of tables or graphical displays. The great advantage of a spreadsheet lies in its ability to store and update information. Further, given its capacity to consistently amend data, using specified formulae, spreadsheets have proved to be a versatile means of constructing databases. By creating such spreadsheets to hold official housing statistics the analytical capacity of such information is enhanced (Bailey and Robertson, 1995; Wilcox, 1995). That said, given that the range of statistics available on a spreadsheet package is limited, for more detailed analysis you will require to invest in a more dedicated statistical analysis software. These packages allow you not only the capacity to work with larger data sets but also subject this data to a broader range of statistical tests. Statistics packages have been around, first on mainframe computer systems, and then on PCs, for a very long time. The names of the leading packages – *SPSS, Minitab, Statsys*, and so on – should be familiar to most with even a basic knowledge of research, even if the packages themselves remain something of a mystery. The range and complexity of these packages cannot be dealt with here, but Bryman and Cramer (1990) provide a useful guide to quantitative analysis using computer software and in particular *SPSS*.

More recently, packages have been developed that, it is claimed, take the tedium out of even qualitative analysis. Information technology can now help with many of the time-consuming but necessary tasks associated with qualitative work, such as data selection, categorisation and indexing through title, location and data type. In the past, this would have been done by hand, using index cards to record and manage information; and of course some researchers still choose to organise their material in this way. Transcribing interviews, note keeping, and basic analysis, as was noted above, can be tackled using a wordprocessor. Anything more complex, however, might best be left to dedicated software specially designed for qualitative work such as *HyperQual, Hypersoft* or *NUD.IST*. There are of course significant differences in what is offered by these various programs and you need to think carefully which, if any, would be most useful for your purposes. In this regard Tesch (1990) offers a useful guide to what is available in the field.

Integrated Packages

While report writing is where the wordprocessing package really comes into its own, a number of integrated packages are now available which combine wordprocessing, a spreadsheet and a database to make the whole process that much easier. *Microsoft Works*, for example, is an integrated package for Apple Macs and PCs which allows the user to copy information between these various software applications in a straightforward manner. Suppose, for example, you were carrying out a small scale survey of customer satisfaction for a housing organisation. Using spreadsheets, you could analyse the results from a questionnaire and then display the findings in both a tabular and graphic form. These tables and graphics, bar charts, pie charts or frequency diagrams can then be imported into the appropriate place within the research report you are preparing using the word processing facility. If, in addition, you had stored the results of your literature search on the database facility, you could import the relevant information into the reference section of the final report. When it then came to presenting your findings you could select the information for overheads and set that up either on a PC slide show facility or have acetates created. Presentational issues are discussed in greater detail in Chapter 15.

The Role of the Computer: a Health Warning

If all this sounds too good to be true, then that's about right. While computers offer a world of automation and ease there is a downside. Computers can be very quick at processing routine tasks and, therefore, they can allow you the capacity to explore a question from a variety of perspectives by re-running the analysis in a number of ways. Where once this would have involved many days work, much of which was spent waiting for the result of the actual computation, these tasks can now be accomplished in a matter of minutes. Graphics can be worked and reworked until you get exactly the arrangement you want, at a size which will fit the page. But such flexibility has its limitations and dangers, particularly where the analysis and interpretation of data is concerned. There is a need to clearly calculate what exactly you are trying to achieve and not get overly enthralled by the technology. It would, therefore, be appropriate to provide a few words of warning:

1. **Don't let the technology drive the research.**
   A computer program will offer you only a limited choice in analysing data and that may not necessarily include the particular approach which you would wish to pursue, or that which is most appropriate for the data. Leave such choices to the computer at your peril. A statistical package will produce a correlation, for example, quickly and relatively easily, but it cannot tell you whether that correlation is either meaningful or relevant to the research question.

2. **Don't try to do too much.**
   While a computer has little difficulty in handling large volumes of data, the question arises, can you? If you have too much information will you have the time needed to prepare the data for analysis and will you have time to get any real 'feel' for the data? Without some understanding of the nature of the data, you may overlook certain important issues or relationships. There may also be a tendency to accept too easily possibly misleading statistics.

3. **Don't trawl through data.**
   The speed and power of computer programs can encourage a mechanistic approach to analysis. Trawling for data and quantification for its own sake, without reference to either theory or the research question being investigated, should be avoided at all costs. There is always the danger that the technology becomes an end in itself, rather than the means to an end.

4. **Remember the adage "garbage in, garbage out".**
   If there are problems then these are likely to lie with you, rather than with the technology. As a researcher your job is to both interpret and to understand, not simply to be technically proficient. Research should always be more about thought than application. To achieve this end as a researcher you must spend time thinking through the key research issues and then assessing what role IT can play in exploring the various relationships that have been considered. You need to recognise not only the advantages, but also the limitations of IT.

The Data Protection Act

If you are thinking about using computers in any aspect of your research, it will be necessary to familiarise yourself with the requirements of the Data Protection Act, 1984. This Act requires that all personal data, namely information which relates to identifiable persons and which is automatically processed, must be officially

registered. The registration requirement covers personal data stored or processed for research purposes, whether on your employer's computer or on your own PC.
It should also be noted that the Act places a responsibility on you to ensure that those using the data other than yourself, namely that your 'servants and agents', conform to the requirements of the Act in exactly the same way as yourself, as the registered Data User. This makes you responsible, for passing on the relevant guidance of the Data Protection Act. You, therefore, need to ensure that the holding, use and disclosure of any personal data for which you are responsible is in accordance with all the requirements of the Act. Broadly speaking, the use of personal data for research should conform to the following principles:

- you should not construct or maintain computer files of personal data, for research purposes, without the express permission of the relevant authority;
- you should be aware of the requirements of the Data Protection Act, 1984 and of the appropriate level of security arrangements which attach to the particular set of personal data you hold; and
- the use of personal data should be limited to the minimum consistent with the achievement of the research objectives. Wherever possible data should be de-personalised so that it is impossible to identify the individual subjects.

For further details of the Act and how it applies to your particular research, contact either your employers' or Institutions' Data Protection Officer.

Advantages of information technology:

- it can greatly reduce the time involved in carrying out complex analytical, as well as routine, tasks;
- it allows for greater flexibility in testing for relationships;
- it can create the space to both think through and test the significance of particular relationships; and
- it can improve the presentational quality of the finished research report.

Disadvantages of information technology:

- information technology can be seen as a substitute for clear thought;
- the researcher can become seduced by the technology and forget that it has a specific purpose to perform, it is not the end in itself;
- you can underestimate the time required to become proficient with software packages;
- IT requires a degree of on-going management to ensure data is not lost, misplaced or corrupted; and
- the time taken to remedy basic data errors can be considerable.

Further Reading

Bryman, A., and Cramer, C., (1990), *Quantitative Data Analysis for Social Scientists*. London: Routledge.

Cawkell, A., (1991), 'Ideal personal information systems', *The Intelligent Enterprise*, 1, 8, 14-18.

Dey, I., (1993), *Qualitative Data Analysis: A User-Friendly Guide for Social Scientists*. London: Routledge.

Kelle, J., (ed), (1995), *Computer-Aided Qualitative Data Analysis*. London: Sage.

Tesch, R. (1990), *Qualitative Research: Analysis Types and Software Tools*. London: Falmer.

Weitzman, E., and Miles, M., (1994), *Computer Programmes for Qualitative Data Analysis*. Newbury Park, CA: Sage.

PART THREE: FINISHING OFF? – ANALYSING, THEORISING AND PRESENTING

When you have collected the information you require, by whatever means, the next problem is what to do with it. How do you make sense of the data, which can resemble a chaotic collection of numbers and text? The data cannot speak for itself and you cannot expect that somehow conclusions will emerge from it; at least not without your help. Data has to be organised and this process is governed by your analytical and interpretational skills. This is where the real skill in researching lies, and this part of the research process takes time. As was pointed out in Chapter 3, you should have given some thought to data analysis and its interpretation at the planning stage. Now is the time to put that plan into action.

This final section deals with these 'finishing off' issues. Chapter 14 explores some of the main points in relation to data organisation, management and its analysis and interpretation, while the final chapter looks at report writing and the presentation of findings.

The Use and Abuse of Research Findings

Housing research, as was noted in Part One, is usually applied, rather than pure or theoretical; that is, it is designed to answer practical questions which have an operational and/or policy focus. Housing researchers will, therefore, be interested in collecting information that will ultimately be used to develop, implement and evaluate a broad range of policies. A critical consideration in this regard is to provide knowledge that helps improve practice and decision-making within housing organisations. Such research work consequently feeds into an active policy area, which operates at a range of levels whether local or governmental. Research findings can, and should challenge accepted practices and norms. At the same time, do not be surprised that in challenging such practices and norms you come into direct conflict with those who hold with the status quo. While researchers have a moral obligation to contribute to public debate on the major issues of the day they must also be aware that alternative arguments and perspectives can and will be ranged against them. Yet, as social scientists we: "… *are de facto part of the social world which we study, and the knowledge which we produce can always potentially be used to some effect; therefore the idea that we can pursue a detached social science which does not engage with public issues is at best very naive.*" (Finch, 1986, 3)

The formation, implementation and evaluation of policy is inevitably a political process. In planning and carrying out policy-oriented research it is necessary to address that political context. In particular, you might consider for whose benefit the research is being conducted, how you would anticipate the findings being used, or perhaps misused, and whether you want them used in this way. Research within this policy environment can always be interpreted in a number of ways. You need to be aware of this fact, and where feasible directly address these possible interpretations.

CHAPTER 14:
Managing, Analysing and Interpreting Data

Objectives of the Chapter

> This chapter is designed to ensure that the reader:
>
> - is conscious of good practice in data management;
>
> - understands the basic means of analysing quantitative and qualitative data;
>
> - appreciates the limitations of statistics; and
>
> - understands the importance of linking theory with data analysis.

Introduction

The data collection phase of any research exercise should provide you with a large amount of information; data which you hope will be both interesting and illuminating. Your specific study may have generated quantitative data, from a questionnaire, and qualitative information from the associated interviews. The goal of any research task is to provide explanation, but the data *per se* cannot provide this. Whether the data is qualitative or quantitative, it needs to be organised, analysed and interpreted by the researcher. This chapter explores some of the main principles of managing, analysing and interpreting the results from quantitative and qualitative data. The limitations of basic statistical analysis are presented and, finally, the relationship between research findings and theoretical concepts is discussed.

Coding, Data Entry and Data management

Given the recent advances in computer software it is feasible to load your data and give the machine the instructions to sort and analyse it in accordance with a standard set of analytical statistical tests. Yet, as was noted in Chapter 13, it is dangerous to abrogate your own thinking and opt to conduct the analysis in a mechanicalistic manner. Certain market research companies, as part of their service, provide a standard analysis of any survey. Avoid using this format and stick to the agreed analysis which has been developed to explore the topic in hand.

To conduct the analysis proficiently it is important that you gain a feel for the data. This is best achieved by investing time in coding, data entry and its subsequent management. Clearly, if there is a very large data set you will need to contract out the coding and data entry operations, but you should still take a keen interest in this operation so that you are confident with the resultant data. In the case of smaller data sets, data preparation can be handled in a PC using a spreadsheet package. In both instances it is the process of categorising and generating coding variables that helps you familiarise yourself with the collected data. Developing such a coding frame also makes it easier to check the accuracy of the processed data. Mistakes will inevitably occur at all stages of data collection, but by spending time on the data preparation side a number can be picked up and amended prior to analysis. Finding such errors later on can be more costly in both time and reputation. Bear in mind, no data set can ever be perfect, but that should not provide an excuse for ignoring the full range of data cleaning exercises.

The data entry process begins with the creation of a code book. Each variable is assigned a unique reference code. The data is then organised by coding each and every response in line with this coding frame. This code book is nothing more than a list of all the variables to be analysed, together with their respective codes. If you are using computer analysis, some instructions which tell the programme where these variables are to be found are also included. Table 14.1 is part of a code book from a local house condition survey.

Table 14.1: Extract from House Condition Survey Code Book

Column	Question No.	Variable Label	Value Label	Code
1-12		Identification (ID) Number	ID number	(code exact number)
13-16		Rateable Value (RU)	RU number	(code exact number)
17	1	House Type	Detached	1
			Semi-detached	2
			Terraced	3
			Tenement flat	4
			Other flat	5
			Maisonette	6
			Converted house	7
			Other	8
			No information	9
18	2	Age of Property	Pre-1919	1
			1919-1944	2
			1945-1964	3
			Post-1964	4
			No information	9

Analysing Quantitative data

Having gone through this coding exercise the data is still in a raw state. It may now be organised, and more easily managed, but as yet it tells you very little. What has to be done now is to examine the information in a variety of ways; in essence, to look at the distribution and patterns or frequencies of the key variables. Producing the range of frequencies is a key data cleaning exercise, as it will be quickly obvious where certain anomalies lie. These can then be traced back to the data set and amended prior to the actual data analysis.

You should not trawl through the data in the hope that something interesting might turn up. Rather your analysis should be informed by the original theoretical concepts and by the research questions which you are seeking to answer. Having applied these concepts to the data, the results are then interpreted against the original assumptions or hypothesis.

If your data is quantitative, or has been reduced to numbers, there is a veritable host of statistical techniques that can be used for analysis purposes. This chapter can do no more than introduce one or two of the most commonly used statistical applications, namely frequency distributions, measures of central tendency and dispersion, and bivariate analysis. There are, however, some very useful texts available if you need more information on quantitative analysis. Rowntree (1981) provides a good introduction to basic statistics, whereas Bryman and Cramer (1990) offer more detailed advice, particularly on using computer-based statistical analysis using *SPSS*.

Frequency Distributions

The most commonly used and the most straightforward descriptive statistic, is the frequency distribution. It is basically a simple count detailing the number of cases in each category, for example, the number of males and females interviewed. This information can be provided as either a table or a graph. Table 14.2 below shows an example of a frequency distribution for house type which you might find in a local house condition survey.

Table 14.2: Frequency Distribution of House Type

Value	Frequency	Percentage
Detached	48	5
Semi-detached	125	13
Terraced	213	22
Purpose built flat	342	36
Maisonette	60	6
Converted house	150	16
Other	16	2
Total	954	100

In this instance the survey area is dominated by purpose built flats and terraces, although converted property and semi-detached dwellings are also significant.

Frequency distributions, however, provide only very limited information. Additional information is needed to tell you something about the 'shape' or variability of the data. The two most common measures of variability are central tendency and dispersion.

Measures of Central Tendency

A measure of central tendency is simply the average of the distribution. In fact, it is not that simple because in statistical terms there is not one 'average', but three, as was noted earlier in Chapter 6: the mean, median and mode. The mean is the arithmetic average, that is the total values in a distribution, divided by the number of observations. Suppose you have an age distribution, as in Table 14.3, from a study of homeless young people resident in a stopover hostel. The mean in this case would be 19 years.

Table 14.3: Frequency Distribution of Stopover Residents' Age

Value	Frequency	Percentage
16	21	21
17	16	16
18	20	20
19	5	5
20	5	5
21	5	5
22	14	14
23	14	14
TOTAL	**100**	**100**

The median, another measure of central tendency, tells us where the mid-point of the distribution lies. In the age distribution above the mid-point is 51 (101/2). The median is the value of the 51st case, that is 18 years. This tells us that 50 per cent of the sample are aged 18 or below. It is lower than the mean, in this case, because the age distribution is skewed towards the younger age groups (57 per cent of the sample are 18 or younger).

The final measure of central tendency, the mode, is simply the value that occurs most often. The mode of modal category for the variable age would be 16 years. This is different from both the median and the mean and again this is because the distribution is skewed.

All three measures of central tendency attempt to do the same thing, to describe the 'average' value of the data. They do so in different ways, however, and if the distribution of the data is not uniform, as in this case, they can produce different outcomes. By employing all three it is evident that a range of issues arise, such as the notable concentration of young people, below 18, and also a cluster at a higher age band. While the former may be explained by the changes in benefit entitlement for young people, the older cohort would require some other explanation.

Measures of Dispersion

Whereas measures of central tendency attempt to summarise the data, measures of dispersion provide information on the amount of variation. The most obvious way of doing this is by examining the range outlined, namely, the lowest and highest values in the distribution. This particular measure of dispersion is susceptible to distortion from outlying or atypical values. If you have information on household income the range might be from less than £4,000 to more than £40,000, as in Table 14.4.

Table 14.4: Frequency Distribution of Household Income

Value	Frequency	Percentage
under £4,000	1	1
£4-10,000	26	26
£11-15,000	38	38
£16-20,000	15	15
£21-25,000	5	5
£26-30,000	9	9
£31-40,000	4	4
over £40,000	2	2
TOTAL	**100**	**100**

Yet, the range is not particularly helpful here since it disguises the fact that there are only a few households in these outlining categories. The inter-quartile range would be a better measure of dispersion for it ignores the extreme values and focuses instead on the 'middle half' of the distribution; that is it discounts those values that fall within the lowest and the highest 25 per cent of the distribution. The inter-quartile range for household income, £4 -10,000 to £16 – 20,000, gives a better picture of the actual data. In calculating the inter-quartile range, of course, half of the available information is lost and this may not be appropriate, particularly if the distribution contains no extreme outlying values.

If you have interval data, the preferred measure of dispersion is the standard deviation. Standard deviation describes the difference between individual observations and the mean of all the observations. It is a sort of 'average distance from the mean' for the whole distribution. Most introductory statistics texts such as Rowntree (1981), discuss how the standard deviation is derived. The actual calculation is more time-consuming than complicated and fortunately can now be easily generated using a computer or a scientific calculator.

Bimodal Analysis

All the above measures describe the characteristics of the data in terms of one variable: they are examples of univariate statistics. As often as not, however, you will want to know something about how two variables are related to each other. Suppose you were interested in any relationship between gender and satisfaction with the services provided by the local housing department. To achieve this end you could make use of a technique called crosstabulation, 'crosstabs' for short, to produce the following two-by-two table.

Table 14.5: Satisfaction with Housing Department by Gender

Value	Satisfied	Dissatisfied	Total
Men	150 (75.0)	50 (25.0)	200
Women	50 (25.0)	150 (75.0)	200
Total	200 (100)	200 (100)	400

This is a much simplified example, but it helps demonstrate the basic idea. In this case there is a clear difference between the satisfaction experienced by men and women. While the housing service was satisfactory to three out of every four men, for women the result was three to one in the opposite direction. This would raise questions about how often and for what reasons men and women make use of the housing department. In practice the 'crosstabs' produced would be more detailed and would usually include a correlation coefficient; a statistic used to express the relationship between the two variables.

Crosstabulations can obviously only deal with a very limited number of categories and, therefore, are not really suited interval data such as income. You could of course re-organise the data into bands, as was done in Table 14.4, but only at the cost of losing some of the detail. One alternative would be to create a scattergram. Suppose, for example your data contained information about the age of a house, this could be plotted against another variable, 'value of house'. The resultant scattergram might look something like Figure 14.6.

Figure 14.6: Scattergram of Value against Age of House

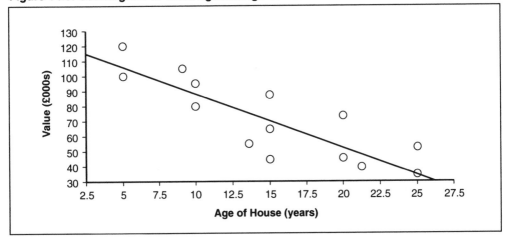

The more dispersed or scattered the points, the weaker the relationship between the two variables. Conversely, the closer together the points, the stronger the relationship. In this case the points seem to cluster around the regression line suggesting that there is a relationship between the age of a house and its value, albeit not a particularly strong one. While there would appear to be an inverse correlation between the age of a house and its value, in that the value tends to decrease with the age of the property, you could not use property age as a reliable guide to price.

Using and Abusing Statistics

Statistics are a powerful tool for analysing data. They are certainly widely used not only in research, but to illustrate many aspects of our daily lives. Next time you read your daily newspaper or watch the news or current affairs on television, note how often statistics are used to support the story. Whether the item is about law and order, homelessness, house prices, or your chances of winning the National Lottery, statistics are invariably quoted. Do you know how these figures are calculated, or exactly what they mean, or indeed if they mean anything at all? For many people the answer to these questions will be an emphatic no. Yet statistics are a powerful and seductive, descriptive tool. Having almost developed a mystical quality it is important to bear in mind that they can be all too easily abused.

A small book, first published in 1954, should be compulsory reading for everyone who intends to use, or to come into contact with statistics. Darrell Huff's *How to Lie with Statistics* provides a humorous insight on some of the more common, *"instances of bumbling and chicanery"* to be found in the world of statistics. Take one example which concerns the dangers of confusing correlation with causation:

> *"You can make an estimate – one that is better than chance would produce – of how many children have been born to a Dutch or Danish family by counting*

the storks' nests on the roof of their house. In statistical terminology it would be said that a positive correlation has been found to exist between these two things. What sounds like a proof of an ancient myth is actually something far more valuable. It is an easily remembered reminder of a useful truth: an association between factors is not a proof that one has caused the other.

In the instance of the storks and the babies, it is not too hard to find a third factor that may be responsible for the other two. Big houses attract big, or potentially big, families; and big houses have more chimney pots on which storks may nest.

But flaws in assumptions of causality are not always so easy to spot, especially when the relationship seems to make a lot of sense or when it pleases a popular prejudice."

(Huff, 1973, 83-85)

The message is clear, always treat statistics, all statistics, with caution and a great deal of cynicism. As was noted in Chapter 10, think clearly about the interpretation put on published statistics and then try and explain the pattern from another perspective. You will find this task is not that difficult.

Analysing Qualitative Data

Not all information comes in a numeric form. Text from interviews or from open-ended questionnaire items, or perhaps data from an observational study also require analysis. How, then, do you deal with such qualitative data. The techniques of data management and analysis may be different, but the problem is essentially the same. It is all about how you organise the information so that it is amenable to a particular approach to analysis.

Exactly how the analysis of qualitative data is conducted often appears to be mysterious or, at least, not clearly articulated.

"Some qualitative researchers still consider analysis to be an art form and insist on intuitive approaches to it. We are left with the researchers telling us of classifications and patterns drawn from a welter of field data, in ways that are irreducible or incommunicable. We do not really see how the research got from 3,600 pages of field-notes to the final conclusions, as sprinkled with vivid illustrations as they may be."

(Miles and Huberman, 1994, 2)

Content Analysis

One way of addressing the problem, of course, would be to quantify the data in some way. This 'content analysis' approach involves counting the frequency with which keywords or phrases associated with the main variables appear within the text. You could then present the information in the form of a frequency distribution, table or graph. It takes time of course to reduce qualitative information in this way. To code an open-ended interview, for example, would involve reading and re-reading the text, developing categories and indexing the material. This technique is commonly used where open items occur within an essentially closed questionnaire, or structured interview context. Suppose you were to ask students why they decide to study for a diploma in housing. It could be framed as an open-ended question, with respondents being free to answer in the own words. Nevertheless, it should not be too difficult, reading through the range of responses to break them down into five or six key themes. You could then construct a coding sheet with these themes on one axis and the interview numbers on the other, as in Table 14.7 below. Using this framework, you could then simply count the number of times each theme was mentioned in an interview.

Table 14.7: Example of Content Analysis Coding Frame

Theme	Interview No.						Total
	1	2	3	4	5	6	
Improve promotion chances	I		卌	II	III	I	12
CIH membership	I	II	I	III	II	I	10
Improve qualifications	II	I	III	I	II	I	10
Financial incentive		III	II	I	I		7
General interest	I		II			I	4
Intellectual challenge		I		I		I	3
Job requirement		I	I				2
Help with career change						I	1

The obvious difficulty in 'condensing' data in this way, is that you will lose something of its essential meaning and richness. Content analysis is, consequently, criticised because it cannot deliver the holistic perspective that is such a crucial part of qualitative research.

Grounded Theory

The grounded theory approach, developed by Glaser and Strauss (1967), takes a much more open and sceptical view of the analysis and interpretation of qualitative data. Grounded theory proceeds not by imposing a structure on the data, as all quantitative approaches do, but by 'grounding' the categories in the data. The idea is that any structure must come directly from the data, from the concepts and categories used by respondents themselves. It is their interpretation and analysis of their experiences that is crucial, not those imposed by the researcher.

Analysis from this perspective is a dynamic process of data reduction, data display, drawing conclusions and verification (Miles and Huberman, 1994). The analysis is not the end product, rather it is an integral and continuous part of the actual research process.

> *"From the start of data collection, the qualitative analyst is beginning to decide what things mean – is noting regularities, patterns, explanations, possible configurations, causal flows and propositions. The competent researcher holds these conclusions lightly, maintaining openness and scepticism, but the conclusions are still there, inchoate and vague at first, then increasingly explicit and grounded ..."*
>
> (Miles and Huberman, 1994, 11)

Through a process of familiarisation, reflection, conceptualisation, linking and re-evaluation, the researcher develops a 'feel' for the data and the concepts and conclusions 'grounded' therein. Qualitative analysis is not as neat and tidy as quantitative approaches would appear to be. It also does not claim to have the same scientific rigour: some of the tales told of qualitative analysis sound more akin to magic than research. Nevertheless, it can be a very fruitful approach and one which has provided interesting and invaluable insights into the operation of the social world.

There is an increasing literature on analysing qualitative data and some useful texts are included in the further reading at the end of the chapter. Most offer practical advice on issues such as using computer software for analysis. Delamont (1992) provides the following checklist of 'basic rules' that might usefully be borne in mind when analysing qualitative data.

> "• *Never let data accumulate without preliminary analysis.*
> • *Index your data as you go; do not allow the data to pile up without knowing what you have collected.*
> • *Generate themes and categories as you go along, and review them frequently. It is better to have too many categories which you recombine later than to have too few.*
> • *Index and code your data densely: do not try to summarize them under just a few themes. Generate as many codes as you can; be 'wild' if you can.*
> • *Sort your data into files (either physically cutting up copies, or 'cutting and pasting' in the wordprocessor). Keep sorting and reviewing your files, in itself that can be a process of discovery.*
> • *Every now and then stop and think. Do not go on mechanically working on the data without reflecting on where you are going and how you are getting there.*
> • *Write analytical memoranda as often as you can. Analytic memos or short notes to yourself and your supervisor in which you review what you are doing, why you are doing it, where you are going next etc.*
> • *Every time you make a decision, write it down and put it in your 'methods' file.*
> • *Try to enjoy the work. It should be an intellectually engaging and creative exercise, not a chore.*
> • *Read other people's work – for ideas, models, parallels, contrasts, metaphors, models, etc.*

- *Read methodological literature properly and think about how it can inform your work*
- *Do not just read it to justify what you are doing anyway!"*

(Delamont, 1992, 151)

Most of the above also has much to commend it when conducting quantative analysis.

Theorising: Making Sense of Findings

"It is good medicine, we think, for researchers to make their preferences clear. To know how a researcher construes the shape of the social world and aims to give us a credible account of it is to know our conversational partner ... we need to know where each (researcher) is coming from. Each will have diverse views of what is real, what can be known, and how these social facts can be faithfully rendered."

(Miles and Huberman, 1994, 4)

Once the data has be reduced and analysed, by whatever means, you will want to think about what this means in a more general sense; to interpret and perhaps theorise about the findings of your research. The relationship between theory and research has already been touched on in Chapter 3 when discussing research planning. It is only through theory that you have any notion of what to study, or how to research a particular topic. Theoretical concepts should guide all research decisions. Just as importantly, an understanding of your theoretical position, where you are coming from, helps you avoid the pitfalls of *post hoc* explanation; inventing a story to fit the facts after the data has been gathered.

This is not to say that you must have a particular theory in mind, or that theories cannot emerge from data that do not fit existing conceptual models. It does help, however, to be aware of your own epistemological assumptions. Some researchers believe that facts exist independent of the researcher and that all you have to do is to discover this objective reality, much in the same way as you might pick up pebbles from a beach. Others take the view that social reality is constructed and that researchers create rather than discover facts. Ask yourself, what side you are on, and how might this decision effect how you make sense of any research findings? Whatever position you adopt it is important to be both aware and honest. Being both aware and honest, you will be less likely to ignore facts which challenge your general argument, or give too much credence to those that support your work. This, after all, is the crux of all research work.

Further Reading

Bryman, A., and Cramer, C., (1990), *Quantitative Data Analysis for Social Scientists*. London: Routledge.

Delamont, S., (1992), *Fieldwork in Educational Settings: Methods, Pitfalls and Perspectives*. London: Falmer.

Dey, I., (1993), *Qualitative Data Analysis: A User-Friendly Guide for Social Scientists*. London: Routledge.

Huff, D., (1973), *How to Lie with Statistics*. London: Penguin.

Miles, M., and Huberman, M., (1994), *Qualitative Data Analysis*, (Second Edition). London: Sage.

Rowntree, D., (1981), *Statistics Without Tears*. London: Penguin.

Weber, R., (1990), *Basic Content Analysis*, (Second Edition). Newbury Park, CA: Sage.

CHAPTER 15:
Reporting Research and Presenting Findings

Objectives of the Chapter

This chapter is designed to ensure that the reader:

- understands the importance of ensuring a good quality of presentation;

- appreciates the range variety and styles of presentation necessary to accommodate different audiences; and

- is aware of the various technical aspects of presentation.

Introduction

There are at least two major problems when finishing off any piece of research. The first, covered in the previous chapter, is allowing enough time to analyse and interpret the data. The second, that of ensuring the results of the study are made available to other people, is the focus of this chapter. If either of these tasks are not adequately carried out then many of the original objectives set for the research will not be met. This chapter deals with the various aspects of dissemination, which need to be considered in order to address the requirements of different audiences. It also provides an insight into the technical aspects of report writing and making oral presentations.

Presentation and Dissemination

Increasingly, organisations paying for research intend that either their organisation, other organisations, or the general public should be influenced by its results. The presentation of the material and the dissemination strategy are, therefore, of critical importance. As such, these issues need to be considered at the planning stage of any research project. Knowing your likely audience will have a bearing on how you focus the study. It also has an influence upon the type of research output you will produce. Having an appreciation of the likely audience also determines the dissemination strategy.

Given the dominant policy focus of much housing research, presentation and dissemination issues are critical. As such, they are clearly more complex than those that need to be addressed by someone submitting a project on an academic course. In this instance the audience, at least initially, is likely to be no more than two, and the format of presentation will be standardised. When dealing with a larger and, therefore, more diversified audience the nature of both presentation and dissemination alter. The same material may need to be produced in a variety of formats in order to get the results over. That said, the principles of clarity, focus and impact should be the same, no matter the audience for the work. Those engaged in personal research endeavours should also appreciate that their work could, and on many occasions does, receive a wider airing. This chapter will provide an appreciation of a broad range of presentational skills that need to be considered. This, in turn, will ensure that a broader range of research material comes into the public domain.

The Need for Different Forms of Presentation

Different audiences require different forms of presentation. A useful example of this is provided by the *Scottish House Condition Survey* (Scottish Homes, 1993). The dissemination strategy for the results of this survey was designed to produce the maximum impact, given its significance in terms of future housing investment. It was also Scottish Homes' first major public relations opportunity, given this first ever national survey was commissioned just after the new agency came into being. As a result, various types of presentation were used to disseminate the findings to as wide an audience as possible. The presentation material included:

- a summary or précis of the main conclusions and recommendations;
- a main research report, and a series of detailed supporting technical reports;
- a report on the methodology employed, which proved useful to other housing organisations about to embark on similar work;
- committee reports, and associated brief summaries;
- publications in professional and academic journals;
- a one page press release summarising the main points (as the full report would be of little use to journalists); and
- verbal presentations for both internal and external audiences which were provided in a variety of formats (overheads, slides, and video).

Such a range from one piece of research is exceptional, but it does act to illustrate the possibilities that are open to a researcher. It also shows that different audiences demand different types of presentation. Each of the above addresses a specific audience which has a particular interest in the work. Each is, therefore, written and structured in a specific style. Generating a broad interest in your work by relying solely upon distributing the research report itself may not produce the desired impact.

Appreciating who the audience is has a clear bearing on the type and style of presentation. You might usefully consider the following questions:

- Who are the likely 'users' of this research, and how will they utilise the research 'product'?
- What is it they will want to find from your study? Users might be just a few people, or it could well be a wider, more general audience. A general audience would only be interested in the two or three main findings of the study. These could be highlighted by a short press release which comes from the executive summary of the report's findings.
- Would the specialist audience read the report cover to cover, or will they want to get an idea of what it is about and then dip into the parts they consider to be of relevance to their own interests?
- If the research hopes to influence both a professional and academic audience can both interests be accommodated within the one research 'product'?
- Are the audience experts in the field, or do they just have a general knowledge of the topic?
- What relation does the audience have to the research?
- Did they write the brief and commission it, or will your publication be the first contact they have with the study?

All this has a bearing on the type and style of presentation you adopt when writing up the study. All these questions need to be carefully considered at the planning stage. Knowing your audience and their specific requirements helps focus the research and the resulting presentational material. In some instances, such as commissioned research, the audience, the focus of the study and the expected outputs will be clearly stated within the brief. On other occasions you will need to think this aspect through for yourself. In the case of press releases, you have to boil the results down to just two or three main points, which can be typed on one side of A4, usually double spaced. Ensuring that the press release has a contact number, at which you can be found, will allow any interested journalist to follow up and expand the story. On the subject of press releases and dealing with the media, this is a specialist and potentially dangerous area, so advice should be sought. Most organisations will have policies for dealing with the press and larger bodies will employ their own Press Officers.

There is also a requirement on the researchers to be clear about what they want to get from conducting the research. What is it that you want to get across to the reader? What is it you want them to understand, and how best can this be achieved? Written style and the way the material is presented can reveal a lot about the writer and how they conceptualise issues. There is undoubtedly a real skill involved in presenting material to best effect, for a given audience.

The production of the research output throws up a number of constraints or obligations that need to be considered when planning the research study. Accommodating these issues has a knock-on effect on the actual research timescales. For example:

- When does the final product need to be presented, and what is the standard expected?
- In order to produce a final report, to an agreed format, what timescales are involved?

Getting a typed final draft into a well designed published report, ready for distribution, can take a great deal of time if designers, typesetters and graphic artists are involved. Production timescales can be short if only a few copies are required, and you are in control of the process. The minute you need a large number of copies, production moves into the hands of others and it is harder to keep control of both the time and eventual product. Production can also cause other presentational problems. While small production runs can accommodate colour graphics, the cost on larger runs could be prohibitive. Black and white graphics are often dull and on occasions difficult to read. They do not necessarily have to be so. Designing your output with the eventual production standards in mind can reduce such difficulties.

The basic points to bear in mind when getting a report designed and printed are:

- contact at least two typesetters who will need to know whether the whole work needs re-keying, or what computer software you are using, the format for the pages, typestyles and layout considerations such as the number of graphs, boxes, illustrations, tables; they will also need to be asked whether they charge for the whole job or by the page; ask about likely timescale for proving a proof copy, corrections and a final output;
- do you need a designer to produce art work for the cover? what do you require? ask for quotes based on the specification you come up with;
- determine the print run; number of pages (the extent); the page size (format); the paper and the cover card to be used, one or two colour printing for text and cover, and the type of binding – burst bound, perfect binding, wiro etc.; printers may also need to liaise with the typesetter and/or designer about specifics such as tint boxes, colour separations;
- ask for estimates from at least two printers, and ask them about turnaround time and delivery arrangements (you don't want ten pallets of books arriving at your front door!);
- and, don't forget that someone other than yourself will probably be needed for the copy edit (before typesetting) and the proofread (after typesetting) to make sure that spellings are consistent and correct, and that the text has been organised in the most accessible manner;
- if your presentation requires an index, this is best done at the proofing stage, but you may have previously 'tagged' keywords for inclusion in the index.

The above list provides the basis both for a production timetable and the creation of a production budget.

Presentational issues also have to confront the key tensions that can arise in conducting any research study. Policy makers or policy customers like to be presented with clear evidence and conclusions. They may also wish to have certain aspects of the research given greater prominence over other aspects. Researchers, knowing the constraints and limitations of their data, are inclined to be less dogmatic. Consequently, there is often a tension between the researcher and the policy customer. It is crucial that the researcher holds onto their integrity and ensures the research reflects their views rather than those who have an influence on the work.

To get a feel for such tensions, and to ensure you are aware of the interests of potential research users, it can be helpful to have an advisory group to report on progress. Many research commissioners now insist that such a body is established, although the title of steering group may indicate an expectation of greater control over the work. Obviously, for some types of research such an approach is not feasible. Whatever the name given to the body its function is to assist with the execution of the research through offering advice, helping to gain access to data, and in formulating the eventual conclusions. For the researcher it has the added advantage of sensitising a group of informed and potentially influential people to the various nuances of the research work. Through working with such steering or advisory groups you can gain an insight into user perceptions, which can be helpful when framing arguments when writing up. Key themes and issues from the research can be rehearsed and refined through circulating working documents and holding internal presentations. Working with such groups can also help greatly in formulating dissemination strategies.

Presenting Research Results

No matter the type of output, or product, from your research it has to be able to communicate effectively with the intended audience. In essence what you should be seeking to achieve is, in effect, a conversation with that audience. To promote such a conversation, and to take on board the known requirements of your audience, you need to consider a variety of issues (Orna, 1995). These should include:

> "• *Showing the structure of the product.*
> • *Helping readers find their way around the structure by means of 'signposts' of various kinds.*
> • *Directing attention to key points.*
> • *Telling readers what they are about to encounter, and summarising what they have just been told ('previews and reviews').*
> • *Telling the 'story' of the research.*
> • *Defining terms.*
> • *Presenting relevant material from the sources we have used.*
> • *Explaining the methods used in the research.*
> • *Presenting sequences and flows of events.*
> • *Distinguishing between parts of text which perform different functions.*
> • *Presenting the results of research – both qualitative and quantitative."*
>
> (Orna, 1995, 114-115)

To accommodate the requirements listed above you need to think carefully about writing style, structure, layout and the use of graphics in relation to both text and diagrams. The issues involved, and how best to address them are well detailed in the above text. Orna (1995) provides an excellent review of presentational issues that need to be considered when trying to get the key information over to the reader. The checklist in Table 15.1, adapted from Orna (1995, 129), illustrates the range of presentational issues that need to be addressed when producing any research product.

Most people have had the experience of having to plough through a dense and lengthy written report. By thinking through the range of issues outlined above you should be able to produce a research report or publication which is accessible, through employing a clear writing style, good layout techniques and the appropriate use of supportive diagrams, tables and illustrations. As the most common output from any research work is the research report, the standard structure of this document is now considered. By focusing on the research report in more detail the above issues of audience focus and information components will be illustrated.

Table 15.1: A Checklist of Information Elements

1. Headings: 'A' level, 'B' level, 'C' level, 'D' level.

2. Signposts: index, cross-references, displayed key paragraphs, emphasis within sentences, previews at the beginning of chapters, recapitulations or summaries at the end of chapters.

3. Narrative: sentences, paragraphs.

4. Definitions

5. Questionnaires

6. Flow-diagrams

7. Diagrams

8. Illustrations and photographs

9. Tables: numeric with text, text only.

10. Lists

11. Detailed text to supplement main text

12. Text commentaries on graphics and/or tables

Structuring the Research report

The basic structure of any research report should be as follows. Obviously, depending on the particular focus of the work this standard structure could be amended. What is important, however, is that a logical sequence is adopted:

- title with terms of reference;
- contents page;
- summary or synopsis;
- method of investigation;
- facts and findings (body of report);
- conclusions and discussions;
- recommendations;
- references; and
- appendices (if necessary).

The summary or synopsis is very important, for it allows a reader to get a measure of the work quickly. It is also important that the method of investigation is clearly outlined, as it is this that allows the reader to assess the reliability and validity of the findings for themselves. Too often, in research studies, the actual method and approach adopted are not made explicit. If other investigators wish to check or compare your findings with a study of their own, there has to be enough information available to replicate the work. Hence, it is good practice to ensure that all relevant information on the type and size of the sample; method used to collect data; date and duration of survey; extent of non-response; and degree of accuracy achieved is properly detailed, either in the text or in an appendix. In essence, all good research reports should provide a detailed description of the survey design. Copies of questionnaire and tabulated results should also be provided in appropriate appendices. Finally, another criticism of research reports is that they fail to provide the tabular information from which any graphic material has been generated. Without this information it is often impossible to check the assumptions or interpretations used by the researcher. The appropriate tabular material should, therefore, also be included within an appendix.

While the research report may be the basic output from a study, as is clear from above, a number of other more targeted outputs or products can be generated. A solid well-considered and well-written research report can ensure such re-packaging operations are relatively straightforward, in that the groundwork for these other products is present and does not need to be created. Two critical aspects for ensuring the production of such a document are ensuring a clear written presentation and the appropriate use of visual material.

Clear Written Presentation

Written text should always be broken down into clear and distinct subsections, which are provided with clear headings and sub-headings. Such 'signposting' tells the reader where the text is leading and, therefore, what to expect next. Style and language should always be as clear and precise as possible. This can only be achieved through practice.

To aid the reader, a standardised text and layout should be employed. Use should be made of different sizes of fonts to illustrate the variations in the importance of headings. Avoid mixing font styles, as this can detract from the overall appearance. While Desk Top Publishing software have opened up new avenues to presentation, they have also brought with them much bad design which can be very distracting for the reader. In relation to design, always try and ensure a fair degree of white space on the page. Avoid the temptation to drop the point size of the type face to save paper in final production.

If the document is destined for wide scale distribution, then text should be professionally typeset. The advances in wordprocessing, discussed in Chapter 13, should ensure a generally good reproduction standard when photocopying, but on large print runs the unit costs are high and quality begins to suffer. Typesetting from disk is now common place. That said, there are major difficulties associated with data transfer from one wordprocessing package to another, or from wordprocessing to the software used by the typesetter. Where possible save text to ASCII format as this is a simpler form, and, therefore, easier to copy. The problem here is that ASCII strips out the hidden codes used by the wordprocessing package and you are likely to lose the complete layout format. Always check the technical requirements of the production process before you set about producing the final version of the report.

Use of Visual Illustration

In the past, both cost and the method of reproduction acted to constrain the use of visual material within research reports. Yet, such material can provide valuable evidence to substantiate key arguments within the report. If used well they can inform without recourse to substantial amounts of explanatory text. Graphic material also acts to lighten the overall visual impact of the report. Graphics can, however, be a distraction if they are not properly thought through and well-designed. The advent of cheap and more accessible printing and the development of high quality graphic technology, through spreadsheets and DTP systems, should ensure a better use of graphic material.

The use of a table or a diagram is in large part determined by the intended audience for the report. Bear in mind that bar charts and other forms of graphic presentation can be very confusing to an untrained eye. To minimise such problems always ensure both tables and graphics:

- are simple and unambiguous;
- have a clear and concise title;
- include a statement about the source of data;
- have column and row headings that are brief and self explanatory;
- have clearly shown units of measurement;
- have logical changes in units of approximations; and
- have a layout that emphasises the vertical, not the horizontal.

Finally, always ensure that all graphics are clearly tied into text, and are placed at the most appropriate place within the text. The integration of software packages means that it is now easy to place the graphics within the text, rather the previously unsatisfactory practice of placing them together at the end of a chapter or in an appendix.

Design is far more than a cosmetic exercise, it is critical to reader understanding. This basic point is now more widely accepted, given the improving quality of so much research material. In particular, the Joseph Rowntree Foundation has set a high standard in the way it designs its key research outputs. Unfortunately, there are still those who believe that design quality is an expensive irrelevance and continue to produce typewritten reports pressed between coloured cardboard covers.

Making Presentations

While the production of written material is the major output from any research exercise, there is often an expectation that some type of verbal presentation will also be made. This is a typical prerequisite in many research contracts. When such a presentation is made at a conference or workshop it could encourage more people to take an interest in the published material.

Verbal presentations are different from written reports in a number of important respects. When people read reports, they can either choose to pay attention or not, because they always have the opportunity to re-read. If part of the report is unclear, they can go back over it more slowly, and attempt to puzzle it out. This is not an excuse for sloppy writing, but rather a clear illustration of the advantages of written communication. Yet, when an audience is listening to a presentation, they are denied these advantages. As they generally hear the message only once, they have to pay close attention at all times. While most presentations allow an opportunity to ask questions, either the audience fails to use it or the time left is limited and only one or two points are made. That said, it is clearly easier to ask questions of a speaker than a book.

Given these limitations, verbal presentations need to be clear. Prior organisation is a must. The audience, in order to understand the message, must see how the speaker gets from point A to point B at all points within the presentation. This is no easy task, but there is a systematic way to approach it. The system detailed below will not make your presentations spellbinding, for content and personality have much to contribute in that regard. It will, however, ensure that your presentations are focused on an intended audience, that the information is both clear and logically developed, and that you do nothing to distract from that message. That said, practice and skill will also be required to put a final polish on your presentations.

Preparation

In any presentation you need to offer the audience something important or interesting early on in the talk. This needs to reassure the audience that they made the right decision in coming to your presentation. In this regard, it is also critical to let the audience know about your credentials to speak on the topic. In any presentation you have about three minutes to convince the audience that you have something important to say. Miss the mark and your audience's attention drifts, or in some cases the audience itself drifts away. This initial stage in the presentation can be partly eased by a good clear introduction from the person chairing the session. When asked to provide speakers notes, don't ignore the request or quickly scribble something up, but rather think about what information would enhance your credibility in the eyes of that audience.

When thinking through your presentation be clear about what your audience knows about the specific topic of your presentation. Do they have any emotional ties to the subject? For example, speaking about anti-social tenants at a housing conference almost guarantees a polarisation into two camps, one representing the 'liberal' housing professionals and the other being the 'reactionary' tenants. Knowing or suspecting the attitudes of an audience is therefore an important consideration. If you can anticipate problems, you can act to address or defuse them as part of your presentation. This is a skill that transfers well into the organisation of meetings, where problems tend to be rife and fixed attitudes tend to be more easily predicted.

Focusing on the Topic

Check that sufficient time has been allocated for your presentation. Will questioning be permitted during the presentation, or afterwards, and how will this affect the time for the presentation? The time allocated influences the type of presentation and its focus: a ten-minute speech is vastly different from a two-hour training session.

When organising the information for any presentation, first determine the number of key points you wish to make. These should be either points of information, which you want the audience to understand, or items which support your argument. Ensure each point is distinct, and that each is similar in scope or level of importance. Once you have determined these key points you need to arrange them. As with written communication, this arrangement needs to make sense not only to you, but to the audience. While the topic will suggest a range of ways to order the main points, you need to decide which arrangement is best. Starting with the conclusions, and then explaining how you got there is often a better approach than working your way through the contents of a research report. Normally, these key points are the basis for visual aids.

When outlining a presentation it is useful to follow certain guidelines. First, make sure that each level of the outline is similar in scope. This applies to sub-points as well as to main points. Limit each section of the outline to one idea, using a short phrase to remind you of the point you want to make. Always ensure that sections do not overlap, as this will cause audience confusion. The outline should act as a primer for your presentation notes, so that with practice your notes become redundant.

Focus on the transitions within any presentation. Transitions are what audiences require to follow your train of thought. Realise that introductions and brief summaries act as transitions, for they connect an audience to the topic and also tie the main points and sub-points together. This point was also made previously in relation to written presentations.

Finally, don't overlook conclusions. They are what brings a presentation to a successful completion. Too often a presentation comes to an abrupt halt, without the audience knowing whether it had finished or not. Such presentations do not conclude; they just die.

Types of Delivery

There are four possible ways to deliver a presentation, each of which has its advantages and disadvantages. Choose a method that makes you comfortable, but ensure it also produces an effective presentation. With the manuscript method you essentially read out the paper. It has the advantage of determining the speaker's words beforehand, hence it minimises concerns about losing the thread, or forgetting what to say next. It also has advantages for rigid time limits, given the entire presentation can be practised until it fits the allotted time. The disadvantage is that without training and practice most people cannot read out loud. Reading a manuscript also limits eye contact with the audience, allowing the audience's attention to wander. While this problem can be overcome by including 'look up' instructions in the manuscript, this does not address all the limitations of the approach.

An alternative approach is to memorise the presentation. The advantages are exactly the same as they were for the manuscript method. In addition, memorisation is also good for eye contact with the audience. Unfortunately, the disadvantages are more serious. First, memorising text, as any actor will vouch takes a great deal of time. If you find reading aloud difficult, then recitation is likely to be worse. The most serious disadvantage, however, is loss of memory. For these reasons, memorising a presentation should be avoided. At the other extreme the impromptu method, that is making it up as you go along, should also be avoided.

Most speakers opt for what is called the extemporaneous method, which means making a presentation from either an outline and/or associated notes. It has all the advantages of good eye contact, naturalness of language, rhythm, pace, and voice modulation. It does require practice, because it is easy to get caught up in the occasion and either talk too long or wander off the subject. These disadvantages notwithstanding, you should get into the habit of using the extemporaneous method of presentation delivery most, if not all, of the time.

Practising the Presentation

Practice is essential for ensuring successful presentation. The objective should be a conversational delivery, and the practice should refine the actual presentation. It is only with practice that you see what works and what does not. After six attempts a presentation is usually quite polished. This means you should:

- practise out loud;
- practise the entire presentation, not just key points;
- practise in front of someone you trust to give you critical feedback;
- practise in the actual presentation environment, if possible, or in one that is similar;
- practise using the visual aids; and
- practise movement and voice modulation.

Bear in mind the stress in a speaker's voice is important, because it changes the meaning of what is being said, as well as calling attention to particular points in the presentation. Try not to mumble or run words together. This is another reason for avoiding the manuscript method, given that when reading a manuscript, you spend most of the time addressing the table or podium. Volume is also important: you must be heard by everyone in the room. This is one reason why you should, if possible, examine the presentation environment before making any presentation. If you have a light voice, or poor vocal projection, you may want to consider an amplification system.

The Presentation Environment

The actual location of the presentation is another issue that needs to be carefully considered. If possible, always try to examine the venue prior to making the presentation. Is it a large auditorium, or a small conference room? How will the audience be seated, theatre-style or around tables? Such factors will influence the types of visual aids you may wish to use, as well as your freedom of movement. It may even affect the formality of your presentation.

Take a note of any potentially distracting elements, such as bright sunlight, lawn mowers running outside the window or a humming fluorescent light. Such distractions can make it difficult for you to gain the audience's attention. Most distractions can be tackled or avoided, and in the case of those you cannot do anything about, then at least you are prepared for them. It is also worth knowing what the audience will be doing before and after the presentation. The slot immediately after lunch does not always produce the most attentive audience.

Finally, clarify what arrangements have been made for you, as the speaker. Will there be a podium, a microphone, a table, an overhead projector or a slide projector? Do you have what you need, and are they all in working condition? You will be nervous anyway, so it is better to avoid unexpected surprises that might make it worse. For a useful review of the issues involved in organising training events or conferences see Dearling (1992).

Using Visual Aids

Visual aids are an important part of any presentations, but they are not a substitute for a clearly thought out presentation. They should be used to highlight presentation points, a means of focusing the audience's attention on key aspects of the material. Correctly designed and used, visual aids should support and expand the content of a presentation. They should help illustrate what you mean, as you speak. If they are to do this, then they must meet certain criteria:

- they must be visible, large enough for the whole audience to see and that includes those people who sit right at the back;
- they must be clear, in that the meaning must be obvious at a glance without recourse to explanation. Too often the flow of a presentation is marred by the speaker having to explain the overheads, in detail, rather than providing the audience with the information they came to hear; and
- they must be controllable, that is easy to use at the presentation.

Good visual aids add a polish to any presentation, and to achieve that shine some basic rules should be considered.

Using Words and Phrases

The words and phrases should be representative of the key topics from which the presentation is constructed. They also need to be both short and straightforward. The trick is to make sure the audience does not have to do too much reading; for while they are reading they will not be listening to you. It is common practice for speakers to start by outlining their presentation. This approach orientates the audience to the topic and to the order of the presentation. Given the importance of the first few minutes of any presentation, for getting and holding the attention of the audience, this is a useful method to adopt.

Flipcharts

Flipcharts, or marker boards, are a popular medium for informal, small group presentations. Yet, in spite of their popularity, most people misuse them. If you are planning to provide information on a flipchart, during the course of a presentation, write it up prior to the talk and cover it. As you progress through the presentation the information can be revealed at the appropriate time. When you are ready to reveal the information it is important to prime the audience. Let them know what is coming up and why it is important before you show it to them. Such repetition helps reinforce the key points of the presentation.

Again writing or graphics must be clear, and neat. Detailed work, even on a large chart, is almost impossible for the audience to see. Bear in mind, flipcharts should be limited to fairly small presentation environments. People seated some distance away from the board will not be able to see what is written. Finally, if you need to write on the chart as part of a presentation, try to avoid turning your back on the audience. Talking as you write is a guaranteed way of distracting an audience. Successful use of these charts or boards requires a little practice, for it is not as easy as it looks.

Overhead Transparencies and Slides

Overhead transparencies are a useful means of presenting information to relatively large audiences. By adjusting the projection distance, the image can be made quite large, without a discernable loss of quality. You can overlay transparencies to add information, as the presentation progresses. Another approach is to cover part of them, only revealing the information as it becomes appropriate to the topic. It is also possible to write directly onto them, but this is not that effective given the act of writing can be highly distracting. Also avoid placing a page of solid typed text, typically copied directly from the report, onto a transparency. The audience cannot and will not read it.

The main disadvantage of these type of visuals is the fact that they can be difficult to manipulate. They have a tendency to stick together, and if you drop them their transparent nature often makes them hard to read and therefore re-order. They are also largely restricted to black and white image, because it is hard to project in colour. To get round this problem you can opt for slides. Slides are excellent for presenting information to large audiences. They make it possible to organise the entire presentation visually, store it in a carousel, and use it over and over again. The use of a remote control is another distinct advantage, in that it allows you to move about when giving the presentation. Almost all other visual systems act to limit your movement.

Slides can only be used in a completely darkened room. If you, as the speaker, are not lit then the sound of a voice in the darkness can be off-putting to an audience. A warm room, the darkness and a presentation after lunch can result in many in the audience taking a nap. To get round these potential difficulties break the presentation into segments of six to ten slides. In between these segments, bring the lights up and continue with the presentation, focusing on the transitions, and finally the conclusion. This helps to combat any rigidity or tedium a slide presentation might have. As with all visual material prime the audience and then let them know what each slide means. Repetition acts to reinforce the key points.

As will be obvious from what has been said above, there is no perfect visual aid for presentations. Each approach has its advantages and disadvantages, both in their ability to present information and, perhaps more importantly, in an individual's ability to use them. Visuals can add greatly to a presentation, but equally they can detract from it, especially if the presenter is uncomfortable with their use. It is, therefore, crucial that you select visual aids which will add to your presentation; that the medium fits into the presentation environment; and, that you feel comfortable with it. Having made the choice, ensure you make time to practice so it runs smoothly.

Conclusions

Hopefully this chapter has illustrated that a great deal can be done to heighten the impact of your research. As with everything in research the potential impacts can only be realised with careful planning. It is, therefore, important to consider early on how and to whom the work is to be presented. This information helps focus the final presentational dimensions of the work.

Written presentation now requires not only good writing skills, but also a knowledge of typographical presentation and the appropriate use of visual illustrations. The advent of wordprocessing and DTP may help, but these are skills which the researcher needs to master. Good design should not be dismissed, because a well presented report is more likely to be read.

Further Reading

Allen, D., (1989), *In Your Own Voice: A Manual for Public Speaking*. Boston: American Press.

Callahan, R., (1990) *How Executives Overcome the Fear of Public Speaking and Other Phobias*. Homewood, IL: Dow Jones-Irwin.

Dearling, A., (1992), *How to Organise Conferences and Training Events*. Harlow: Longman.

Nelson, R., (1989), *Making Effective Presentations*. Glenwood IL: Scott-Foresman.

Orna, E., with Stevens, G., (1995), *Managing Information for Research*. Buckingham: Open University Press.

CHAPTER 16:
Concluding Remarks

This book has been about viewing research as a process, about seeing the research task not as a collection of stages that you need to pass through but as a complete operation which needs to be considered as an entity. The focus has been to highlight the key questions that have to be addressed when planning any research project. The intention has been to demystify research and make it clear that it does not require a high degree of specialist knowledge. Housing research is not the preserve of academic experts. Rather it is an essential tool for improving the quality of all aspects of housing work, whether at an operational or strategic level. As housing research impacts on the day-to-day work of practitioners it is important that they understand how such material is generated and, in doing so, assess its relevance to their own work. Practitioners should also be able to conduct or commission studies to their own research agenda, as opposed to those imposed by others. As the saying goes, knowledge or information is power.

The book has stressed the importance of adopting a systematic and disciplined approach to research. If there is any 'trick' to doing research it lies in ensuring that adequate time is spent on planning. Planning should involve focusing on the questions you wish to explore and figuring out how best to answer these questions given the time and resources available. What is it you want to know and how can you gain an insight into this issue? What sort of information will need to be collected? What methods require to be adopted to provide the data and how will the research assumptions be tested against this information? What sort of interpretation can be taken from the results and how does this relate to our previous understanding of the issue? How are the results of this work to be presented, and what pressures need to be accommodated? All these questions need to be considered in the planning of any research. This book seeks to remind you of these questions and illustrate the range of answers you could employ.

Experience also plays a part. Like many things in life the best way to learn is by doing. But it does help if, as a novice, you have some pointers. The book has provided a range of insights into the research process built up from years of previous experience. The task of accumulating that experience may not be as traumatic as it could be, by taking cognisance of others' insights. Research has been likened to mapping out an unexplored territory, in that it is a matter of, *"... aiming in the right direction, getting your bearings right (from previous studies) and making sure you are adequately equipped to get there and back."* (Hakim, 1987, 171). Hopefully the book will have helped fill in some blanks on your research map. Yet, as Hakim also points out, Columbus set sail to find the East Indies and came across the West Indies and America instead. Columbus was lucky, but research that is not clearly thought out or is poorly planned is unlikely to succeed. One sad fact about research, which is at variance with its popular image, is that you are unlikely to discover anything of real interest by mistake.

That is not to say well-planned research does not go wrong. In reading this book, you may be left with the impression that conducting research is a rather orderly and predictable process. If you follow the instructions carefully enough you will eventually reach the desired goal. Unfortunately, housing research, in common with all social research, deals with a variety of complex interactions any one of which can go wrong. You might be wise to remember Murphy's Law: if something can go wrong, it will go wrong. No amount of planning, for example, can guarantee you achieve a good response rate from a postal questionnaire, or that the policy you are researching will not be amended during the study. The best you can do is to plan carefully for any foreseen problems and make contingency plans. It may also be helpful at times to keep your fingers crossed.

What then is the future for housing research? The demand for the sorts of information outlined in this book are likely to be sustained, and in certain areas demand is likely to grow. The recent growth in diverse housing providers, the increased focus on professional standards, and the need for public accountability in all aspects of policy and planning will continue to provide the impetus. Current demand for information within housing organisations is unprecedented. The same is true for the barrage of research information being provided by government, government agencies, research foundations and pressure groups. Yet, are the right questions being asked? Performance information tends to provide a checklist of activities but fails to say much about actual performance. Housing needs studies can generate a large amount of data but do not always provide much insight into predicting future housing needs. There is also a tendency for major studies to focus on issues that do not appear to be of that much interest to those outwith a very closed policy community. While housing organisations need good quality information if they are to provide an improved service, they also need to be asking the right research questions. Given the domination of research agendas by a few interests, it is critical that more practitioners engage with the research process. Through this mechanism a broader and more responsive research agenda for housing should emerge. That said, whether you are doing it yourself, commissioning others to do it, or simply making use of the findings, dealing with research is going to be an increasingly important part of a housing professional's job, if it is not already.

Housing research, by itself, can never provide the complete answer: you always need to be aware of the limitations of research. Much of the recent, and no doubt future, output of housing research has been policy focused. Policy makers tend to have unrealistic expectations, seeing the research effort in terms of providing solutions and/or predictions of future events, rather than merely explaining the present situation. As a researcher you should be careful not to be seduced by overly ambitious expectations. You also have a responsibility to make it clear to those who are commissioning and/or using the results of your research work what interpretations the information will bear. Having said that, good quality research can and does make a meaningful contribution in many areas of housing policy and practice. Hopefully this book will help ensure an improvement in the quality of that housing research.

Appendix One

Commissioners and/or Funders of Housing Research

Central Government:
- Commissioned or contracted research by government departments such as Department of the Environment (DoE), Scottish Office Development Department (SODD), or the Welsh or Northern Ireland Office.
- Indirectly through quangos such as Housing Corporation, Northern Ireland Housing Executive (NIHE), Scottish Homes or Tai Cymru.
- Audit Commission (covering England and Wales) and the Accounts Commission (covering Scotland).
- Indirectly through Government-funded research bodies such as the Economic and Social Research Council (ESRC) which gives grants to academic researchers under agreed themes.

Local Government:
- Commissioned or contracted research either by an individual local authority or through a representative body, such as the Association of Metropolitan Authorities (AMA), Association of District Councils (ADC), Convention of Scottish Local Authorities (CoSLA), or through a local authority body with a specific interest, such as the Local Government Management Board (LGMB) or the Local Authority Research and Intelligence Organisation (LARIA).
- London Borough Grants Unit.
- Association of London Government.

Professional Associations:
- Chartered Institute of Housing (CIH).
- Chartered Institute of Environmental Health (CIEH).
- Royal Institute of British Architects (RIBA) and the Royal Incorporation of Architects in Scotland (RIAS).
- Royal Institution of Chartered Surveyors (RICS).
- Royal Town Planning Institute (RTPI).

Representative Bodies:
- Council for Mortgage Lenders (CML).
- National Federation of Housing Associations (NFHA); National Housing Forum (NHF); Scottish Federation of Housing Associations (SFHA); Welsh Federation of Housing Associations (WFHA); Northern Ireland Federation of Housing Associations (NIFHA).
- Housebuilders' Federation.

Philanthropic Bodies:
- Joseph Rowntree Foundation.
- Cadbury Bournville Trust.
- Sainsbury's Trust.
- Leverhulme Trust.
- Nuffield Foundation.
- Carnegie Trust.
- Tudor Trust.
- The Bridges Trust.
- London Housing Foundation.

Pressure Groups:
- Shelter; Shelter Scotland; Shelter Wales.
- Consumers' Association; Scottish Consumer Council; Welsh Consumer Council; Northern Ireland Consumer Council.
- CHAR Campaign for Single Homeless; Scottish Council for Single Homeless.
- Child Poverty Action Group (CPAG).
- Council for the Protection of Rural England (CPRE); Rural Forum.
- National Housing and Town Planning Council (NHTPC).
- Tenant Participation Advisory Service (TPAS).
- Town and Country Planning Association (TCPA).

Lenders:
- Halifax Building Society.
- Nationwide Building Society.

Universities:
- There are too many to name individually, but they are important as a major source of research commissioning

Appendix Two

Information Sources on Housing

Books:
  Use bibliographies for pointers to further reading.
  Consult journals for reviews of new books.

Journals (Academic):
  *Housing Studies, Habitat International, Environment and Planning A,
  Environment and Planning D, Urban Studies, International Journal of Urban
  and Regional Research, Urban Affairs Quarterly, Built Environment, Journal of
  Social Policy, Critical Social Policy, Policy and Politics, Area, Town Planning
  Review, Journal of the American Planning Association, Netherlands Journal of
  Housing and the Built Environment, Scandinavian Housing and Planning
  Research.*

Journals (Professional):
  *Housing, Housing Review, Inside Housing, Roof, Roof Briefing, Voluntary
  Housing, HA Weekly, Housing and Planning Review, Municipal Journal, Social
  Housing, Architects Journal, Community Care, Housing Finance, Search
  (published by the Joseph Rowntree Foundation) Scottish Homes Housing
  Research Review.*

Abstracts:
  Applied Social Science Index and Abstract (ASSIA), *British Humanities Index*
  (BHI), *Social Science Citation Index* (SCCI).

Research Summaries:
  JRF Findings; DoE Housing Research Summaries; Scottish Homes Precis.

Newsletters / In-house journals:
  Scottish Council for Single Homeless, Scottish Federation of Housing
  Associations (SFHA) *Federation Focus*, Age Concern News, CHAR Housing
  Campaign for Single People, Housing Studies Association Newsletter, European
  Network of Housing Research (ENHR) Newsletter.

Occasional Papers Series:
  Centre for Urban and Regional Studies (CURS), University of Birmingham.
  Centre for Housing Research and Urban Studies (CHRUS), University of
  Glasgow.
  School for Policy Studies (previously the School for Advanced Urban Studies),
  University of Bristol.
  Centre for Housing Policy, University of York.
  London Research Centre, NHTPC.

Planning Exchange:
Bibliography, Weekly List, Urban Development Digest, Housing Digest.

Previous Dissertations:
Universities and Colleges with housing courses.

Parliamentary Sources:
Acts (Housing Act 1988, Housing (Scotland. Act 1988).
Bills (Housing Bill 1987, Housing (Scotland. Bill 1987).
Command Papers (White and Green Papers).
Select Committee Reports (Environmental, Scottish Affairs).
Transcripts of Debates (Hansard and Committee Reports).
Parliamentary Questions and Answers (Oral and Written).
Shelter Parliamentary News

Government Sources:
Research Reports (CRIU).
English Survey of Housing; Scottish House Condition Survey; Welsh House
Condition Survey; Northern Ireland House Condition Survey
Circulars and Letters.
DoE; Scottish Office; Welsh Office; Northern Ireland Office Press Notices.
DoE; Scottish Office; Welsh Office; Northern Ireland Commentary on Housing
Programme.
Public Expenditure White Paper and each Government Department's
Commenting on on Annual Programmes.

Official Housing Statistics:
Housing and Construction Statistics (annual/quarterly).
Scottish Housing Statistics (annual).
Scottish Office Statistical Bulletin, Housing Series (regular).
Local Housing Statistics (quarterly).
Annual Reports of individual Building Societies and Banks.
Northern Ireland Housing Statistics (annual).

Other Housing Statistics:
Housing Finance Review (annual) (published by Joseph Rowntree Foundation).
CIPFA Rating Review (annual).
Housing Finance (quarterly) (published by CML).
All in One Place (published by CHAR).

Other Official Statistics:
Census.
Annual Report of the Registrar General.
Family Expenditure Survey (annual).
General Household Survey (annual).
National Dwelling and Household Survey.
Social Trends (annual).
Economic Trends (monthly with annual supplement).

Publications of Housing and other Organisations:
Annual Reports of the Housing Corporation; Scottish Homes; Tai Cymru;
NIHE; local authorities, housing associations.
Guidance notes issued to housing associations by the above bodies.

Local authority Housing Departments Housing Plans or Housing Investment Plans.
Local authority Planning Departments Local Plans.
Local authority Social Service/Social Work Community Care Plans.

Other published material:

Housing Strategy Statements and published research reports.
Other publicity material (leaflets on improvement grants, allocations, equal opportunities, and homelessness policy).
Minutes of housing committee meetings.

Unpublished material:

Committee Reports.
Internal research or monitoring reports covering waiting lists, lettings, cuts, benefits, arrears, repairs, improvements.
Housing association business plans.
Housing association annual accounts.

Appendix Three

A Sample Research Brief

Boosting Housing Investment Through Capital Receipts

Proposal for a research project on behalf of the Chartered Institute of Housing to explore the potential for boosting investment in affordable rented housing through the use of unused capital receipts

Overall Objective

To consider the feasibility and implications of adopting in England and Wales the same principle of recycling capital receipts into new housing investment that applies in Scotland, and the particular effects of allowing the re-use of accumulated receipts.

Background

The sales of council houses through the Right to Buy has been the Government's biggest privatisation initiative. It has generated around £30 billions of capital receipts, or more than the sale of any single public corporation. Yet these proceeds have largely not been explicitly recycled to produce new social housing investment.

The Chartered Institute of Housing, along with other organisations, has long advocated the explicit recycling of receipts. An important part of this proposal is the re-use of existing receipts that local authorities have had to set aside against debt in accordance with capital finance rules. The Labour Party is publicly committed to 'release' of such receipts, and the CIH wishes to examine the practical implications of such a policy, together with the implications of moving towards the explicit recycling of future receipts in the way that already occurs in Scotland.

Scope of Project

1. To estimate the extent of set-aside capital receipts which either exist as cash or have been lent internally to finance other borrowing, and the availability of such receipts to support additional capital expenditure in the event of a decision to release them for this purpose.

2. To consider the distribution of such receipts in relation to housing need, and the extent to which redistribution of resources might be feasible to remedy any imbalance.

3. To assess the financial effects of such a policy change in terms of the overall impact on resource availability for housing investment and the detailed effects at the local authority and central government level, in terms of subsidy, capital controls and measures of the public sector deficit.

4. To assess the potential for use of future receipts, and their possible impact on levels of housing investment.

5. To consider measures for the ring-fencing of capital receipts for housing purposes.

6. To outline the changes necessary in primary legislation or capital finance rules.

7. To make recommendations on future data collection and accountancy practice in relation to capital receipts, to facilitate the policy changes under consideration.

8. To provide a lay-person's description of the treatment of capital receipts, and its implications (in terms of both capital and revenue) for central and local government and for tenants of local authority housing.

Approach

Because of the paucity of data on receipts, the starting point of the project will be a survey of all local housing authorities in England and Wales seeking relevant information.

The data received will be compared with indices relating to the need to invest in housing. These could include measures relating to investment requirements in relation to HRA stock condition and the need for new building. Relevant indices would be management and maintenance allowances, or corresponding calculations for capital purposes or the GNI itself, data from the Index of Local Conditions and the HNI.

The extent of mal-distribution would be measured and redistribution mechanisms considered and assessed, with particular regard to the potential and limitations of the RTIA mechanism.

Local financial effects will be measured through the loss of income on surplus set-aside receipts, or the extra interest charges that would result from new borrowing.

Advice will be sought on the accountancy treatment of receipts and how this might vary between authorities, and the extent to which such variation might have an impact on the resources that could be released.

The PSBR treatment of receipts and their potential 'release' will be assessed through discussions with the Treasury and others. If possible, alternative options will be examined.

Interviews with selected authorities will be used to explore such issues as:
   • why the variation in published figures (on PCL set-asides) is so great, including definitional interpretations;

- how local authorities could actually 'release' their receipts, including whether they are locked in for particular periods;
- whether the authority would be likely to take up the option, given its local impact; and
- whether the authority has or is about to change its policy, given the Labour Party's stated position on the issue.

Account will be taken of experience in Scotland, where receipts have always been explicitly recycled, to provide some guide to the possible implications of adopting such a system in England and Wales.

Reference will be made to the evidence presented to the Environment Committee's inquiry into housing need, to assess the overall contribution release of receipts could make to meeting investment requirements, in the light of the study's findings.

Advisory Group

It is intended that a small advisory group be established, including LAA representation and a representative of CIPFA, and a local authority treasurer.

Timescale

The study will be announced and the survey initiated immediately after Christmas. An initial report of findings will be prepared for limited circulation by the end of February. A final report will be published in April.

Chartered Institute of Housing
November, 1995.

Appendix Four

A Sample Research Contract

SCOTTISH HOMES RESEARCH & INNOVATION SERVICES: CONDITIONS OF CONTRACT FOR APPOINTMENT OF CONSULTANTS

Contractor's General Responsibility

1. Unless otherwise agreed in writing, the Contractor shall provide the accommodation required for the project.

2. The Contractor shall be responsible for monitoring the progress of the project and preparing a final report or other form of output by the completion date as specified in the letter of appointment.

3. The project finance as defined in the letter of appointment shall be used only for the purpose specified in the letter of appointment and not for any other project or purpose.

4. The Contractor and any consultancy staff employed on the project shall ensure that they have no obligation to any other body under conditions incompatible with Scottish Homes' requirements and they may not undertake any other contract which may produce, in the sole opinion of Scottish Homes, a conflict of interest in relation to the project. The opinion of Scottish Homes regarding the matter will be final.

5. Before questionnaires, or other forms may be circulated to, or telephone or interview surveys undertaken, with 25 or more commercial or business concerns, including housing associations, or local authorities, the Contractor shall obtain the prior written approval of Scottish Homes. In these cases, clearance is required by Scottish Homes from the Central Statistical Office's Survey Control Unit. The Contractor shall take into account the extra time required for these additional procedures. Permission is not required for surveys of individuals.

6. Scottish Homes' representatives or any person authorised by Scottish Homes shall be entitled to inspect and review all records and correspondence relating to the project during normal working hours, on reasonable notice given.

7. The Contractor shall submit to Scottish Homes progress reports (either by verbal presentation or a written report) stating the progress achieved to date at such intervals as Scottish Homes may specify. Scottish Homes may specify the requirement for an oral presentation of the final results by the Contractor to its Departmental Officers.

8. The Contractor is not and shall not hold himself out as being the servant or agent of Scottish Homes for any purpose other than those expressly conferred by this contract and shall not use Scottish Homes' name in relation to the project in any press release, public information or other release of information without the prior written approval of Scottish Homes. It is specifically prohibited for the Contractor to use Scottish Homes' name in any matter or context not directly related to the project.

9. The Contractor and any specialist staff employed on the project shall not accept any fee or any other form of renumeration whatsoever from any third party in relation to the project. The Contractor shall take all appropriate steps to ensure that neither the Contractor nor any consultant or employee is placed in a position where there may be an actual conflict or potential conflict between the financial or personal interests or such persons and the duties owed to Scottish Homes under the provisions of this contract. The Contractor will disclose to Scottish Homes full particulars of any such conflict which may arise. The Contractor will also disclose to Scottish Homes any interests he may have in any other contracts to which Scottish Homes is a party.

10. The Contractor shall keep Scottish Homes informed immediately of any delay or anticipated delay which may occur once the project has commenced. The Contractor shall obtain the prior written approval of Scottish Homes to any change in the time limits or expenditure limits.

11. The Contractor shall keep the estimates of the cost of the project under review throughout. In the event of the estimates being exceeded or likely to be exceeded, the Contractor shall notify Scottish Homes immediately in writing, stating any revised estimate and an explanation for the proposed increase. The limit of Scottish Homes' liability shall not be exceeded without its prior written approval. For the avoidance of doubt Scottish Homes shall not be liable for any expenditure incurred without its prior written approval first having been obtained by the Contractor.

Equipment

12. Equipment such as computers and software as well as books and other similar material required for furtherance of the project and purchased with project funds shall be deemed to be the property of Scottish Homes. On satisfactory completion of the project, arrangements for disposal of the said equipment shall be agreed with Scottish Homes.

Research Findings

13, The copyright of all outputs, to include data and research findings, reports, information programs and data provided, and the format in which the results are produced for the project, shall be the property of Scottish Homes unless otherwise agreed in writing by Scottish Homes. All information provided by Scottish Homes for the purpose of the study shall be returned to Scottish Homes on completion of the project.

14. The data, research findings reports, programs and any other material related to the project shall not be communicated or reproduced, in whole or in part, by the contractor, or any party, to any third party without Scottish Homes' prior written approval. The Contractor shall not communicate, with the media or any other third person, about the work carried out for the project nor publish the results of the project in any report or article without prior written consent of Scottish Homes, which consent shall not be unreasonably withheld.

15. Scottish Homes shall be entitled to use the outputs and the form in which results are produced in any way in which it sees fit, and to authorise or assign other such rights or uses as Scottish Homes in its sole discretion considers appropriate. The Contractor shall not be entitled to receive any additional payment in respect of any such use.

Staffing

16. Only persons with the appropriate qualifications, expertise, skill, care and diligence in carrying out projects of a similar size and scope and complexity to the project and capable of carrying out efficiently the duties to be undertaken by them shall be employed by the Contractor in the research team on the project.

17. The Contractor shall inform Scottish Homes in writing of any intended changes in the project team personnel from that specified in the Contractor's tender/proposal document.

Early Termination of Appointment

18. If any of the conditions of contract contained in these presents are not complied with, Scottish Homes shall be entitled to terminate the Contract. Without prejudice to the foregoing generality Scottish Homes reserves the right to terminate the contract if the Contractor submits on more than one occasion, material to Scottish Homes of a quality which does not meet its requirements, of which Scottish Homes shall be the sole judge. It is further specified that the following conduct (which is not exhaustive) by the Contractor shall result in the immediate termination of the contract.

   – Submission of false invoices.
   – Unauthorised publication of project findings.
   – Excessive delay in providing reports to Scottish Homes.
   – Use of unqualified staff on the project.
   – Non-approved use of project funds.
   – Plagiarism.
   – Bankruptcy or insolvency.

Consequences of Early Termination

19. In the event of early termination of the Contract:

    a) The Contractor shall be deemed to be in breach of contract and shall forthwith cease the work on the project.

    b) Scottish Homes shall retain any sum of whatever nature due to the Contractor and shall be under no obligation to make any further payment to the Contactor. When Scottish Homes has assessed the cost, damage, and loss incurred as a result of the early termination of the contract, it shall be entitled to deduct the full amount of such cost, damage and loss from the total sum due to the Contactor and the payment of any balance after such deduction shall be in full and final settlement of all debt owed by Scottish Homes to the Contractor. In the event that such cost, damage and loss exceeds the total sum due to the Contractor, Scottish Homes shall be entitled to recover the difference as a debt owed by the Contractor to Scottish Homes.

    c) Scottish Homes shall not be liable for damages in respect of any loss of fees which the Contractor might have been expected to earn.

    d) Where Scottish Homes is satisfied that there is evidence of misapplication of project finances by the Contractor, Scottish Homes shall be entitled to recover such monies from the Contractor

20. Where Scottish Homes is satisfied that there is evidence of misapplication of project finances by the Contractor, but where the appointment is not terminated, Scottish Homes shall be entitled to deduct such monies from future payments due to the Contractor.

Breach of Contract

21. Breaches of the general conditions above or of any of the other conditions contained in these presents are material Breaches of Contract.

Disputes

22. In the event of any dispute arising between Scottish Homes and the Contractor the same shall be referred to mediation by either party in accordance with the mediation procedures laid down by the Law Society of Scotland. In the event of the parties failing to reach agreement through mediation, other than on a matter where the decision of Scottish Homes under this Contract is final and conclusive, then the dispute or difference shall be referred to a single Arbiter to be mutually agreed between the parties to this Contract, or if the parties are unable to agree on the appointment of an Arbiter, chosen by the President of the Law Society of Scotland for the time being, on the application of either party. The cost of referral to such mediation or arbitration shall be borne equally between the parties.

Governing Law

23. These presents shall be construed and all rights and obligations hereunder shall be regulated according to the Law of Scotland.

Interpretation

24. In these presents words imparting the singular shall include the plural and vice versa and words imparting the masculine shall include the feminine and vice versa.

Indemnity

25. The Contractor shall ensure that all consultants or sub-contractors or others employed on or in connection with the project are paid timeously and the Contractor shall keep Scottish Homes indemnified from and against all actions, proceedings, claims, losses, expenses and damages occasioned by any breach by the Contractor of any obligation, undertaking or stipulation

Bibliography

Abercrombie, P., (1945), *The Greater London Plan, 1944*. London: HMSO.

Abercrombie, P., and Matthew, R., (1949), *Clyde Valley Regional Plan, 1946*. Edinburgh: HMSO.

Adelman, C., *et al*, (1977), 'Re-thinking case study: notes from the second Cambridge Conference', *Cambridge Journal of Education*, 6, 139-50.

Allen, D., (1989), *In Your Own Voice: A Manual for Public Speaking*. Boston: American Press.

Anderson, I., Kemp, P., and Quilgars, D., (1993), *Single Homeless People, A Report for the Department of Environment*. London: HMSO.

Anderson, I., and Quilgars, D., (1995), *Foyers For Young People: Evaluation of a Pilot Initiative*. York: Centre for Housing Policy, University of York.

Bailey, N., (1996), 'The de-regulated private rented sector in four Scottish cities: 1987-94.' *Research Report, 50*. Edinburgh: Scottish Homes.

Bailey, N., and Robertson, D., (1995), 'Investment in housing in Scotland', *Working Paper*. Edinburgh: Scottish Homes.

Bales, R.F. (1970), *Personality and Interpersonal behaviour*. London: Holt, Rinehart and Winston.

Bassett, K., and Short, J., (1979), *Housing and Residential Structure*. London: Routledge.

Baxter, J., (1995), *The Internet and Local Authorities: Local Government Information Service*. Bedford: Bedford County Council.

Bell, J., (1993), *Doing Your Research Project - A Guide for First Time Researchers in Education and Social Sciences*, (Second Edition). Buckingham: Open University Press.

Berry, R., (1986), *How to Write a Research Paper*, (Second Edition). London: Pergamon.

Bines, W,. Kemp, P., Pleace, N., and Radley, C., (1993), *Managing Social Housing*. Report to the DoE. London: HMSO.

Blackwell, J., and Kennedy, S., (eds), (1988), *Focus on Homelessness. A New Look at Housing Policy*. Dublin: Columba Press.

Blalock, H., (1984), *Social Statistics*, (Second Edition). London: McGraw-Hill.

Boddy, M., and Snape, D., (1995), *The Role of Research in Local Government*. Wokingham: Local Authorities Research and Intelligence Association.

Booth, C., (1889), *The Labour and Life of the People*. London: Macmillan.

Borg, W., (1981), *Applying Educational Research*. New York: Longman.

Bowes, A., and Sim, D., (forthcoming), *'Life histories in housing research: the case of Pakistanis in Glasgow'*, *Quality and Quantity*.

Bowley, M., (1945), *Housing and the State, 1919-44*. London: Allen and Unwin.

British Standards Institution, (1978), *Citing Publications by Bibliographical References,* (BS 5605). London: British Standards Institution.

Bromley, D., (1986), *The Case Study Method in Phycology and Related Disciplines*, New York: Wiley.

Bryman, A., (1989), *Research Methods and Organisation Studies*. London: Routledge.

Bryman, A., and Cramer, C., (1990), *Quantitative Data Analysis for Social Scientists*. London: Routledge.

Burgess, E., Mckenzie, R., and Park, R., (1925), *The City*. Chicago: University of Chicago Press

Burnett, J., (1986), *A Social History of Housing, 1815 - 1985*, (Second Edition). London: Methuen.

Callahan, R., (1990), *How Executives Overcome the Fear of Public Speaking and Other Phobias*. Homewood, IL: Dow Jones-Irwin.

Carroll, L., (1865), *Alice's Adventures in Wonderland*, London: Norton.

Catterick, P., (1994), *Business Planning for Housing*. Coventry: Chartered Institute of Housing.

Cawkell, A., (1991), 'Ideal personal information systems', *The Intelligent Enterprise*, 1, 14-18.

Central Statistical Office, (1996), *Guide to Official Statistics*. London: HMSO

Centre for Housing Research, (1989), *The Nature and Effectiveness of Housing Management in England*. London: HMSO.

Clapham, D., and Kintrea, K., (1994), 'Community ownership and the break-up of council housing in Britain', *Journal of Social Policy*, 23, 2, 219-245.

Cole, I., and Furbey, R., (1994), *The Eclipse of Council Housing*. London: Routledge.

Committee of Scottish Health Services, (1936), *Report of the Committee of Scottish Health Services*. London: HMSO.

Cox, A., (1994), *Public Housing - A London Archives Guide*. London: Guildhall Library.
Cullingworth, J., (1966), *Housing and Local Government*. London: George Allen and Unwin

Damer, S., (1982), *Rent Strike! The Clydebank Rent Struggles of the 1920s*. Clydebank: Clydebank District Libraries.

Darley, J., (1990), *Octavia Hill: A Life*. London: Constable.

Dearling, A., (1992), *How to Organise Conferences and Training Events*. Harlow: Longman.

Delamont, S., (1992), *Fieldwork in Educational Settings: Methods Pitfalls and Perspectives*. London: Falmer.

Dennis, N., (1970), *People and Planning*. London: Faber and Faber.

Denzin, N., (1978), *The Research Act in Sociology*. London: Butterworth.

Denzin, N. (1983) 'Interpretive interaction', in Morgan, G., (ed), *Beyond Method: Strategies for Social Research*. Beverly Hills, CA: Sage.

Department of the Environment, (1977), *Housing Policy: a Consultative Document*. London: HMSO.

de Vaus, D., (1993), *Surveys in Social Research*, (Third Edition). London: UCL Press.

Dey, I., (1993), *Qualitative Data Analysis: A User Friendly Guide for Social Scientists*. London: Routledge.

Dillman, D., (1978), *Mail and Telephone Surveys: The Total Design Method*. Wiley: New York.
Donnison, D., (1967), *The Government of Housing*. Harmondsworth: Penguin.

Durant, R., (1939), *Watling: A Survey of Social Life on a New Housing Estate*. London: P S King.

Eichler, M., (1988), *Nonsexist Research Methods: A Practical Guide*. Boston: Allen and Unwin.

Englander, D., and O'Day, R., (eds), (1995), *Retrieved Riches: Social Investigation in Britain , 1840-1914*. Buckingham: Open University Press.

Fielding, N., (1993), 'Qualitative interviewing', in Gilbert, N., (ed), *Researching Social Life*. London: Sage.

Finch, J., (1986), *Research and Policy: The Uses of Qualitative Methods in Social and Education Research*. London: Falmer.

Fletcher, C., (1974), *Beneath the Surface: An Account of Three Styles of Sociological Research*. London: Routledge and Kegan Paul.

Forrest, R., and Murie, A., (1986), *'An Unreasonable Act?'*, *SAUS Study*, 1. Bristol: SAUS, University of Bristol.

Forrest, R., and Murie, A., (1991), *Selling the Welfare State*. London: Routledge.

Foulis, M, B., (1985), 'Council house sales in Scotland', *Central Research Unit Paper*. Edinburgh: Scottish Office.

Glaser, B., and Strauss, A., (1967), *The Discovery of Grounded Theory*. Chicago: Aldine Press.

Glasgow Municipal Commission, (1904), *Glasgow Municipal Commission on the Housing of the Poor*. Glasgow: City of Glasgow Corporation.

Gower Davies, J., (1972), *The Evangelistic Bureaucrat*. London: Tavistock.

Gregory, S., and White, J., (1991), *Frontline Housing Management: A Summary of Progress on 21 PEP Partnership Projects*. London: Priority Estates Project Ltd.

Hague, C., (1984), *The Development of Planning Thought*. London: Hutchinson.

Haines, J., (1977), *The Politics of Power*. London: Jonathen Cape.

Hakim, C., (1980), 'Census reports as documenting evidence: the Census commentaries', *Sociological Review*, 28, 3, 551-80.

Hakim, C., (1983), 'Research based on administrative records', *Sociological Review*, 31, 489-519.

Hakim, C., (1987), *Research Design: Strategies and Choices in the Design of Social Research*. London: Allen and Unwin.

Harloe, M., and Martens, M., (1984), 'Comparative housing research' in *Journal of Social Policy*, 13, 3, 255-227.

Haywood, P., and Wragg, E., (1978), 'Evaluating the Literature', *Ready Guide 2: Guides in Educational Research*. Nottingham: University of Nottingham, School of Education.

Heritage, J., (1984), *Garfinkel and Ethnomethodology*. Cambridge: Policy Press.

Hill, J., (ed), (1991), *The State of Welfare: The Welfare State in Britain since 1974*. Oxford: Claredon Press.

Hobbs, D., (1988), *Doing the Business*. Oxford: Oxford University Press.

Hole, V., (1972), 'Housing' in Gittus, E., (ed) *Key Variables in Social Research*. London: Heinemann.

Hole, V. (1979), 'Social research in housing', *Local Government Studies*, November/December.

Holmans, A., (1987), *Housing Policy in Britain: A History*. London: Croom Helm.

Honville, G., and Jowell, R., *et al* , (1987), *Survey Research Practice*. London: Heineman.

Hoyt, (1939), *The Structure and Growth of Residential Neighbourhoods in American Cities*. Washington DC: Federal Housing Administration.

Huff, D. (1973), *How to Lie with Statistics*. London: Penguin.

Jarmain, J., (1948), *Housing Subsidies and Rents*. London: Stevens.

Kelle, J., (ed), (1995), *Computer-Aided Qualitative Data Analysis*. London: Sage.

Kintrea, K., *et al*, (1996), 'An Evaluation of Scottish Homes Gro-Grant Mechanism'. *Central Research Paper*. Edinburgh: Scottish Office.

Knibbs, S., (1994), 'Host from care', *Community Care*, 1028, 10th August, 16-17.

Krueger, R., (1994), *Focus Groups: A Practical Guide for Applied Research*. London: Sage.

Lacey, C. (1971), *Hightown Grammar: the school as a social system*. Manchester: Manchester University Press.

Lawless, P., (1981), *Britain's Inner Cities: Problems and Policies*. London: Harper and Row.

Lincoln, Y. and Gubba, E., (1985), *Naturalistic Inquiry*. Beverly Hills, CA: Sage.

Lodge, D., (1981), *The British Museum is Falling Down*. London: Penguin.

Lofland, J. and Lofland, L., (1984) *Analysising Social Settings: A Guide to Qualitative Observation and Analysis*. Belmont, CA: Wadsworth.

Maclennan, D., Brailey, M., and Lawrie, N., (1982), *The Rehabilitation Activities and Effectiveness of Housing Associations in Scotland*. Edinburgh: Scottish Office Central Research Unit.

Majchrzak, A., (1984), *Methods for Policy Research*. London: Sage.

Malpass, P., (1995), 'Housing studies a critical evaluation', draft paper presented to the Housing Studies Association Education Group.

Manchester University Settlement, (1945), *Ancoates: A Study of a Clearance Area*. Manchester: MUS.

Marsh, D., and Rhodes, R., (1992), *Policy Networks in British Government*. Oxford: Clarendon Press.

Marwick, A., (1977), *Introduction to History*, (Units 3, 4 and 5 of A101, Arts Foundation Course), Buckingham: Open University Press.

Matza, D., (1969), *Becoming Deviant in Eaglewood Cliffs*. New Jersey: Prentice-Hall Orwell.

May, T., (1993), *Social Research: Issues, Methods and Process*. Buckingham: Open University Press.

Melling, J., (1982), *Rent Strikes: People's Struggle for Housing in the West of Scotland, 1890-1916*. Edinburgh: Polygon.

Merrett, S., (1979), *State Housing in Britain*. London: Routledge and Kegan Paul.

Merrett, S., with Gray, F., (1992), *Owner Occupation in Britain*. London: Routledge and Kegan Paul.

Miles, M., and Huberman, M., (1994), *Qualitative Data Analysis*, (Second Edition). London: Sage.

Milne, A., (1926), *Winnie-the-Pooh*, (Second Edition). London: Methuen.

Ministry of Housing and Local Governmennt, (1965), *Report of the Committe on Housing in Greater London*, Cmnd 2605 (Milner Holland Committee). London: HMSO.

Mitchell, C., (1983), 'Case and situation analysis', *Sociological Review*, 31, 2. 187-211.

Morrison, D., and Henkel, R., (1970), *The Significance of Test Controversy - A Reader*. Chicago: Aldine.

Moser, C., and Kalton, G., (1974), *Survey Methods in Social Investigation*. London: Heinemann.

Moser, C. and Kalton, G., (1983), *Survey Methods in Social Investigation*, (Second Edition). London: Heinemann.

Munn, P., and Drever, E., (1990), *Using Questionnaires in Small Scale Research*. Edinburgh: SCRE.

Murie, A., and Wang, Y., (1992), 'The sale of public sector housing in Scotland', *Research Paper*, 43. Edinburgh: School of Planning and Housing, Heriot Watt University.

Nelson, R., (1989), *Making Effective Presentations*. Glenview IL: Scott-Foresman.

Nevitt, A., (1966), *Housing, Taxation and Subsidies*. London: Nelson.

Newall, R., (1993), 'Questionnaires', in Gilbert, N., (ed), *Researching Social Life.* London: Sage.

Oppenheim, A., (1992), *Questionnaire Design, Interviewing and Attitude Measurement.* London: Pinter.

Orna, E., with Stevens, G., (1995), *Managing Information for Research.* Buckingham: Open University Press.

Phillips, E., and Pugh, D., (1987), *How to Get a PhD.* Buckingham: Open University Press.

Pickvance, C., and Pickvance, K., (1994), 'Towards a strategic approach to housing behaviour: a study in the south east of England', *Sociology,* 18, 3, 657-77.

Pimlott, B., (1992), *Harold Wilson.* London: Harper Collins.

Platt, J ., (1981), 'Evidence and proof in documentary research', *Sociological Review,* 29, 31-66.

Power, A., (1987), *Property Before People: The Management of the Twentieth-Century Council Housing.* London: Allen and Unwin.

Power, A., (1991), *Housing Management: A Guide to Quality and Creativity.* London: Longman.

Prescott-Clarke, P., Atkins, J., and Clemens, S., (1993), *Tenant Feedback: A Step-by-Step Guide to Tenant Satisfaction Surveys.* London: HMSO.

Presbytery of Glasgow, (1898), *Report of the Commission on the Housing of the Poor in Relation to their Social Condition.* Glasgow: James Maclehose and Son.

Procter, M., (1993), 'Measuring attitude', in Gilbert, N., (ed), *Researching Social Life.* London: Sage.

Rickford, F., (1994), 'Home at last', *Community Care,* 1009, 24th March, 16-17.

Robertson, D. (1992), 'Scottish home improvement policy, 1945 - 1975: Coming to terms with the tenement', *Urban Studies,* 29, 7, 1115-1136.

Robertson, D., (1996), 'Scotland's new towns : a modernist experiment in state corporatism'. Macinnes, A., Foster, S., and MacInnes, R., (eds), *Scottish Power Centres.* Edinburgh: Cruithne Press.

Robertson, D., and Bailey, N., (1994), 'Redefining housing association business plans,' *Research Report, 38.* Edinburgh: Scottish Homes.

Robertson, D., and Bailey, N., (1996), 'Review of the impact of housing action areas', *Research Report,* 47. Edinburgh: Scottish Homes.

Rosenburg, L., (1995), 'Monitoring low cost home ownership: a longitudinal analysis of housing market trends within the privatised areas of four council-built estates in Scotland', *Housing Studies,* 10, 3, 285-304.

Rowntree, D., (1981), *Statistics Without Tears*. London: Penguin.

Royal Commission on Housing of the Industrial Population of Scotland, (1917), *Report of the Royal Commission on Housing of the Industrial Population of Scotland Rural and Urban*. Cd 8731. Edinburgh: HMSO.

Royal Commission on the Distribution of the Industrial Population, (1940), *Report of the Royal Commission on the Distribution of the Industrial Population*. Cmd 6153. (Barlow Commission). London: HMSO.

Scottish Health Services Committee, (1936), *Report of the Committee of Scottish Health Services*. Edinburgh: HMSO.

Scottish Homes, (1993), *Scottish House Condition Survey 1991: Survey Report*. Edinburgh: Scottish Homes.

Scottish Housing Advisory Committee, (1937), *Report on Rural Housing in Scotland*. Cmd 5462. Edinburgh: HMSO.

Scottish Housing Advisory Committee, (1945), *Planning Our New Homes*. Edinburgh: HMSO.

Scottish Housing Advisory Committee, (1947), *Modernising Our Homes*.Edinburgh: HMSO.

Scottish Housing Advisory Committee, (1947), *Distribution of New Houses in Scotland*. Edinburgh: HMSO.

Schuller, T., (1988), 'Pot-holes, caves and lotusland: some observations on case study research', in Burgess, R., (ed), *Studies in Qualitative Methodology*, (Volume 1), London: JAI Press, 59-71.

Short, J., (1982), *Housing in Britain: The Post War Experience*. Methuen: London.

Sim, D., (1994), *British Housing Design*. Longman's Institute of Housing Series: Harlow.

Smith, S., McGuckin, A., and Knill-Jones, R., (eds), (1991), *Housing for Health*. Harlow: Longman.

Social Research Association, (1994), *Commissioning Social Research: A Good Practice Guide*. London: SRA.

Spradley, J., (1979), *The Ethnographic Interview*. London: Holt, Rinehart and Wilson.

Swennarton, M., (1981), *Homes Fit for Heros: The Politics and Architecture of Early State Housing in Britain*. London: Heinemann.

Tesch, R. (1990), *Qualitative Research: Analysis Types and Software Tools*. London: Falmer.

Twine, F., and Williams, N., (1993), 'Resales of public sector housing in Scotland', *Research Report*, 24. Edinburgh: Scottish Homes.

van Zijl, V., and David Couttie Associates Ltd, (1993), *A Guide to Local Housing Needs Assessment*. Coventry: Chartered Institute of Housing.

Vaughan, J., (1982), 'Searching the Literature: Additional sources of information and how to keep up to date', in Hartnett, A., (ed), *The Social Sciences in Educational Studies: A selective guide to the literature*. London: Heinemann.

Weber, R., (1990), *Basic Content Analysis*, (Second Edition). Newbury Park, CA: Sage.

Weitzman, E., and Miles, M., (1994), *Computer Programmes for Qualitative Data Analysis*. Newbury Park, CA: Sage.

Whitham, D., (1989), 'State housing and the great war', in Rodgers, R., (ed), *Scottish Housing in the Twentieth Century*, Leicester: Leicester University Press.

Wilcox, S., (1995), *Housing Finance Review 1995/96*. York: Joseph Rowntree Foundation.

Williams, N., and Twine, F., (1991), 'A research guide to the Register of Sasines and the Land Register in Scotland.' *Working Paper*. Edinburgh: Scottish Homes.

Wolcott, H., (1981), 'Confessions of a "trained" observer' , in Popkewitz, T., and Tabachnik, B., (eds), *The Study of Schooling*. New York: Praeger.

Worsdsall, F., (1979), *The Tenement: a Way of Life*. Glasgow: Chambers.

Young, M., (1934), *Becontree and Dagenham*. London: Beacontree Social Survey Committee.

Young, M., and Wilmott, P., (1957), *Family and Kinship in East London*. London: Routledge and Kegan Paul.

Name index

Abercrombie, Peter, 23
Abercrombie, P., and Matthew, R., 23
Adelman, C., 133, 140
Allen, D., 176
Anderson, I., Kemp, P., and Quilgars, D., 20,130
Anderson, I., and Quilgars, D., 60

Bailey, N., 9
Bailey, N., and Robertson, D., 144
Bales, R.F., 128, 132
Baxter, J., 57
Bell, J., 36, 42, 54, 63, 124, 138
Berry, R., 42
Best, Richard, 26
Bines, W,. Kemp, P., Pleace, N., and Radley, C., 9, 20
Blackwell, J., and Kennedy, S., 60
Blalock, H., 74, 85
Boddy, M., and Snape, D., 43, 51
Booth, C., 21, 118
Borg, W., 112
Bowes, A., and Sim, D., 20
Bowley, M., 23
Bromley, D., 138, 140
Bryman, A., 74
Bryman, A., and Cramer, C., 85, 145, 148, 153, 161
Burgess, E., Mckenzie, R., and Park, R., 19, 140
Burnett, J., 21, 119

Cadbury, George, 21
Callahan, R., 176
Carroll, L., 39, 42
Catterick, P., 7, 16
Cawkell, A., 143, 148
Chadwick, Edwin, 21
Clapham, D., and Kintrea, K., 20
Cole, I., and Furbey, R., 33
Cox, A., 121
Crossman, Richard, 118
Cullingworth, Barry, 24, 25

Damer, S., 120
Darley, J., 120
Dearling, A., 174, 176
Delamont, S., 62, 63, 131, 132, 160, 161
Dennis, N., 25
Denzin, N., 45, 51, 132
de Vaus, D., 103
Dey, I., 66, 75, 148, 162
Dillman, D., 103
Donnison, David, 22, 23, 24
Durant, R., 22

Eichler, M., 90
Englander, D., and O'Day, R., 21, 118

Fielding, N., 106, 115
Finch, J., 149
Forrest, R., and Murie, A., 33, 117
Foulis, M, B., 33

Glaser, B., and Strauss, A., 159
Gower Davies, J., 25
Gregory, S., and White, J., 8, 16

Hague, C., 120
Haines, J., 120
Hakim, C., 17, 18, 47, 48, 51, 103, 122, 124, 133, 136, 140, 177
Haywood, P., and Wragg, E., 62
Heritage, J., 123
Hill, J., 14
Hill, Octavia, 120
Hobbs, D., 129, 131
Hole, V., 20
Holmans, A., 22, 119
Honville, G., and Jowell, R., 88
Howell, Ebenezer, 21
Hoyt, 19
Huff, D., 157, 158, 162

Jarmain, J., 23

Karn, Valerie, 26
Kelle, J., 148
Kintrea, K., 14, 20
Knibbs, S., 56
Krueger, R., 108

Lacey, C., 126
Lever, William, 21
Lawless, P., 25
Lodge, D., 14
Lofland, J. and Lofland, L., 131, 132

Maclennan, Duncan, 26
Maclennan, D., Brailey, M., and
    Lawrie, N., 20, 26
Macmillan, Harold, 23
Majchrzak, A., 17, 18
Malpass, P., 22, 27
Marsh, D., and Rhodes, R., 29
Marwick, A., 119, 124
Matza, D., 128
May, T., 106, 115
Melling, J., 22, 120
Merrett, S., 23, 119
Miles, M., and Huberman, M., 148,
    158, 160, 161, 162
Milne, A., 65, 75
Mitchell, C., 121, 133, 140
Morrison, D., and Henkel, R., 18
Moser, C., and Kalton, G., 75, 76, 85,
    103
Munn, P., and Drever, E., 103
Murie, A., and Wang, Y., 33

Nelson, R., 176
Nevitt, A., 24
Newall, R., 103

Oppenheim, A., 103, 115
Orna, E., with Stevens, G., 167, 176
Orwell, G. 129

Phillips, E., and Pugh, D., 42
Pickvance, C., and Pickvance, K., 56
Pimlott, B., 24

Platt, J ., 123, 124
Power, A., 8, 16, 20
Prescott-Clarke, P., Atkins, J., Clemens,
    S., 10, 16, 103
Procter, M., 103

Rachman, Peter, 24
Rickford, F., 56
Robertson, D. 23, 61, 111
Robertson, D., and Bailey, N., 7, 120
Rosenburg, L., 33
Ross, Stephen, 28
Rowntree, D., 85, 153, 156, 162
Rowntree, Joseph, 21
Rowntree, Seebohm, 21

Schuller, T., 136, 139, 140
Short, J., 24
Sim, D., 59
Smith, S., 118
Spradley, J., 106
Swennarton, M., 119

Tesch, R., 145, 148
Titmuss, Richard, 24
Townsend, Peter, 24
Twine, F., and Williams, N., 33

Unwin, Raymond, 21

van Zijl, V., and David Couttie, 11, 16
Vaughan, J., 55, 63

Weber, R., 162
Weitzman, E., and Miles, M., 148
Whitham, D., 117
Wilcox, S., 144
Williams, Peter, 26
Williams, N., and Twine, F., 11
Wilson, Harold, 24, 118, 120
Wolcott, H., 131

Young, M., 22
Young, M., and Wilmott, P., 22, 23

Subject index

A

abstracts, 55, 56, 117
access, 35, 36, 38, 46, 130
  gatekeepers, 35, 36, 38
action research, 20
advisory committee, 116, 167, 186 *see*
  project management, steering
  committee
Advisory Housing Panel, 21
affordability, 9, 10, 12
analysing data
  qualitative, 158-161
  quantitative, 151-158
applied research, 17-18
Applied Social Science Index and
  Abstract (ASSIA), 56, 181
ASLIB Index to theses, 56
averages, 67, 154 *see* measures of
  central tendency

B

Barlow Commission, 23
Bath Information and Data Services
  (BIDS), 56
Bethnal Green, 22, 23
bibliography, 61, 117, 181
bimodal analysis, 156-157
  crosstabs, 156
  scattergram, 156-157
British Humanities Index, 56
British Library, 56, 120-121
British National Bibliography (BNB),
  56
Building Research Establishment, 22
building societies
  house price data, 11
business plans,12, 26, 117, 134, 183

C

card index, 61
case study approach, 133-140
  comparative analysis, 137
  policy evaluation, 137
  practical considerations, 137-140

CD-roms, 56, 57
census, 7-11
  problems with, 7
  of employment, 12
Central Statistical Office, 187
Centre for Environmental Studies
  (CES), 24, 25
Centre for Housing Research, 15, 26
Centre for Urban and Regional Studies
  (CURS), 24
Chartered Institute of Housing (CIH)
  code of conduct, 50
  sample research brief, 184-186
citizens charter, 10
coding, 151-152
  codebook, 152
  frame, 159
commissioning research, 43-51
commissioners and funders
  of housing research, 179-180
community care, 12, 44, 134
  for single homeless, 28
  plans, 183
Community Care, 181
community development projects
  (CDP), 25
comparative research, 137
competitive tendering, 26, 46, 48-50,
  189
consumer satisfaction surve ,*see* tenant
  satisfaction survey
content analysis, 158, 159
Continuous Recording System
  (CORE), 9
cost-benefit analysis, 13-15
cost-centered accounting, 8
council housing,
  sales, 30, 33, 34, 35, 117, 120, 184
  right to buy, 11, 33, 34, 76, 184

D

databases, 49, 56, 61, 142, 144, 145
data,
  analysis of, 141, 151-159 *see*
  information technology

collection, 36, 37 *see* methods,
  methods toolkit
entry, 151-152
management, 15, 107, 141, 149-162
official statistics, 11, 57, 182
recording of, 30, 113, 116, 126-128,
  129, 130, 144
use and abuse, 149, 157-158
Data Protection Act, 146-147
Department of Social Security (DSS),
  92
Department of the Environment (DoE),
  25, 179
Dewey decimal system, 55, 59
diaries, 118
dissemination, 38-39, 163-164
dissertation, 1, 38, 141, 182
documentary research, 116-124
  primary sources, 116, 117, 119, 123
  secondary sources, 117, 119
  tertiary sources, 117
documents
  archives, 9, 120, 121
  external criticism, 123
  internal criticism, 123, 124
  historical housing studies, 119-120
  official records, 116, 118, 119, 121-
    122
  restricted access, 55, 122
  searches, 120-121
  unwitting sources, 119, 123
  witting sources, 119

E
Economic and Social Research Council
  (ESRC), 26, 179
Economic Trends, 57, 182
electoral register, 78, 79
Environment and Planning, 55, 181
ethics, 5, 33, 49, 63, 129
  confidentially, 36, 48, 51, 88, 109,
    122
European Network of Housing
  Research (ENHR), 27
exit polls, 81, 84

F
field notes, 131, 143, 158
findings
  relationship to theory, 38, 63, 151,
    161
frequency distributions, 153-155, 158
funders, 13, 18, 29

and the research agenda, 28
values of, 19, 27

G
garden cities, 2, 59, 120
General Household Survey, 182
Glasgow Municipal Commission, 21
Glasgow rent strike, 22
globalisation, 18
going native, 131
government and research, 15, 21, 22,
  24, 25, 28, 149, 179
  political, 28
  rational, 28
graphics, 144, 145, 146, 166, 169, 170,
  171, 175
grounded theory, 159
Gro-Grants, 14
Guide to Official Statistics, 57

H
Halifax house price index, 11, 20
Hansard, 121, 182
Home Office, 25
homeless, 7, 10, 13, 20, 33, 53, 60, 67,
  71, 72, 74, 101, 129, 130, 134, 137
Housing, 38, 55
housing,
  and central government, 21-29
  house condition surveys, 12, 71-73,
    77-79, 99, 152, 153, 164
  needs assessment, 10-11
  planning and public health, 21-22
Housing Act, 1988, 9
Housing (Homeless Persons) Act, 28
Housing (Scotland) Act, 1988, 9
Housing and Planning Review, 55
housing associations, 9, 10, 12, 78, 117,
  122, 134
Housing Campaign for Single People
  (CHAR), 28
Housing Corporation, the, 26
housing investment plans (HIP), 10
housing plans, 12, 13, 25, 26, 118
  checklist, 12
  local authority, 12
housing research
  history and development of, 5, 17-29
  nature of, 5, 18-19
Housing Review, 55
Housing Studies, 55
housing studies association, 27
housing systems analysis, 13
hypotheses, 6, 34, 62, 137

I
independent variables,
information,
  interpreting, 15
  monitoring, 7-9
  operational, 7-10
  strategic, 10-13
  uses of, 7-14
information and housing research, 4-16,
  181-183
information technology, 27, 141-150
  Data Protection Act, 147
  desk top publishing, 143, 169
  e-mail, 57
  integrated packages, 145
  Internet, 57
  literature searches using the Internet,
  142-143
  Mailbase, 57
  statistical packages, 145
  strengths and weaknesses, 145-147
  survey software, 143
  qualitative analysis packages, 145
  wordprocessing, 142, 143, 145, 160,
  169, 176
  World Wide Web, 57
inner area studies (IAN), 25
intellectual property rights, 49
interpretivist tradition, 131
interviewing
  bias, 112
  recording, 113-114
  situation, 109
interviews, 104-115
  as rich source of data, 105
  focus group, 108
  group, 108-109
  semi-structured, 107-108
  structured, 106
  strengths and weaknesses, 114
  unstructured, 106

J
Journal of Social Policy, 55
journals, 55-60, 116, 181 *see* individual
  journals

K
key word searches, 55, 56, 58, 142,
  143, 166

L
labour force survey, 12

levels of measurement, 67-69
  interval, 69
  nominal, 67-68
  ordinal, 68-69
  ratio, 69
libraries
  access to, 55
  catalogue, 55
  copyright libraries, 56, 121 *see*
  British Library
  inter-library loan, 58
literature,
  computer searches, 56-57, 141, 142-
  143
  locating published material, 54-56
  planning a search, 58-62
  review, 61-62
  searches, 54, 55, 56, 62

M
making a presentation, 170-174
  conclusions, 172
  environment, 173
  focusing of topic, 171
  key points, 171-172
  outlining, 172
  preparation, 171, 173-174
  transitions, 172
Manchester University Settlement, 22
market research, 37, 77, 80, 152
measurement, 64-75
  and meaning, 65
  and theory, 74
  quantitative versus qualitative, 65-66
measures of central tendency, 154-155
  mean, 67, 68, 69, 154
  median, 68, 69, 154
  mode, 68, 69, 154
measures of dispersion, 155-156
  inter-quartile range, 155
methods toolkit, 52-53
Milner Holland Committee, 24
Ministry of Health, 22
monitoring, 5, 7-9, 13, 15, 20, 22, 27,
  33, 39, 41, 86
  operational systems, 8
  performance measures, 8
  problems of, 7
  purpose of, 8
  quality of service *see* tenant
  satisfaction survey

N

National Federation of Housing
  Associations, 26
national on-line manpower information
  system (NOMIS), 12
naturalistic paradigm, 128
non-verbal communication,
Northern Ireland Housing Executive, 26

O

observational methods, 19, 36, 52, 107,
  125-132, 137 *see* participant
  observation, structured observation
observer effect, 126
official statistics, 7, 11, 12, 57, 144, 182
option appraisal, 13-15

P

participant observation, 53, 66, 129-130
  generalisability, 66, 131-132
  interpretation, 130
  note taking, 130-131
  finding a setting, 130
  sampling, 130
  complete observer, 129
  complete participant, 129
  problems with, 131-132
Planning Exchange, the, 24, 56
planning research, 5, 32-34
  establishing a focus, 33
  hypotheses, 34
  research question, 34
  resources, 34-35
  timescale, 39-40
Policy and Politics, 55
policy community, 27, 28, 29, 178
policy networks, 29
policy research, 17-18, 19, 24, 26
poverty, 21, 64
presenting research, 163-176
  audiences, 165
  forms of presentation, 164
  press release and the media, 165
  timetable, 165-166
pressure groups, 17, 26, 28, 175
priority estates projects (PEP), 8-9, 20
private rented sector, 9, 58, 79
  problems researching, 9, 79
project management, 39, 46 *see*
  advisory committee, steering
  committee
pure research, 17-18

Q

questionnaires, 86-103
  administration of, 99-100
  bias, 93, 99, 100
  computer based, 97, 98, 143
  design of, 97-98
  face-to-face survey, 87
  layout of, 97-98
  piloting, 98-99
  postal, 87
  response rates in, 100-101
  strengths and weaknesses of, 101
  telephone, 87-88
  uses of, 89
question types, 92-97
  category, 94-95
  closed item, 92-93
  grid, 96
  Likert scale, 96
  multiple response, 94
  open-ended, 92-93
  quantity, 95-96
  rank order, 95
  semantic differential, 97
  single answer list, 93

R

referencing, 61
  British Standard BS5605, 61
  Harvard system of, 61
Regional Trends, 57
Register of Sasines, 11
reliability, 70, 72-74
  alternate forms, 73
  item-total, 73-74
  inter-rater, 72
  split-half, 73
  test-retest, 72-73
Rent Restrictions Act, 22
research
  appraisal of existing, 40-41
  briefs, 44-47, 184-186
  contract, 187-191
  design, 5, *see* planning research
  funding, 47 *see* commissioners and
  funders
  process, 31-32
  question, 5, 30, 31, 70, 74, 116, 126,
    153 *see* planning research
  research reports, 167-169
  structure of, 168-169
Roof, 38
Rough Sleepers Initiative, 28

Rowntree Foundation, the Joseph, 24, 26

S
sample, 76-85
  bias, 78, 80, 81, 87
  representative, 77, 78, 79, 82, 83, 84
  cluster, 79-80
  confidence level, 82-83
  non-random, 80
  purposive, 81
  quota, 80
  reputational, 81
  simple random, 78
  error, 82
  size, 83
  snowball, 81
  stratified, 79
  systematic, 78-79
School of Advanced Urban Studies (SAUS), 25
Scottish Continuous Recording System (CORE), 9
Scottish Homes, 13, 14, 26, 79, 89, 135, 164
  sample research contract, 187-191
Scottish Housing Advisory Committee, 27
Scottish Office, 20, 22, 26, 89, 120
  housing statistics, 20
Shelter, 28
slum clearance, 22
Social and Community Planning Research (SCPR), 24
Social Science Citation Index (SSIC), 56
Social Trends, 57
steering committee, 46 *see* advisory committee, project management
structured observation, 126-128
  Bale's interactive process analysis system, 127-128
  schedules, 143

styles of presentation, 172-173
  extemporaneous method, 173
  impromptu method, 172
  memorising, 172
  manuscript method, 172

T
Tai Cymru, 26
taking notes, 58-61
tenant satisfaction surveys, 1, 9-10, 33, 36, 45, 79, 89, 111, 145, 156
theoretical research, 17-18
theory building,
timetable, 39, 40
  time sheet, 8
town planning, 23
triangulation, 53, 132, 138
Tudor Wallers Report, 21

U
units of analysis, 65, 67, 77
Urban Studies, 55

V
validity, 70-72
  concurrent, 71
  construct, 72
  criterion related, 71
  face, 70-71
  predictive, 71
valuation roll, 11
value free research, 19, 28, 113
value relevant research, 19
variables, 18, 34, 79, 83, 140, 152, 153, 154, 156, 157, 158
visual aids, 170-175
  acetates, 170, 175
  flipcharts, 174-175
  slides, 170, 175
Voluntary Housing, 38, 55

W
Welsh Office, 26
writing-up, *see* presenting research